JEFFREY J. SCHOTT, EDITOR

COMPLETING THE URUGUAY ROUND:

A Results-Oriented Approach to the GATT Trade Negotiations

INSTITUTE FOR INTERNATIONAL ECONOMICS
Washington, DC

September 1990

AKM 6901 - 2/1

Jeffrey J. Schott, a Research Fellow at the Institute for International Economics, was a Senior Associate at the Carnegie Endowment for International Peace (1982–83) and an International Economist at the US Treasury (1974–82). He is the author or co-author of several recent books on trade, including *Free Trade Areas and U.S. Trade Policy* (1989), *The Canada-United States Free Trade Agreement: The Global Impact* (1988), *Auction Quotas and United States Trade Policy* (1987), *Trading for Growth: The Next Round of Trade Negotiations* (1985), and *Economic Sanctions Reconsidered: History and Current Policy* (1985, rev. ed. forthcoming).

INSTITUTE FOR
INTERNATIONAL ECONOMICS
11 Dupont Circle, NW
Washington, DC 20036
(202) 328-9000   Telex: 261271 IIE
UR   Fax: (202) 328-5432

C. Fred Bergsten, *Director*
Linda Griffin Kean, *Director of Publications*

The Institute for International Economics was created by, and receives substantial support from, the German Marshall Fund of the United States.

RECEIVED

Printed in the United States of America 92 91 90   5 4 3 2 1

**Library of Congress
Cataloging-in-Publication Data**

Completing the Uruguay round: a results-oriented approach to the GATT trade negotiations / [edited by] Jeffrey J. Schott.
p. 256 cm.
Includes index.
1. Tariff. 2. General Agreement on Tariffs and Trade (Organization) 3. Foreign trade regulation. 4. Uruguay Round (1986–   )
I. Schott, Jeffrey J., 1949–
HF1713.C624   1990   90-5297
382'.92—dc20   CIP
ISBN 0–88132–130–3

Contents

Acknowledgments   vii

Preface   *C. Fred Bergsten*   ix

1 **Uruguay Round: What Can Be Achieved?**   *Jeffrey J. Schott*   1
2 **Agriculture**   *Dale E. Hathaway*   51
3 **Textiles**   *William R. Cline*   63
4 **Safeguards**   *Colleen Hamilton and John Whalley*   79
5 **Subsidies**   *Gary Clyde Hufbauer*   93
6 **Antidumping**   *Patrick A. Messerlin*   108
7 **Services**   *Brian Hindley*   130
8 **Trade-Related Investment Measures**   *Edward M. Graham
   and Paul R. Krugman*   147
9 **Intellectual Property**   *Keith E. Maskus*   164
10 **Dispute Settlement**   *Robert E. Hudec*   180
11 **Reflections on Restructuring the GATT**   *John H. Jackson*   205

Index   225

Tables
3.1 Projected consumer costs of alternative apparel liberalization
    proposals, 1992–2000   71
4.1 Cases of administered protection by type of action and country,
    1980–86   82
4.2 Key proposals and positions in the GATT safeguards negotiations   86
6.1 Import relief measures initiated, by type and country, 1979–88 110–111
6.2 Extent of proposed changes in the GATT Antidumping
    Code, by article   113

Figures
3.1 Predicted and actual US apparel trade, 1978–89   69

Acknowledgments

The Uruguay Round will likely succeed if negotiators work as hard as my colleagues at the Institute in assisting me on this volume. Special thanks are due Michael Treadway for his major contribution to the editing of the chapters, Linda Griffin Kean and Vilma Gordon for preparing the manuscript for publication, and Trisha Jessee for helping to organize the initial conference where the papers were presented.

J.J.S.

Preface

The Uruguay Round of multilateral negotiations in the General Agreement on Tariffs and Trade has become the focal point for world trade policy in the late 1980s and early 1990s. As the successor to the Kennedy Round of the 1960s and the Tokyo Round of the 1970s, the outcome of the round will go far to determine the future of the global trading system. This study analyzes each of the major issues under discussion, reviews the results of the negotiations to date, and recommends a final outcome for both the individual components of the round and its overall package.

The Institute has conducted extensive previous research on the Uruguay Round and its constituent issues. In response to a request from then–US Trade Representative William E. Brock, Gary Clyde Hufbauer and Jeffrey J. Schott developed one of the initial blueprints for the negotiations in *Trading for Growth: The Next Round of Trade Negotiations*, published in September 1985. Hufbauer and Joanna Shelton Erb proposed new initiatives in one of the most controversial areas addressed by the round in *Subsidies in International Trade* (1984). William R. Cline analyzed *The Future of World Trade in Textiles and Apparel*, including (in the revised edition of June 1990) a review of the detailed proposals made for this sector in the round. Dale E. Hathaway addressed a central topic of the negotiations in *Agriculture and the GATT: Rewriting the Rules* (September 1987) and, along with William N. Miner, followed up with *World Agricultural Trade: Building a Consensus* (1988). In connection with that volume, the Institute cosponsored *Reforming World Agricultural Trade: A Policy Statement by Twenty-nine Professionals from Seventeen Countries*, which sought to advance the negotiations at a key point (May 1988).

Our new assessment derives in large part from a conference held at the Institute on 25 June 1990 at which experts from a number of countries presented papers on each major topic being negotiated. As with several earlier Institute projects, we are releasing our findings in two different formats in an effort to meet the needs of different readers. This book includes all of the papers presented to the conference. Chapter 1 presents an analytical summary of conclusions and policy recommendations from each paper along with proposals by Jeffrey J. Schott for a successful completion of the round; this chapter is also being released separately as number 29 in our POLICY ANALYSES IN INTERNATIONAL ECONOMICS series, entitled *The Global Trade Negotiations: What Can Be Achieved?*

The Institute for International Economics is a private nonprofit research institution for the study and discussion of international economic policy. Its purpose is to analyze important issues in that area, and to develop and communicate practical new approaches for dealing with them. The Institute is completely nonpartisan.

The Institute was created by a generous commitment of funds from the German Marshall Fund of the United States in 1981, and now receives about 15 percent of its support from that source. Major institutional grants are also being received from the Ford Foundation, the William and Flora Hewlett Foundation, the Alfred P. Sloan Foundation, and the C. V. Starr Foundation. The Dayton Hudson Foundation and the General Electric Foundation provide support for the Institute's program of studies on trade policy. A number of other foundations and private corporations are contributing to the increasing diversification of the Institute's financial resources. About 15 percent of the Institute's resources in our latest fiscal year came from outside the United States, including about 4 percent from Japan.

The Board of Directors bears overall responsibility for the Institute and gives general guidance and approval to its research program—including identification of topics that are likely to become important to policymakers over the medium run (generally one to three years) and which thus should be addressed by the Institute. The Director, working closely with the staff and outside Advisory Committee, is responsible for the development of particular projects and makes the final decision to publish an individual study.

The Institute hopes that its studies and other activities will contribute to building a stronger foundation for international economic policy around the world. We invite readers to let us know how they think we can best accomplish this objective.

C. FRED BERGSTEN
Director
August 1990

COMPLETING THE URUGUAY ROUND:

**A Results-Oriented Approach to the
GATT Trade Negotiations**

1

The Uruguay Round: What Can Be Achieved?

Jeffrey J. Schott

With the December 1990 target date fast approaching for completion of the Uruguay Round of multilateral trade negotiations under the auspices of the General Agreement on Tariffs and Trade (GATT), the outcome of the talks is still very much in doubt. Will the round yield agreements that significantly liberalize existing trade barriers and expand the coverage of GATT rules to new areas such as services, investment, and intellectual property? Will the results instead be relatively modest, focusing more on rulemaking than on liberalization? Or will the talks break down entirely over such intractable issues as agricultural subsidies, leaving the GATT trading system in disarray?

In the aftermath of the Houston economic summit in July 1990, the prospect of abject failure has greatly diminished. The leaders of the major industrial countries undertook a political commitment to make the Uruguay Round succeed: the summit declaration states their "determination to take the difficult political decisions necessary to achieve far-reaching, substantial results in all areas of the Uruguay Round by the end of this year."[1] However, the declaration did not

---

1. Economic Declaration of the Summit of Industrialized Nations, Houston, Texas, 11 July 1990, paragraph 19.

address two crucial questions: what constitutes "substantial results"? and will the round be extended if those results are not achieved by year's end?

How much has to be achieved in the Uruguay Round to allow the results to be characterized as a success? Either a big or a small package of agreements could (and almost surely would) be so presented; however, the effects on the multilateral trading system would be markedly different.

At a minimum, the Uruguay Round needs to reinforce confidence in the multilateral trading system and make a significant contribution to trade liberalization. By promoting solutions to long-standing trade problems as well as reinforcing GATT rules and enforcement mechanisms, a big package of agreements could achieve such a result. In contrast, a small package that merely supplements existing GATT rules would likely paper over major ongoing trade disputes, exacerbating the restiveness of key trading nations with the multilateral process. The result could be a Pyrrhic victory for the GATT system and actually undermine its future prospects. Therefore, a successful round requires a big package of agreements.

This thesis is admittedly controversial: the economist's reach for a big package may well exceed the politician's grasp. Yet it still seems possible, despite the constraints established by the negotiations so far, to achieve what politicians and economists alike would deem to be substantial results in three major areas: trade liberalization, rulemaking, and institutional reform of the GATT system.

In other words, the GATT negotiators should not settle for a minimalist package of agreements in the rush to meet the December deadline. If the negotiators need to extend the round, either to wrap up final details of a comprehensive package or to prevent the talks from collapsing altogether, they should do so.[2] Regrettably, the lack of progress in the talks immediately after the Houston summit makes it increasingly difficult for the negotiators to meet the December dead-

2. Concern about concluding and ratifying the Uruguay Round results during a recession (a distinct prospect for the United States) could be another reason to consider an extension. Moreover, the crisis in the Middle East could also complicate the timetable for the negotiations.

line, and it is conceivable that talks could continue into early 1991, or even longer.

There are no insuperable institutional barriers to extending the talks. The GATT ministers themselves set the deadline of December 1990 for the conclusion of the round, and they can extend it for good cause (as was done in the Tokyo Round to work out the terms of the Subsidies Code). A more inflexible deadline is the expiration on 1 June 1991 of US fast-track implementing authority, which requires the President to notify the Congress at least 90 days prior to entering into trade agreements. As a practical matter this means that, without an extension, the fast-track authority cannot be used after 1 March 1991. However, the 1988 Omnibus Trade and Competitiveness Act provides for a two-year extension of the fast-track authority if the President demonstrates that "progress [in the round] justifies the continuation of the negotiations" and if neither the House nor the Senate disapproves before 1 June 1991. It would be far preferable to complete the negotiations as scheduled by the end of December 1990, but that deadline should be extended if necessary to achieve the desired substantive outcome.

The objective of this volume is to suggest how the GATT talks can succeed in achieving a big package of agreements. Experts in each of the key areas of the round discuss the critical issues under negotiation and the interlinkages among them, analyzing both the substance of each issue and the differing national interests at work, and identify what they consider the most desirable outcome (or range of potential outcomes) that could be achieved in each area. In addition, they examine important issues in each area that should be included on the post-round GATT agenda.

The purpose of this overview chapter is to mold the various pieces of the negotiations into a coherent package. To that end, it addresses four specific issues: why a successful Uruguay Round is important; why a big package of agreements is critical to its success; what should be included in the big package in the areas of market access, new issues, and institutional reforms; and what is in the package for the major trading countries. In so doing, it sets out an ambitious, yet feasible, target for negotiators to aim at, and a standard against which the final Uruguay Round results can be judged.

Why Is a Successful Uruguay Round Important?

The Uruguay Round was conceived with two interrelated goals in mind: to blunt protectionist pressures that were eroding support for the multilateral trading system and to bring the GATT up to date by extending the coverage of its rules to important areas of international trade not subject to, or inadequately covered by, existing GATT provisions.[3] To be successful, the Uruguay Round needs to contribute to both strengthening and modernizing the GATT. To achieve such results, the negotiators face two critical challenges.

The first challenge is to renew confidence in the efficacy of the multilateral disciplines of the GATT and to provide a viable alternative to unilateral actions and to bilateral and regional trading arrangements (primarily by the United States and the European Community). Since the conclusion of the Tokyo Round the GATT system has been buffetted, in developed and developing countries alike, by strong protectionist pressures generated by the second oil shock, global recession, debt crises, and massive trade imbalances. The difficulties in dealing with these problems led to allegations that the multilateral process with its broad membership and agenda was too slow and complex, and too hampered by inadequate rules that were inadequately enforced, to counter the drift toward protection.[4] These perceived weaknesses in the GATT system, coupled with the reluctance until 1986 of many countries to engage in new multilateral negotiations, led the United States and the Community both to deploy unilateral measures (such as US Section 301 and antidumping actions) in attacking foreign trade barriers and practices, and to pursue bilateral and

---

3. These objectives are particularly important for the United States, the *demandeur* of the round, which needs to reconstitute its export-oriented free-trade coalition to bolster domestic support for international trade agreements. That coalition was fragmented in the 1980s by dollar overvaluation and huge trade deficits, agricultural trade disputes, and a growing concern that US competitiveness in high-technology industries was being undercut by unfair foreign trade practices.

4. For a fuller discussion of this point, see Schott (1989, 7–10).

regional trade pacts initially as complements to, but also as potential substitutes for, the multilateral system.[5]

These policies contributed to allegations, primarily in the United States and the Community, that the GATT was "dead." Yet on the contrary the GATT is still held in great respect in most corners of the world, and it is considered, even with its present limitations, to be a valuable forum. The best evidence of this is the ongoing procession of new members into the GATT: more than a dozen countries (including Mexico) have joined in the last decade, and new requests for membership have come from Venezuela, Taiwan, China, the Soviet Union, and Bulgaria.

The second challenge for the Uruguay Round is to make the GATT system more relevant and responsive to the changing nature and scope of international commerce. The credibility of the GATT depends in large measure on its ability to address the emerging issues of the 1990s—especially the problems of sunrise industries (such as microelectronics and telecommunications) and the barriers confronted by firms engaged in trade and investment in goods and services on a world scale. To do so requires progress not only on the "new issues" on the Uruguay Round agenda, but also on traditional trade issues such as subsidies and dumping, where rules need to be adapted to deal with evolving patterns of trade and investment and the disputes that will inevitably arise. This task is complicated further because trade policy considerations often are inextricably linked to industrial policy concerns, often with national security overtones (such as in disputes about semiconductors and high-definition television).

Failure to meet these challenges could reinforce the growing doubts about the multilateral system and lead to increased resort to unilateral actions as well as bilateral and regional trading arrangements. This in

---

5. In the 1980s, the United States negotiated bilateral free trade pacts with Israel and Canada (it will soon start similar talks with Mexico) and special preferences for the Caribbean Basin. The European Community began a process of deepening its integration, through its historic 1992 initiative, and broadening its scope, through the accession of Greece, Spain, and Portugal as well as through ongoing negotiations to create a "European Economic Space" with countries in the European Free Trade Association and in Eastern Europe.

turn would likely contribute to the further erosion of multilateral discipline over time, for several reasons.

First, weak GATT rules open the door to the aggressive use of unilateral measures, which can mask protectionist intent and undermine the multilateral process. This was demonstrated in the 1980s by actions taken by both the United States and the European Community, which often broke or bent GATT rules. Conspicuous examples are the overzealous use of antidumping and countervailing duty actions, the imposition of quotas under "voluntary" export restraint (VER) arrangements, and (in the United States) the use of Section 301. To be sure, such measures often can be justified as ways of constraining protectionist impulses, breaking down trade barriers, and disciplining unfair trade practices; for example, the use of Section 301 so far has led to trade reforms in Japan, Korea, and Taiwan.[6] Yet granting national authorities unlimited discretion to interpret multilateral rules increases the risk that the policemen, not the legislators (i.e., the GATT negotiators), will make the law instead of simply enforcing it.

In the absence of a stronger GATT system, unilateral measures could easily be deployed with increasing fervor and frequency. In the United States, this could lead to the proliferation of VERs (especially if the US economy slips into recession) and increasing resort to antidumping actions. In addition, resort to Section 301 is likely to increase, since many cases have been deferred pending solutions in the Uruguay Round: the complaint against Japanese import controls on rice is the most prominent example. In the European Community, unilateralism would mean the continued aggressive use of antidumping measures and possibly the emulation of Section 301 actions. The main target would probably continue to be the East Asian countries, with a particular focus on problems of high-technology trade as well as agriculture.

Second, unless GATT rules are strengthened, countries will continue to pursue bilateral and regional trading arrangements, substituting regional discrimination for the most-favored-nation (MFN) principle that is the foundation of the GATT system. The dynamic trend in this

---

6. See especially the provocative case for strengthening GATT law through acts of civil disobedience, including the use of Section 301 in certain circumstances, in Hudec (1989).

direction, already evidenced in Europe and North America, could extend both geographically and along sectoral lines. The regional and bilateral accords concluded to date have been generally consistent with the lax standards of GATT Article XXIV, which allows exceptions to the MFN principle for free trade areas and customs unions.[7] However, in the absence of a stronger GATT, the extension of such arrangements—both within Europe and in the Western Hemisphere—could lead to their becoming substitutes for rather than complements to the multilateral system. This in turn could lead to the devolution of the multilateral system into regional trading blocs.[8]

Finally, and perhaps most importantly, if the Uruguay Round fails to strengthen the multilateral system, trade disputes could proliferate and spill over to political and security relationships (see Bergsten 1990). Such spillover effects were limited during the Cold War period because of overriding security concerns among the main industrial countries. With the end of the Cold War, trade battles could become more intense and impede the international cooperation needed to pursue both economic and political objectives, such as reforms in the Soviet and East European economies and the maintenance of US troops in Europe.

To sum up: a stronger and modernized GATT is needed to prevent a surge in new trade frictions, generated by increasing resort to unilateral trade actions and the proliferation of discriminatory bilateral and regional trading arrangements. Either the GATT will emerge from the Uruguay Round strengthened, or it will be progressively weakened as the major trading nations seek alternatives to deal with pressing trade issues.

---

7. The Wisemen's report on the GATT issued in 1985 warned about the dangers to multilateralism already evident in the abuse of provisions of GATT Article XXIV, which have not prevented the spread of regional preferences (see Leutwiler et al. 1985).

8. Movement toward such arrangements might not lead, as is commonly assumed, to a tripolar world, but rather to one where the growing EC bloc would be confronted with a Pacific Basin bloc. Despite current US–Japan trade tensions, a bipolar world would likely emerge, driven by closer trade and investment ties among *firms* in each region, which could generate tensions of both an economic and a political nature between the two blocs. See Schott (1990a) and Krause (1990).

Why Is a Big Package Needed?

The Uruguay Round seeks to achieve what the past seven rounds of GATT negotiations have not: the liberalization of hard-core trade barriers in such areas as agriculture and textiles, and the establishment of new rights and obligations in areas not yet subject to GATT discipline, such as services, investment, and intellectual property. These two sets of objectives have been closely linked during the negotiations—progress on the "old" issues will be required to achieve broad-based participation in the "new" areas.

The task is ambitious: decades of protection have nurtured strong domestic interests that profit significantly from trade controls and energetically resist liberalization. Moreover, both the "old" and the "new" trade problems are rooted to a large extent in national economic policies that have overlapping and sometimes conflicting domestic and international trade objectives. Even if the economic case for reform is clear, liberalization may present very difficult political problems.

The success of the round depends on the ability of the major trading nations both to exchange concessions on liberalization of existing barriers and to agree to new and stronger GATT trading rules, including more-effective dispute settlement procedures. Only a big package of agreements can facilitate the needed trade-offs and generate enough new trading opportunities to overcome the opposition to reform from entrenched protectionist interests.

Such a bargain will not be struck easily. Even the wide-ranging Tokyo Round package did not include reforms in such sensitive areas as agriculture and textiles, because the proffered payoffs were not large enough to overcome political opposition to change in the major trading nations. The success of the round thus needs to be predicated on an "almost-all-or-nothing" strategy. Substantive results will have to be reached in almost all the contentious areas under negotiation—including agriculture and textiles. It is unlikely that a package that omits significant reforms in both these areas will generate the payoffs needed to catalyze support for major changes in existing barriers.

A big package would produce two important dividends. First, it would demonstrate that the GATT is a "results-oriented" institution.

It would enhance the credibility of the multilateral process as a means to secure liberalization of long-standing trade barriers and to safeguard existing market access through comprehensive and enforceable rules. This is especially important for the United States, which needs to maintain and broaden its export drive, particularly in manufactures, to reduce its large trade deficit.

Second, a big package is needed to secure the implementation of major reforms by national governments. A big package would mobilize political coalitions to lobby for the Uruguay Round results. Indeed, in the United States, it will be very difficult to get support from the business community and other domestic constituencies for reforms needed to implement GATT agreements without the promise of substantial new trading opportunities in such areas as agriculture and financial services, and new rules on protection of intellectual property.

By facilitating major reforms, a big package would demonstrate that the multilateral process can be an effective and viable alternative to unilateralism. This is especially important at a time when many in Congress point out that unilateral pressure has been highly effective. Congress is most reluctant to limit US discretion to take unilateral action, and only significant concessions from other countries will temper this position.

Because of the close coordination between the Congress and the executive branch on US negotiating positions, it is unlikely that Congress would fail to ratify a Uruguay Round package that US Trade Representative Carla A. Hills presents to it. Whether Congress will agree to change existing US laws, however, will depend on the expected payoff: the concessions offered by other countries. In other words, a small package is easy to ratify because it requires few changes in US law, but a big package should also be acceptable because it will require major changes in the laws of other countries that will promote US trade objectives.

The Uruguay Round Package: What Should Be Included?

The agenda of the Uruguay Round is comprehensive and complex, involving 15 separate negotiating groups. The chapters in the rest of this volume provide detailed analyses of the key issues under negotiation. In this overview, I will try to tie the individual issues together into a coherent package, referring as appropriate to the proposals set forth in those chapters.

A big Uruguay Round package needs to contain agreements in three main areas: market access for traditional products, the new issues (services, investment, and intellectual property) coupled with dispute settlement, and other institutional reforms. Compressing 15 groups into three areas is designed to simplify the analysis and to illustrate the trade-offs needed to achieve substantive results. The following sections highlight the maximum results that can be achieved in each area, given the constraints so far imposed on the negotiations.

MARKET ACCESS

The market access negotiations involve two sides of the same coin. The first side is liberalization: a big package requires, *inter alia,* a reduction in trade barriers in agriculture, textiles and apparel, tariffs, and government procurement. The flip side, equally integral to this part of the negotiations, is the safeguards complex: the range of measures that countries use to unravel existing market access and to roll back previous liberalization. The safeguards complex includes the traditional safeguards issues under GATT Article XIX as well as so-called gray-area measures (those measures not subject to GATT rules, such as VERs), antidumping and countervailing duty actions, and government subsidies (which are often used to offset or counteract commitments to liberalization).

The two sides of the market access coin are integrally linked. Commitments to liberalize trade are valuable only if disciplines exist to ensure that the reform will not be offset by other actions. This is a paramount concern, for example, in the debate about transitional safeguards during the process of phasing out of quotas under the Multi-Fiber Arrangement. On the other hand, countries will be less anxious to commit to reform if they are denied recourse to remedies against unfair trade practices and to temporary import relief for domestic industries facing severe adjustment pressure.

TRADE LIBERALIZATION

Agriculture

The linchpin of the trade liberalization part of the Uruguay Round is agriculture, even though that sector today accounts for only about 13 percent of world trade (see Hathaway 1987). Unlike in past rounds, in which agriculture was shunted aside before the final package of agreements was concluded, the negotiation of significant reforms in agricultural policies is crucial to the overall success of the Uruguay Round, for several reasons:

□ Agricultural subsidies are expensive: they create large distortions in world markets for farm products and act as a drag on overall economic growth. Agricultural policies in industrial countries alone cost consumers about $245 billion in 1989.[9] International pressure through the GATT talks, coupled with domestic budget pressures, provides the best way to gain support for domestic farm reforms, since a significant part of the cost of national farm programs is inspired by the need to offset the policies of other countries.

□ Agricultural trade disputes have proliferated, increasing international frictions, which have led to the imposition of trade restrictions. The escalation of such disputes can catch manufactured goods in the retaliatory crossfire. More generally, such trade disputes impugn the credibility of the GATT process—a key point for US domestic politics, since agriculture is an important component of the free-trade coalition.

□ Agricultural liberalization offers the potential for increases in US exports of grains, oilseeds, and beef; substantial export gains can

---

9. This was more than in any year prior to the start of the Uruguay Round, although less than the $280 billion cost in 1988. See Organization for Economic Cooperation and Development (1990) and *Financial Times*, 15 June 1990, 3.

also be expected for many developing countries (including Argentina, Brazil, and Thailand), particularly in rice and sugar.[10]

□ The Uruguay Round may be the last chance to reform the European Community's Common Agricultural Policy (CAP) before its geographic sphere is extended to the countries of the European Free Trade Association (EFTA) and to Eastern Europe. Agricultural protection is even higher in EFTA than in the Community; closer relations between the two blocs would tend to strengthen support for existing CAP programs. The competitiveness problems of much of Eastern European agriculture could also create a strong vested interest against reforms of protection in the agricultural sector.

□ Substantive results are needed in agriculture to get the support of the 14 agricultural exporting countries in the Cairns Group, as well as that of other developing countries, for agreements in the new issue areas. These countries are driven primarily by their export interests and have threatened to walk away from the negotiating table if the Uruguay Round package does not include new disciplines on agricultural export subsidies, internal support measures, and border measures.[11]

The Uruguay Round negotiations need to achieve fundamental reforms in agricultural policies, not merely restraint in the use of farm subsidies. The draft text prepared by Aart de Zeeuw, the chairman of the Negotiating Group on Agriculture, provides ample scope to achieve such a result. Such an accord could track the outline of reforms proposed by Dale E. Hathaway in chapter 2 of this volume, which crafts a compromise between the US and the EC positions that would

---

10. Roningen and Dixit (1989) estimate that comprehensive farm trade liberalization would have a positive *net* trade balance effect for the United States, although trade volume in several product sectors would fall. Overall, the US economy would also experience a large welfare gain from agricultural liberalization.

11. The communiqué issued after the ministerial meeting of the Cairns Group in Santiago, Chile, on 6 July 1990, stated: "Ministers renewed their determination that the Round cannot and will not conclude, in whole or in part, without a substantial outcome on agriculture" (paragraph 14).

achieve significant reforms in the three major areas under negotiation: price supports, export subsidies, and market access.

In essence, the agricultural package should incorporate a sharp (say, 50 percent) reduction in current levels of export subsidies and domestic subsidies (including deficiency payments), conversion of quotas into tariffs or tariff rate quotas, and significant liberalization of import protection from existing levels.[12] The reductions in domestic subsidies could be based on an aggregate measure of support (AMS), as proposed by the European Community, with two important provisos. First, support for each product must be capped at existing levels in the agreed base period; there should be no "rebalancing," as the Community proposes, by which support for some products could be increased even as the overall level of support was reduced. Second, in addition to the overall commitment to reduce the AMS, there should be a separate commitment for cuts in export subsidies by product (on a phased basis, say, 10 percent per year for five years).

All existing border measures should be converted to tariffs, with limited exceptions where tariff rate quotas are required to maintain domestic support programs during a transition phase. In the case of the Community, the converted tariff could have a flexible or variable component, based only on the percentage change of the ECU–SDR exchange rate. Although this is not in itself a desirable feature, it would be a pragmatic bow to the Community, acknowledging its difficulty in accepting a tariffication plan without some protection against exchange rate fluctuations.

The farm package should also include two less controversial components relating to food security and to sanitary and phytosanitary regulations (e.g., relating to the use of hormones in meat), as well as special safeguard measures to protect against import surges and extraordinary price movements. The food security section should *not* be used to preclude import liberalization (for example, for rice); instead

---

12. The base year for calculating such reductions should be 1988, as proposed in the de Zeeuw text. Using 1986 as a base year, as proposed by the European Community and Japan, or even an average of support in 1986–88, would yield lower *additional* reductions from current 1990 levels for products such as cereals, meat, and dairy products. Reforms taken since the start of the round should receive credit but should not substitute for additional steps. See *Financial Times*, 31 July 1990, 1.

it should encourage stockpiling in lieu of trade protection to the maximum extent possible.

In sum, such a package would result in major changes in current farm programs in the United States, the European Community, and Japan, and require:

☐ The United States and the Cairns Group to temper their demands for the phase-out of export subsidies, and to recognize that half a loaf can still be very nourishing;

☐ The United States to sharply reduce its level of price supports[13] and to abandon its Section 22 waiver—these measures would significantly reform US sugar and dairy programs;

☐ The European Community to accelerate the pace of its own reforms, and sharply reduce its use of export subsidies, to abandon its unsubtle attempt to raise barriers to oilseeds imports through rebalancing, and to constrain the range of variation of its variable levy; and

☐ Japan to open its market to rice imports by establishing a tariff rate quota (although the quota level could be linked to some minimum level to satisfy food security considerations).

Textiles and Apparel

Liberalization of trade in textiles and apparel is another key component of the market access negotiations. Above all, the Uruguay Round accord must include a commitment to phase out the Multi-Fiber Arrangement (MFA), as agreed in the Punta del Este declaration that launched the round.[14] William R. Cline, in chapter 3 of this volume and in the revised edition of his 1987 study of this sector (Cline 1990),

---

13. Since the mid-1980s, the United States has cut its price supports less than has the Community, and the 1990 farm bill would freeze supports at existing levels for five more years.

14. The objective set forth in the Punta del Este declaration was "the eventual integration of this sector into GATT on the basis of strengthened GATT rules and disciplines" (GATT 1986).

analyzes the three approaches that have been suggested to achieve that result:

□ Annual expansion of existing quotas until they become redundant (that is, "growing out" of the MFA);

□ Conversion of existing quotas into tariff rate quotas coupled with annual reductions in the surcharge rate on imports above the quota; and

□ Creation of global quotas to be phased out over a period of several years.

Any of these proposals would be preferable to the maintenance of the MFA.[15] The preferred solution put forward by Cline is a tariff rate quota system based on existing, country-specific quotas. Surcharge rates for shipments above the quota level could initially be set as high as the Smoot-Hawley levels incorporated in column 2 of the Tariff Schedule of the United States,[16] yet still provide for an orderly phase-out of the quantitative restriction within 10 years. The elimination of the quotas should be accorded higher priority than the reduction of existing levels of tariff protection.

Alternatively, countries could agree simply to expand their existing quotas each year until the restrictions become redundant (that is, when the supply of quota "tickets" exceeds the demand for imports). However, according to Cline's calculations, the annual quota growth rate would have to be above 7 percent just to prevent the quotas from becoming more restrictive over time. If a 10-year phase-out period were adopted, the annual growth rate would need to be considerably higher, averaging 9 percent, to avoid a political backlash in the final year when the industry would face going "cold turkey."

Even the global quota approach, which has been almost universally criticized by all countries except the United States and Canada, could

---

15. Of course, some textile-exporting countries with relatively uncompetitive industries benefit from the guaranteed market access afforded by MFA quotas, and thus strongly disagree with this assessment.

16. For apparel, the median column 2 rate is 70 percent; this would represent a tariff surcharge of about 39 percent on top of the basic tariff of 22½ percent (see Cline, chapter 3 in this volume).

lead to the desired liberalization over time if large annual growth rates are adopted. The opposition to it reflects the odd nature of the scheme: the global quota approach is essentially a devil's compact, increasing protection in the short term in return for a long-term commitment to liberalization by phasing out the quotas.[17] The rationale for this approach is that political opposition to reform is so great that industry support can only be gained by "back-loading" adjustment.[18] Although suboptimal, if the devil's compact proved enforceable, it would still be better than the present situation.

Tariffs

The basic issue in the tariff negotiations in the Uruguay Round is whether countries should opt for liberalization through a formula or through a request-offer approach. In the end, either could yield the same degree of tariff cuts, mandated by the ministers at the Montreal midterm review of the Uruguay Round to average about 30 percent (GATT 1989). For the major industrial countries, whose average tariffs already have been reduced to low levels during previous rounds of GATT negotiations, the effect of such liberalization would be quite modest.[19] Neither approach would deal effectively with the problem of tariff escalation: high tariffs would remain in some areas, providing high levels of effective protection for advanced processing activities. More extensive tariff cuts, particularly by the industrialized countries, should be sought to rectify this problem.

---

17. The US global quota approach derives from a proposal for MFA reform contained in Hufbauer and Schott (1985), which included the use of auctions to allocate quota rights in order to generate revenues to finance adjustment programs for domestic industry and workers. The US proposal in the Uruguay Round makes no reference to this self-financing adjustment feature of the proposal, and is silent on quota allocation methods.

18. Such commitments should be incorporated in domestic legislation to reduce the risk that the liberalization will be called off in future years.

19. For example, the EC proposal would cut its average tariff from 5.44 percent to 3.86 percent in incremental steps over a multiyear period. See *Financial Times*, 21 February 1990, 8.

Furthermore, although tariff cuts may be significant for some products, the impact will be minimized because the cuts will be phased in over an extended period, and there will undoubtedly be exceptions. A notable candidate for exception might be textiles, where in return for the phase-out of MFA quotas one might see less done toward cutting the existing high tariffs.

Government Procurement

In the government procurement area, substantial liberalization could be achieved by expanding the number of entities subject to the GATT Government Procurement Code. Priority in extending coverage should be given to procurement by telecommunications, transport, and electric power authorities, as well as to the provision of services. The effectiveness of code disciplines could also be improved by lowering the contract threshold above which code rules apply (as was done bilaterally between the United States and Canada in their free trade agreement).

In August 1990, the European Community increased the ante in these negotiations by offering to open much of its newly integrated internal procurement market to competitive bidding by code signatories in return for reciprocal access to foreign markets. The EC proposal also would extend code rules to state, regional, and local governments, and "to enterprises, public or private, which have special rights or privileges granted by a public authority."[20] Such an offer could prompt the Japanese to take further steps to open their procurement process to foreign suppliers, particularly in the telecommunications sector. However, coverage of procurement by subfederal entities could prove difficult for both political and constitutional reasons in the United States and other countries. If so, the Community is likely to reduce the scope of its offer to match the new opportunities offered by other GATT members in this area. Nonetheless, substantial levels of procurement in particular sectors could be opened up to competitive bidding, contributing importantly to the overall package.

---

20. For a discussion of the proposal, see *Financial Times*, 3 August 1990, 16.

THE SAFEGUARDS COMPLEX

The safeguards complex comprises escape clause and other unilateral measures deployed to provide import relief to troubled domestic industries. Talks in this area form an essential complement to the trade liberalization component of the market access negotiations; indeed, safeguards rules provide the lubricant for all the market access reforms that could be achieved in the Uruguay Round. Safeguard rules need to be flexible enough to encourage countries to stretch the limits of trade reforms to which they will commit themselves, yet rigorous enough to prevent countries from resorting to them so freely that they render the original trade concession meaningless (see Hamilton and Whalley, chapter 4 in this volume). Such concessions have less value the easier it is for countries to reverse their reforms:

□ By invoking the GATT safeguards clause;

□ By misusing other GATT exceptions that have a similar effect (namely, the balance of payments safeguards of GATT Articles XII and XVIII, and the health and safety and national security exceptions of Articles XX and XXI); and

□ By overzealous use of the antidumping and countervailing duty provisions of Article VI (particularly with regard to price undertakings and suspension agreements incorporated in the Tokyo Round codes).

GATT negotiations traditionally deal with these issues separately, even though the measures are intertwined in the import policies of GATT member countries. Weaknesses in the safeguards clause of GATT Article XIX have led to its disuse; instead countries have deployed a rash of extra–GATT controls (particularly VERs) and often have used countervailing and antidumping duties overzealously (most notably the European Community and the United States, but also more recently some developing countries).

The safeguards complex is a hydraulic system: demand for import relief "flows" toward those safeguard mechanisms that offer the least resistance. If it is tough to use Article XIX and easy to get relief through VERs or through countervailing or antidumping actions, an industry seeking relief will choose one of the latter. For this reason, negotiators need to design integrated solutions in all these areas and ensure that the results are mutually consistent.

Agreements on the safeguards complex of issues should focus both on reform of the GATT safeguards clause and on revisions to the Antidumping Code and the Subsidies Code (which governs the use of countervailing duties).

Article XIX Safeguards

Reform of GATT Article XIX should incorporate two main provisions: a requirement that safeguards be accompanied by structural adjustment measures for the industry seeking the relief, and strong constraints on the use of VERs and other so-called selective measures that discriminate among countries.

First, safeguards rules are needed to promote adjustment so that demand for import relief does not become quasi-permanent, as it has in textiles, clothing, and steel in the last few decades. A commitment to adjustment is critical to reduce the demand for protection that has remained unsated for decades. Adjustment requirements should be flexible, allowing the adjustment measures to be developed by the industry that is seeking the import relief (along with its workers, with or without the participation of government), and monitored and enforced adequately at home and by the GATT (using the proposed new trade policy review mechanism described below).

An adjustment requirement would be an added burden for countries seeking Article XIX relief and might further discourage its use, as the experience with US Section 201 shows: that law has hardly been used since an adjustment provision was added to it in the 1988 trade act. The safeguards system therefore needs to provide incentives to industries to opt for import relief through an adjustment-oriented Article XIX approach instead of seeking other GATT remedies (countervailing duty or antidumping actions) or going outside the legal statutes entirely and getting political support for negotiating VERs. To induce countries to use Article XIX, and thus to self-select for industrial adjustment, new safeguards rules need to:

□ Lower the injury standard from one requiring serious injury to a material injury test;[21]

□ Bar the imposition of quotas except for those who opt for adjustment-oriented safeguards;

□ Eliminate authorization for retaliation and bar compensation claims; and

□ Plug the loopholes in other areas of the hydraulic safeguards complex, especially the use of VERs.[22]

Second, safeguards rules should prohibit or at least severely constrain the use of selective actions. Such provisions should encompass VERs, the most common form of selective action, as well as the old-fashioned import quotas that are still in vogue in some sectors (particularly agriculture).

There are two main reasons to constrain the use of selective safeguard measures. First, selective actions initially cover less trade than do MFN actions but often become globalized as coverage is extended to all significant suppliers to prevent leakage (e.g., those affecting US imports of textiles, steel, and machine tools); trade coverage then loses its selective character even though selectivity made it easier to take the first step to impose safeguard actions. Second, selective actions usually take the form of quotas rather than tariffs.

The most desirable solution to the VER problem would be a new safeguards code that simply prohibits both exporting and importing countries from adhering to such agreements. With the support of the United States, the European Community, and Japan—the three main practitioners of the VER art—such an obligation could be easily

---

21. To GATT purists this may sound like heresy, but the choice is not between safeguards and no safeguards but between Article XIX safeguards and assorted unfair trade remedies with, at best, a material injury test.

22. VERs are dangerous because they create a "coalition for protection" between the exporters and the import-competing industries. The former reap the windfall profits generated by the artificial scarcity caused by the trade restraints; both parties benefit from a guaranteed market share. Thus, the economic incentives on both sides support the continuation of the restraints over time (as evidenced in textiles, steel, and automobiles). See Bergsten et al. (1987, chapter 9).

enforced. This step would stop the spread of VERs in new and even more pernicious forms.[23]

In the event that an outright ban on VERs is unobtainable, the preferred fallback approach should be to sharply limit their application by subjecting them to stringent multilateral surveillance under the safeguards code. This seems to roughly comport with the compromise on selectivity reportedly discussed bilaterally by the United States and the European Community at the informal ministerial meeting in April 1990 in Puerto Vallarta, Mexico.

Such reforms would yield an additional benefit: tightening rules applied to the import relief actions taken by developed countries (including extra–GATT safeguard actions) would make it easier to argue for tightening in those areas where developing countries use safeguards actions (primarily GATT Article XVIII:B, which allows developing countries to apply safeguards measures for balance of payments [BOP] purposes). Indeed, the value of developing-country participation in trade negotiations is often discounted because of doubts about the sustainability of trade reforms that—even when bound in GATT schedules—can be voided by BOP safeguards. This provision has been greatly abused over the years, generating strong concern about the problem of developing countries as free riders.[24]

As part of the overall package of safeguards reforms, GATT rules on BOP safeguards should also be revised to prevent such measures from masking sectoral protection, and to ensure that they are time-limited. If BOP safeguards remain in place for more than two years, they should be linked to structural adjustment policies adopted pursuant to Inter-

---

23. For example, the European Community is in the process of negotiating a VER to limit Japanese automobile sales in the EC market, with two added twists. First, it is seeking to supplement external border controls with internal EC border controls that monitor sales of Japanese cars *between EC member states;* second, such controls do not differentiate between cars built in Japan and cars built in Japanese subsidiaries in the Community. As Richard N. Cooper has pointed out to me, this would establish a dangerous precedent of setting quotas based on the site of corporate headquarters rather than on the production site.

24. Because of the broad-based exemptions sanctioned by Article XVIII:B, GATT discipline on the trade policies of developing countries is quite weak and prone to abuse. Although such safeguards are supposed to be temporary, most controls notified under Article XVIII have been in place for more than 10 years.

national Monetary Fund and/or World Bank programs. Developed countries should go further and waive the right to invoke Article XII; this would provide useful insurance against the possible invocation of Article XII by developed countries that run current account deficits.[25]

Antidumping, Subsidies, and Countervailing Duties

Under the GATT, antidumping and countervailing duties (CVDs) are legitimate measures that countries can apply unilaterally to offset the injurious effects of imports benefiting from unfair trade practices. However, GATT rules governing these measures have not been able to keep up with the changing and increasingly complex nature of international production and trade. As a result, both exporting and importing nations have been able to exploit vague GATT rules to protect national firms through the overzealous use of subsidies as well as of antidumping and CVD actions.

The two areas are interrelated: CVD cases are brought against countries that grant subsidies; those same subsidies can also cause price discrimination between export goods and those sold in the home market, and thus trigger dumping complaints; industries often "forum shop" between the two remedies when deciding how to pursue import relief. Such linkages underscore the need in the Uruguay Round to develop complementary reforms in rules on the application of antidumping and CVD actions, as was done in the Tokyo Round.

The current negotiations on subsidies and CVDs are essentially working toward the same trade-off as in the Tokyo Round: greater multilateral discipline on trade-distorting subsidies by all countries, in return for greater discipline on the use of CVDs (primarily by the United States). Unlike the Tokyo Round code, however, the Uruguay Round results will have to impose strong discipline on the use of domestic subsidies such as regional aids (in addition to improvements

---

25. For example, waiver of Article XII would preclude consideration by the United States of an import surcharge to deal with its twin deficits, as was done in 1971 and was again actively debated in Congress as recently as 1984–85.

in existing code obligations on export subsidies), to convince Congress to make further changes in the US CVD law.[26]

An accord on subsidies and CVDs should build on the draft proposals put forward by Michael Cartland, the chairman of the Subsidies Negotiating Group. In particular, the agreement should expand the scope of subsidies prohibited by the GATT,[27] introduce the concept of nonactionable subsidies for a limited number of practices (such as support of precompetitive research and development) that are deemed *a priori* to be noninjurious, and revise CVD rules by, among other things, adding a *de minimis* test and barring recourse to price undertakings. In addition, as Gary Clyde Hufbauer recommends in chapter 5 of this volume, code disciplines should be extended to subfederal and parastatal entities.

In contrast, the antidumping negotiations pose a new trade-off: tighter controls on the "old" rules relating to the determination of dumping in return for new rules to protect against the circumvention of antidumping duties. The former would address concerns relating primarily to the administration of US and EC antidumping laws, particularly the procedures that result in the calculation of high antidumping duties. The latter would deal with the problem of exporters attempting to avoid antidumping duties by means of slight product alterations or by shipping components of the dumped product for minor assembly ("screwdriver") operations in the importing country or a third country.

Reforms of the GATT Antidumping Code should impose tighter criteria for the calculation of dumping (covering the range of adjustments permitted to be made to price data in comparing export and home-market prices) and bar the use of price undertakings (i.e., minimum price commitments) to resolve antidumping cases. As Patrick A. Messerlin argues in chapter 6 of this volume, such undertakings can

---

26. In the Tokyo Round, the main US concession was the incorporation of an injury test in the US CVD law.

27. In this area, code revisions should include, *inter alia,* prohibitions on mixed credit subsidies as well as subsidies contingent on export performance or domestic sourcing. Coverage of the latter would have the added benefit of constraining the use of subsidies to distort investment flows, and thus would reinforce the provisions of a prospective agreement on trade-related investment measures (see below).

generate substantial anticompetitive effects. He cites several examples where industries have sought to reduce price competition in the domestic market by pursuing antidumping actions to coerce foreign suppliers to maintain minimum import prices. In the absence of strict antitrust regulations, such practices can promote soft cartels in the protected market.

New provisions also should be added to the code relating to the enforcement of dumping duties, so that unfairly traded products cannot avoid penalty duties. However, safeguards should be added to ensure that such "anticircumvention" provisions—much like price undertakings—do not encourage "soft" cartels.

Messerlin strongly opposes the adoption of anticircumvention rules, on the grounds that they reinforce antidumping measures that are often used by firms to cartelize the importing market. However, failure to include such provisions would reduce the prospects for other, more desirable changes in the Antidumping Code, and would likely result in any event in the proliferation of unilateral actions to stop the circumvention of antidumping duties.

Both Hufbauer and Messerlin offer some suggestions on how to reform the rules on CVD and antidumping actions, or at least discourage the overzealous use of those provisions. The hard part is to tighten the rules and limit the use of VERs at the same time. The hydraulic nature of the safeguards complex exacerbates this task: the easier it is to use selective actions on the safeguards side, the easier it is to tighten up the rules in antidumping, and vice versa.

Given the concern cited by Messerlin about the use of antidumping actions to promote soft cartels, the preferred solution would be to allow more flexibility to use selective safeguards (which, if covered by a new safeguards code, would be subject to multilateral surveillance, would be sharply time-limited, and would require adjustment) rather than allow more flexibility in the administration of antidumping rules. This trade-off would tend to limit the duration of import relief and thus lessen the risk that protection would promote the cartelization of the import-competing industry.

Such results would improve the Antidumping Code at the margin, but would not resolve the problem of how to adapt national antidumping disciplines to multinational corporations, where it is hard to discern the scope of arm's-length transactions. To deal with this problem,

GATT rules should begin to focus more on antitrust considerations than on the discriminatory pricing issues of GATT antidumping rules. This idea was introduced in the US–Japan Structural Impediments Initiative (SII) but is clearly beyond the pale of the Uruguay Round.

NEW ISSUES AND DISPUTE SETTLEMENT

The new issues (services, investment, and intellectual property) and dispute settlement go hand in glove. Countries find it hard to agree to new rules if they perceive that the rules will not be enforced. A stronger dispute settlement mechanism is therefore needed to gain credibility and acceptance for stronger rules, in old and new areas alike. Similarly, stronger GATT rules facilitate acceptance of stronger multilateral dispute settlement; both, in turn, lessen the scope for unilateral actions taken to enforce national rights under the trading rules.

A package of agreements involving the new issues and dispute settlement will require three difficult trade-offs. First, solutions to long-standing problems in such "traditional" trade areas as agriculture and textiles will have to be offered in exchange for rules in the new areas of services, investment, and intellectual property. Many developing countries (particularly those in the Cairns Group) will likely abstain from agreements in areas previously not subject to GATT discipline if developed countries refuse to liberalize merchandise trade barriers affecting their primary export interests.

The second trade-off is between the strength of the new rules and the breadth of their application. Weaker rules will promote broader membership, but can they provide a basis for effective multilateral discipline? The experience of the past decade, in which vague rules on agricultural subsidies contributed to numerous trade disputes that could not be resolved by expert panels, suggests that weak rules can actually have perverse effects, contributing to a growing dissatisfaction with the efficacy of both GATT discipline and GATT dispute settlement procedures.

Stronger rules, by comparison, probably would limit participation in the new agreements. Either nonsignatories would have to be accorded full rights under the agreements, even though they assume no obligations, or the pacts would have to be applied only to signatories, on a conditional MFN basis. In the elaboration of trading rules, the conditional MFN principle is often preferable, as it avoids the free-rider and foot-dragger problems and yields stronger GATT rights and obligations.[28]

The third trade-off involves the issue of cross-retaliation in dispute settlement cases: the right to retaliate against unfair practices applying to both goods and services, by restricting either the goods or the services of the offending country, would be granted in exchange for constraints on unilateral actions. Cross-retaliation would strengthen the GATT dispute settlement system and offers a strong argument to tighten up on unilateral measures. Recognition of this principle implies acceptance of the new issues as part of the GATT system, a point on which most GATT members have yet to agree.[29]

Cross-retaliation is regarded by some countries as a means for the United States to threaten actions against their merchandise exports if they do not open their services markets to US participants. However, it could also lead countries to press for further liberalization of US service sectors, especially financial services, where the Glass-Steagall and McFadden acts limit the scope of banking activity in the US market, and in transportation, where foreign competition is limited by a host of trucking, maritime, and air transport laws.

Because the Uruguay Round marks the first time that trade negotiations have focused on these issues, a key objective of the negotiations in each case is to establish multilateral trading rules to discipline international transactions, and to promote liberalization of trade barriers over time. These rules should take the form of codes of conduct, open to all GATT members but applying only to signatories (as with the Tokyo Round codes). Agreements in the new issue areas are important for three reasons.

First, the rules incorporated in the prospective framework codes establish a "standstill" commitment: a baseline from which future

---

28. For a discussion of these problems and arguments favoring the conditional MFN approach, see Hufbauer and Schott (1985).

29. However, such a step is likely to occur either at the end of the Uruguay Round or with the graduation of the GATT into a full-fledged World Trade Organization (see below).

policy must evolve in a nondiscriminatory and liberalizing direction. This standstill commitment is critical, as it was in the US–Canada Free Trade Agreement, because it removes an important cause of uncertainty that can act as a potent trade barrier. That argument was made very clearly in the US–Canada case; it applies at least as strongly in a multilateral context. Given such a commitment, even if the Uruguay Round agreements focused primarily on rulemaking, with limited liberalization of specific barriers initially, the standstill result would be quite important.

Second, all three accords should promote more-open investment policies. The certainty created by a standstill agreement would spur investment as well as trade; indeed, that is why countries interested in foreign investment (such as Mexico) have been pursuing reforms unilaterally in the new issue areas. Investment reforms would apply obviously to an agreement on trade-related investment measures, but also to services, because cross-border investment is critical to the provision of many services. In addition, such reforms are important for negotiations on intellectual property (especially for developing countries), since technology transfer is effected primarily through foreign direct investment.

Interestingly, the United States could become the exception to the trend toward welcoming foreign investment, if Congress applies new restrictions on foreign direct investment in the United States. Although little action has been taken to date,[30] continued pressure for such restrictions provides all the more reason for GATT members to support a new accord on trade-related investment measures that commits the United States to maintain its present open policy toward foreign investment.

Finally, agreements in the new areas are important because they cover the trade problems faced by many sunrise industries. The credibility of the GATT in the 1990s depends on addressing the problems of these sectors more prominently (especially in the subsidies area, as well as in the new issue areas). New rules on services need to

---

30. The Exon-Florio amendment to the 1988 US Omnibus Trade and Competitiveness Act relating to national security concerns is one of the few new constraints on foreign direct investment in the United States, and so far that law has been applied only as a light screening mechanism (see Graham and Krugman 1989).

promote the further development of, and ensure open access to, global financial and information networks essential for the conduct of world trade. New rules on investment need to ensure that investment controls do not substitute for trade protection of high-technology industries. And new rules on intellectual property need to be crafted to promote innovation as well as the diffusion of new technologies in both developed and developing countries.

SERVICES

A General Agreement on Trade in Services (GATS) should meet two objectives. First, it should establish a framework of rights and obligations to guide the formulation of national laws, policies, and regulations affecting services, and to ensure that foreign suppliers have access to markets and receive national treatment. The framework should also include dispute settlement provisions, preferably as part of the GATT mechanism, to permit cross-sector linkage between goods and services. Second, the GATS should liberalize trade through an evolutionary process, sector by sector, starting from the baseline of existing policies (see Hindley, chapter 7 in this volume).

To accommodate special conditions that apply in specific service industries, the GATS framework should be supplemented by sectoral annotations elaborating how the principles enunciated in the framework should be interpreted for particular industries. Such provisions will need to be quite detailed with regard to financial services and telecommunications. For example, inclusion of financial services will require a prudential safeguard clause to ensure that national regulators are not inhibited from imposing controls to protect the integrity of the financial system, and some provision to ensure that dispute panels have sufficient financial expertise to judge cases.

The coverage of the GATS should be as comprehensive as possible. The principle set forth in the Houston summit declaration that "no sector should be excluded from the GATS a priori" should be strengthened. Any exceptions from GATS rules should take the form of time-limited reservations rather than permanent exemptions. GATS rules should apply to all services except those specifically named in an annex listing industries for which countries reserve the right temporarily to maintain practices that discriminate against foreign service providers.

The rationale for a no-exemptions policy is to avoid a process in which the exclusion by one country of one industry triggers comparable withdrawals by other countries, thus reducing the effective coverage of the GATS. Problems in specific industries, particularly transportation services, should be handled by specific GATS provisions,[31] sectoral annotations, and time-limited reservations, recognizing that the difference between a long-term reservation and an exemption is fuzzy indeed.

Over time, the GATS should promote significant liberalization of barriers to services trade through request-offer negotiations. Such a process is unlikely to yield a large harvest in the Uruguay Round, however, since the December 1990 deadline means that time is running short for the fashioning of sweeping trade-offs. However, the threat by the Community and the United States to invoke the nonapplication provision—by which signatories can deny the rights of the agreement to other countries at the time of their accession—could be used to coerce reluctant trading partners to lower barriers to their service markets on an ad hoc basis. This tactic was used successfully during the Tokyo Round to ensure that Japan committed itself to opening its procurement market to foreign competition.

INVESTMENT

The Uruguay Round negotiations on trade-related investment measures (TRIMs) should reinforce the growing trend in developed and developing countries toward more-open investment policies. New GATT obligations would help lock in reforms in countries that already have reduced investment protectionism, encourage further liberalization, and protect against the erection of new barriers. This last point is

---

31. Such provisions could be drafted to effectively exempt a sector from GATS rules. Although bending the no-exemption policy, it may be the only feasible way to deal, for example, with the threat by the US maritime industry to scuttle US participation in the entire round (as it threatened to scuttle the free trade agreement with Canada, with the result that all transport services were excluded from that agreement).

particularly important at a time when congressional concerns about the rapid buildup of foreign direct investment in the United States threaten to divert the United States from its traditionally open investment policy (Graham and Krugman 1989).

That said, a TRIMs accord would only be a first step toward more effective multilateral discipline on investment policies. As noted by Edward M. Graham and Paul R. Krugman in chapter 8 of this volume, the TRIMs accord is unlikely to deal with the basic issue of right of establishment. In addition, the problem of investment incentives has been delegated to the subsidies negotiations, where new discipline will be difficult to attain. Nonetheless, a TRIMs agreement would open the door to future discussions within the GATT and would achieve some important progress in limiting distortions caused by local-content and export performance requirements (which require investors to incorporate a fixed value of domestic components in their final products, and to export a fixed share of their production, respectively).

For these reasons, it is important that the TRIMs accord contain substantive rules, even if they keep some developing countries from joining right away. The United States, the European Community, and Japan, which together are both home and host to the greater part of the world stock of foreign direct investment, are already committed to a TRIMs accord; they comprise the critical mass of participants needed to make the agreement work. Additional signatories from the newly industrializing countries (for example, Korea and Mexico) are likely. The agreement should be open-ended, however, so that new signatories may be added in the future, when they decide to take on the code obligations.

Together, this group of countries should be able to agree on the prohibition of at least the first six types of TRIMs identified by Graham and Krugman, namely, local-content, export performance, local manufacturing, and trade-balancing requirements, as well as production mandates and foreign-exchange restrictions. In addition, the accord should include a commitment to continue GATT negotiations on other investment issues after the conclusion of the Uruguay Round.

The presence of distortions caused by existing TRIMs may require that such measures be phased out in incremental steps. For example, the prohibition of new performance requirements would put existing subsidiaries of multinational firms, which have previously agreed to TRIMs as a condition of establishment, at a disadvantage relative to new entrants. The preferred solution would be to set a firm date for the phase-out of existing TRIMs, thus constraining and eventually eliminating such requirements for all investors. An incremental process would have the added benefit of allowing differential treatment for developing countries, which could facilitate their participation in the agreement.

INTELLECTUAL PROPERTY

The negotiations on trade-related intellectual property rights (TRIPs) is the one area of the Uruguay Round in which increasing protection is the solution, not the problem. It is also the area most closely associated with the needs of sunrise industries, and thus is critical to the overall success of the Uruguay Round package.

The TRIPs negotiations have wrestled over the classic problem of intellectual property rights: how to balance the objective of promoting innovation with that of facilitating the diffusion of technology. As Keith E. Maskus explains in chapter 9 of this volume, developed countries generally seek strong protection of intellectual property to safeguard the competitiveness of their rightsholders (especially high-technology firms). Developing countries argue that strong rules would limit their ability to persuade rightsholders to transfer technology to their economies.[32] These differing views have generated the most prominent North-South confrontation of the round.

However, weak intellectual property protection in developing countries could actually divert technology transfer. Such transfers are most likely to be effected through foreign direct investment, which could be inhibited rather than promoted by national intellectual property regulations that require compulsory licensing of patents or that implicitly condone the misappropriation of technology through lax enforcement.

New GATT rights and obligations are needed to supplement existing international treaties, administered primarily under the World Intellectual Property Organization (WIPO). Strong GATT rules are needed to improve upon the weak standards, as well as limited enforcement, of

---

32. Some countries promote the appropriation of foreign technologies through compulsory licensing; requirements to "work" patents (which force patentholders to manufacture locally rather than import to maintain exclusive right to the patent); and administrative delays, which increase the risk of misappropriation of intellectual property and reduce the effective period of protection.

the WIPO conventions. The two bodies should work together to improve standards for the protection of intellectual property, so that new GATT disciplines reinforce the objectives of the WIPO conventions.[33]

GATT rules should provide protection against two basic problems: commercial counterfeiting (involving the sale of goods with false trademarks) and the misappropriation of technology (involving both patent and copyright infringement). The latter problem is particularly significant, given the growing importance of high-technology products in international trade.

First, the TRIPs accord should contain provisions that embody nondiscrimination and national treatment principles to guide the formulation and implementation of national intellectual property policies. These provisions should establish a framework of rights and obligations similar to codes in the other new issue areas.

Second, a GATT agreement on TRIPs should develop minimum standards and enforcement procedures to bolster protection of patents, copyrights, trademarks, and trade secrets. GATT rules should follow the example of many national laws and regulations by extending intellectual property protection to new areas (e.g., patents for biotechnology products and processes, and copyright protection for software), to areas now inadequately protected (e.g., process patents for pharmaceuticals), and to *sui generis* areas such as semiconductor chip mask designs.

In the area of patents, a standard term of effective duration dating from the time the patent was first granted (say, 20 years) should be accepted. Compulsory licensing of patents should be discouraged; in those limited cases in which it would be allowed, countries should not prevent the rightholder from receiving full value for the license. Copyright protection should be extended to computer software and databases, and should be crafted to extend to new forms of expression that may result from technological developments. Trademark protec-

---

33. For example, the European Community has suggested that the GATT agreement on TRIPs commit its members to comply with the Paris and Berne conventions (relating to patents and copyrights), even if they are not signatories to those treaties. See *International Trade Reporter*, 4 April 1990, 478.

tion should derive from use or registration and be renewable indefinitely.

Third, enforcement procedures should apply to domestic commerce as well as international trade, since lack of enforcement in the home market could easily allow infringement of intellectual property rights. To be sure, not all developing countries now have the capacity to implement controls within their home markets, but they should at least intercept trade in counterfeit goods at the border and commit themselves to broader enforcement measures over time.

Overall, a GATT agreement on TRIPs should establish strong rules and enforcement procedures, even if it means losing some potential member countries. Indeed, the GATT talks were established expressly to broaden the scope of international obligations that could not be agreed elsewhere; watering down the provisions to attract broad membership would defeat that purpose. It follows that proposals to incorporate a TRIPs accord into the GATT by amendment rather than as a code of conduct are less likely to achieve the necessary rigor because of the need to accommodate the views of the two-thirds of the GATT membership needed to approve amendments.

A conditional MFN code, on the other hand, could achieve both strong discipline and relatively extensive membership. Although countries could not be compelled to participate in the accord, the likelihood that some countries would continue to apply unilateral pressure (for example, the United States via Section 301) when problems arise with nonsignatories could provide a powerful incentive to join. The participation of developing countries could be further encouraged by code provisions that recognize their technical problems regarding enforcement and allow them to continue certain practices (e.g., compulsory licensing) under limited conditions.

DISPUTE SETTLEMENT

Weak and vague trading rules are a prime cause of international trade disputes and make it difficult for the multilateral dispute settlement process to function effectively. The bulk of the proposed Uruguay Round package detailed thus far is designed to strengthen GATT rules;

strong rules reduce the scope for dispute and thus facilitate acceptance of stronger GATT dispute settlement procedures.

Reform of the GATT dispute settlement process should encourage the use of, and compliance with, multilateral procedures, and thus lessen the need for GATT members to resort to unilateral trade actions. In particular, the rulings of expert panels convened to resolve disputes need to carry greater weight. To that end, the Uruguay Round negotiations need to resolve three main problems:

□ How to obtain acceptance of panel findings in a timely fashion;

□ How to promote expeditious compliance with GATT rulings; and

□ How to limit the use of unilateral measures.

The three are interrelated and involve essentially the enforcement of national rights under multilateral trade agreements. The perceived slowness of the GATT process (partly remedied by interim reforms agreed at the Montreal midterm review),[34] the ability of disputants to block the consensus needed for the GATT to approve panel findings and authorize retaliation, and the difficulty in securing compliance with GATT rulings have generated sharp doubts regarding the efficacy of the multilateral process and encouraged the use of unilateral measures (whether by stretching the existing rules on unfair trade practices, going outside the rules to negotiate VERs, or invoking national statutes such as US Section 301).

The first two problems should be dealt with through procedural reforms of the GATT dispute settlement process that expedite the process and automatically allow affected countries to retaliate if GATT recommendations are not implemented. Reforms should establish an automatic right to convene a panel on any GATT–related issue, provide for the expeditious formation of the panel, and make panel rulings binding, subject to review by a new appellate tribunal (see the discussion of these issues by Robert E. Hudec in chapter 10 of this

---

34. At that time, countries agreed on an interim basis to expedite, among other things, the formation of panels and to set strict time limits for panel deliberations, with final reports normally due within six months. For the full text of this agreement, see GATT (1989, 24–31).

volume). Panel rulings should include recommendations on the maximum period to be allowed for compliance, after which affected countries could retaliate without further multilateral authorization.

Implementation of these reforms would promote a convergence between the GATT process and US Section 301 cases. Under the 1988 trade act, the US Trade Representative can defer action under Section 301 if the GATT rules that US rights have not been impaired. Speedier processing of cases, binding acceptance of panel findings, and a fixed period for compliance should allow the United States to take Section 301 cases to the GATT, and avoid the need to make unilateral determinations on foreign trade practices. If countries do not abide by GATT decisions, the United States would then be authorized by the GATT to invoke retaliatory measures using Section 301 authority.

For most cases, reform of GATT dispute settlement procedures would allow the United States to continue to use Section 301 in conformity with its GATT obligations (since US domestic and GATT procedures would proceed in tandem). However, certain cases filed under Section 301, notably those involving alleged "unreasonable" practices by foreign governments, could cover practices that US law deems actionable (that is, subject to US retaliation) even though they are not censured by the GATT. In such situations, the approach suggested by Hudec seems appropriate and could be implemented through two changes in US law: to make retaliation discretionary in Section 301 cases involving "unreasonable" measures, and to require that Section 301 retaliation be applied only after the President has taken account of "both international obligations and the outcome of GATT dispute settlement proceedings."

In sum, reform of GATT dispute settlement procedures need not require the renunciation of, or even major changes in, Section 301. The improved multilateral process should make resort to unilateral actions unnecessary, and turn Section 301 into a procedure for channeling US complaints to the GATT and implementing multilaterally authorized retaliation.

INSTITUTIONAL ISSUES

The third part of the Uruguay Round package involves institutional issues other than dispute settlement. Three issues merit particular mention: the trade policy review mechanism (TPRM), proposals for a new World Trade Organization (WTO), and relations among the GATT, the International Monetary Fund (IMF), and the World Bank.

TRADE POLICY REVIEW MECHANISM

The Montreal midterm review authorized the GATT Secretariat to inaugurate, on an interim basis, periodic reviews of the trade policies of member countries to provide greater transparency of national laws and practices and "to contribute to improved adherence. . . to GATT rules, disciplines and commitments" (GATT 1989, 33). By the end of 1990, reviews of the policies of all the major industrialized nations and a few developing countries will have been held; these initial reviews, however, have pointed out a number of problems with this fledgling mechanism, and the need for a stronger and more permanent TPRM.

First, the quality of the information generated by TPRM reviews needs to be upgraded. The reports are more narrative than analytical (partly because countries avoid self-incrimination), and the staff of the GATT is much too small to do the task; as a result, the TPRM process does not provide the incisive analysis needed to provide a good public airing of national trade policies. The TPRM staff should supplement their reliance on governmental reports with information and analysis generated by nongovernmental bodies, including research institutions.[35]

Second, the TPRM needs to deal with policy development as well as review of existing measures, as the IMF and the OECD do in their national economic reviews. Under its interim mandate, the TPRM process is limited to a review of policies in place because it is charged solely to ensure conformity of national policies with GATT rules. But to promote continued conformity as trade policies evolve also should be an important function for the TPRM. To do that, the TPRM would have to be associated with domestic surveillance bodies in each country (perhaps along the lines of the Australian Industries Commis-

---

35. Indeed, a good model for a TPRM report would be the comprehensive analysis of US trade protection in Hufbauer, Berliner, and Elliott (1986).

sion) that could monitor policy developments at home and link up with the GATT review. In particular, a domestic surveillance body could serve three important purposes:

☐ It could provide independent and objective analysis of existing trade measures and advise on the formulation of new policies;

☐ It could promote adjustment by educating the public on the costs of protection; and

☐ It could monitor domestic adjustment programs established pursuant to safeguards actions, and work with the TPRM or the GATT safeguards code committee to ensure that GATT commitments are being followed.

This last point is an item for the post–Uruguay Round agenda, but as a prerequisite, the Uruguay Round package should reinforce the TPRM so that it can take on more important tasks in the future.

A WORLD TRADE ORGANIZATION

The GATT was originally conceived as an interim trade arrangement to be superseded by the International Trade Organization (ITO), with its comprehensive multilateral charter of rights and obligations negotiated immediately after World War II. However, the ITO charter was never ratified, and the GATT has effectively served in its place, despite its limited institutional structure.[36]

Both the European Community and Canada have put forward proposals for a new World Trade Organization (WTO), essentially based on the model described by John H. Jackson (1990). As proposed, the WTO would not be a substitute for the GATT, but rather an institutional reinforcement for it. Unlike the ITO, the proposed WTO would not involve substantive trade obligations; rather it would deal

---

36. Interestingly, the Uruguay Round agenda encompasses many of the issues covered by the ITO but left out of the GATT (e.g., services and investment), as well as many of the issues dealt with inadequately in both the ITO and the GATT (e.g., BOP safeguards and agriculture). See Schott (1990b) and Diebold (1952).

with the legal issues involved in restructuring the GATT into a membership organization, strengthening the secretariat, removing the provisional character of some GATT obligations, and various administrative reforms.

Although these proposals have been put forward to emphasize the commitment to strengthening the GATT, they do not substitute for solutions to the substantive trade problems that have weakened the GATT system far more than its institutional shortcomings. For this reason, a WTO will only make sense if the Uruguay Round achieves major new trade reforms, which then would need to be incorporated in a revised GATT framework.[37] Extensive consideration of such proposals during the round could deflect attention away from substantive tasks, and thus should be deferred until all the key Uruguay Round bargains have been struck.

RELATIONS AMONG THE BRETTON WOODS INSTITUTIONS

The subject of GATT–IMF–World Bank relations has received the least amount of attention of the items on the agenda of the Functioning of the GATT System (FOGS) negotiating group. Essentially, the negotiating objective in this area is to ensure the consistency and compatibility of the three organizations in their respective efforts on trade, monetary, and development issues. Important linkages exist among these issues that can complicate international economic management and generate pressures for trade protection.[38]

For both bureaucratic and substantive reasons, neither national governments nor international institutions adequately deal at present with the problems created by the overlap of macroeconomic and trade policies. Currency imbalances—both overvaluation and undervaluation—generate pressure for trade protection (see Bergsten and Williamson 1983). In turn, trade barriers can impede the effectiveness of

---

37. This point is particularly relevant to the prospective agreements in the new issue areas, which (unlike the Tokyo Round codes) do not elaborate or interpret existing GATT provisions.

38. Some refer to these as trade-finance linkages, although the scope of the subject matter really deserves the broader heading of macro-micro linkages.

exchange rate changes in promoting the macroeconomic adjustments necessary to correct trade imbalances (see Bhagwati 1989). Among developing countries, debt problems often prompt the imposition of new trade controls.

The FOGS group clearly cannot resolve these vital but complex issues by the December deadline for the round. Yet GATT members should continue to explore whether cooperative efforts among the international institutions would be desirable to promote better coordination of macro- and microeconomic policies in the member countries. To this end, the Uruguay Round package should include a declaration designed to expand the dialogue among the international institutions after the Uruguay Round. With the reforms of the TPRM and a better GATT institutional structure, one could then see the GATT becoming a full and desired partner in discussions with the IMF and the World Bank.

What Is in the Package for the Key Trading Countries?

Acceptance and ratification of the Uruguay Round package will require that each member country assess whether the overall results are in its best interests. Traditionally, countries have judged GATT negotiations from a mercantilist perspective, balancing their own concessions against those of other countries. However, as academics are anxious to emphasize, the results of the round can also be calculated in broader economic welfare terms, where a country's own trade concessions often are the most beneficial part of the package for its domestic economy. This section attempts to bridge the semantic gap between mercantilists and academic economists. Instead of referring to concessions and gains, it summarizes the national objectives of the major players in the round and the changes that would be required in their current policies to achieve them.

The United States, as the *demandeur* of the round, has multiple objectives involving the main areas of the Uruguay Round package. Among the market access issues, the key objectives are agricultural reforms, new disciplines on subsidies and antidumping policies, and more-open public procurement practices. In the new issues, agreements on services, intellectual property, and investment are needed, along with improved dispute settlement procedures. In addition, progress needs to be made to control the GATT's free-rider problem, particularly with respect to the newly industrializing countries (NICs), which has contributed to the GATT's credibility problem.

The changes required of the United States would be (first and most difficult) the phase-out of textile and apparel quotas (but probably without significant tariff cuts in those sectors); circumscription of the use of Section 301, antidumping practices, and VERs; agricultural reforms; and tariff cuts. On balance, such results should be considered in the US interest, even in mercantilist negotiating terms.

The EC list of objectives is a little shorter, which may tend to explain the reticence of EC negotiators. For the Community, the objectives are new rules on services (especially financial services) and intellectual property rights; acceptance of the principle of selective application of safeguards measures; progress on institutional issues, including dispute settlement reforms that place limits on US Section 301; and progress on the broader GATT reform issues (including establishment of a new multilateral trade organization) discussed by Jackson in chapter 11 of this volume.[39] The EC objectives focus mainly on rulemaking rather than liberalization, and suggest a willingness to weaken the rules as necessary to encourage broad-based support for agreements in new areas.

The changes required for the Community are agricultural reforms, including much larger subsidy cuts than the EC negotiators have been willing to agree to so far; the phase-out of MFA quotas; circumscription of their use of safeguards and antidumping measures; and tariff cuts. These are quite extensive changes, especially in comparison with the Community's more limited rulemaking objectives, and explain in part the problem in getting the Community to accept broad reforms in agriculture and textiles.

What should balance the equation for the Community, and thus prompt acceptance of substantive reforms in these sensitive areas, is

---

39. A traditional EC goal, reform of rules on countervailing duties, has been less actively pursued because of a growing ambivalence toward subsidy reforms: the granting of regional aids and other adjustment subsidies to the Mediterranean members of the Community pursuant to the 1992 process runs directly counter to efforts in the GATT to discipline the use of such subsidies.

the importance of maintaining a strong GATT system for both economic and political reasons. As the United States did in the earlier postwar period, the Community needs to regard GATT concessions as an investment in the economic health and political stability of its friends and neighbors. This is important for both the overall US–EC relationship and for EC relations with the Eastern European countries that are now turning to the GATT to help them restructure their economies.

The paucity of Japanese objectives is even more suggestive of the problems in putting a Uruguay Round package together. The Japanese objectives are decidedly narrower than the Community's: reform of antidumping rules and limits on US Section 301, the latter as part of a strengthened multilateral dispute settlement process; and new rules on services, investment, and intellectual property.

Interestingly, Japan is one of the main beneficiaries of a strong multilateral trading system and should contribute much more in terms of both concessions and leadership in crafting solutions to problems in such areas as safeguards and antidumping. Yet despite the frequent complaints about barriers to entry in the Japanese market, the list of formal government trade barriers is quite limited. As a result, little is being asked of Japan in the round: some tariff cuts; agricultural reforms, particularly with regard to rice; and a further opening of its government procurement market. This, of course, raises the question of whether the GATT agenda should be expanded to focus on structural impediments issues after the Uruguay Round, including competition policy and barriers to foreign investment.

The interests of the developing countries are harder to summarize. It is too simplistic to treat all the developing countries as a single homogeneous group; for example, the NICs stand to both reap more gains from and provide more concessions in the round, whereas relatively few demands will be placed on the least developed countries. Overall, however, there are a number of important gains for developing countries, the most important of which derive from agricultural and textile and apparel liberalization in the industrial countries.[40] Develop-

---

40. In some cases those developing countries that likely would lose export market share if there is liberalization of textile and apparel quotas would be the same ones that should increase exports as a result of agricultural liberalization, and vice versa. For example,

ing countries would also benefit from stronger GATT dispute settlement procedures, tariff cuts, liberalization of trade in tropical products, tighter standards for the determination of dumping, and a broader, more effective safeguards code that is based on the nondiscrimination principle and that disciplines VERs.

The changes required of the developing countries are acceptance of rulemaking in the new areas (perhaps at first without new liberalization), liberalization of their import restrictions on textiles, and constraints on their use of BOP safeguards. The burden posed by such changes is not onerous, except in the textiles sector (where it would be commensurate with the adjustment required by the developed countries in phasing out MFA quotas). For example, in the new areas many NICs such as Korea do not have major problems with adopting new rules on investment and intellectual property, provided those rules are (as is likely) compatible with changes in national laws and regulations instituted during the past decade. Similarly, reform of BOP safeguards would only limit the abuse of Article XVIII:B; it would not forbid appropriate recourse to such temporary protection. Thus, for most developing countries the practical effect of such changes would be modest, requiring them simply to bind in the GATT reforms taken in recent years.

In sum, the prospective bargain for the developing countries is heavily weighted in favor of supporting a big package. Concerns that were once raised about a North-South confrontation now seem quite exaggerated. Indeed, developing countries should be more concerned about the possible failure of the developed countries to deliver a big package of agreements, with its consequent adverse implications for the future of the multilateral trading system.

Conclusions

The Uruguay Round is the most comprehensive and complex negotiation ever undertaken in the GATT. Its success would reinvigorate the multilateral trading system, yielding both political and economic

---

Korea would gain from textile liberalization in return for more opening of its market for agricultural imports.

benefits for GATT member countries and enabling the GATT to keep pace with rapidly changing developments in international trade.

The concluding stages of the round come at a critical time. The end of the Cold War has eliminated the "security blanket" that linked the Western countries together throughout the postwar period and muted economic disputes in deference to shared security interests. The risk of trade confrontation thus becomes greater, underscoring the need for greater cooperation on trade and other economic policies to prevent such conflicts from adversely affecting political relationships. A stronger GATT system would help deflect those pressures and thus contribute to more harmonious international relations.

THE ALMOST-ALL-OR-NOTHING APPROACH

The task before the GATT negotiators is daunting, but not insurmountable. Following an "almost-all-or-nothing" approach, negotiators still could achieve a big package of agreements, along the lines presented in this study, by the December 1990 deadline, or by early in 1991. However, they should not sacrifice content for the sake of achieving results within that time frame; it would be better to extend the round than to accept inadequate agreements. Indeed, the press of both economic and political events (e.g., the threat of recession in the United States, the Iraqi crisis, the German election) may necessitate an extension into 1991 or even beyond.

The success of the Uruguay Round depends on achieving a big package of agreements, for three main reasons:

☐ A big package would provide the scope for the broadest range of trade-offs among issues, which in turn could generate extensive reform of existing trading rules, the development of rules in new areas, and significant liberalization of trade barriers;

☐ A big package would demonstrate that the multilateral process is a viable and preferable alternative to the unilateral trade actions and bilateral and regional trading arrangements that the United States and the European Community among others have increasingly undertaken in the past decade; and

☐ A big package would "modernize" the GATT by addressing the concerns of the sunrise industries, the dynamic new players in world trade, particularly with regard to protection of intellectual property, subsidies for research and development, and issues of antidumping and competition policy. Although the Uruguay Round package is likely to only scratch the surface in some of these areas, positive results would provide the basis for more extensive negotiations in the future.

The United States and the European Community hold the key to negotiating a big package of agreements. Essentially, the success of the round depends on their willingness to liberalize their long-standing barriers in agriculture and in textiles and apparel that have proved immune to reform in past negotiations. To do so, they will first have to resolve their own differences, particularly regarding agricultural reforms, Section 301, and industrial subsidies.

If the United States and the Community take the lead, other countries will follow and commit themselves to the expansion and extension of GATT disciplines across the board (including in the contentious area of intellectual property). If instead they opt for more modest changes, the results of the round in other areas will be limited as well. Agriculture and textiles are thus the linchpins of the Uruguay Round package. Modest results in these areas mean a small Uruguay Round package overall.

The GATT system could be seriously weakened if the Uruguay Round achieves only a small package of agreements. Such a result would provide little inducement for countries to substantially reform existing discriminatory practices in "old" and "new" trade areas alike. As a result, a small package would confirm the status quo: a growing restiveness on the part of the United States and the Community with present multilateral trading rules, leading them toward a further use of unilateral trade actions and an elaboration of bilateral and regional trading arrangements.

COMPLETING THE URUGUAY ROUND

The preceding sections have laid out an ambitious array of agreements that could be crafted in the concluding stages of the Uruguay Round.

Together they would fulfill the mandate of the Houston summit declaration "to achieve far-reaching, substantial results in all areas of the Uruguay Round." The ability of GATT negotiators to achieve this package of agreements is thus a good standard for judging the success of the round.

In the area of trade liberalization, the package should include:

☐ A 50 percent reduction in agricultural protection from 1988 levels— both export and domestic subsidies—as well as the conversion of border measures to tariffs or tariff rate quotas;

☐ A firm commitment to phase out the Multi-Fiber Arrangement;

☐ At least a 30 percent cut in tariffs; and

☐ A substantial increase in access to public procurement markets through the extension of the GATT Government Procurement Code to telecommunications and services, among other areas.

With regard to the safeguards complex, reforms should include:

☐ A new safeguards code that encourages import-competing industries to use Article XIX by lowering the injury threshold and barring retaliation or compensation, but requires users to adopt adjustment measures;

☐ Prohibition or strong constraints on the use of voluntary export restraints, but limited provision for selective actions under Article XIX, subject to strict time limits and adjustment requirements; and

☐ Tighter discipline on the use of subsidies and on the calculation of antidumping and countervailing duties, including the proscription of price undertakings and the introduction of carefully circumscribed anticircumvention rules.

In the new issue areas, the package should include:

☐ Framework agreements on services, investment, and intellectual property, incorporating extensive rules and dispute settlement mechanisms to be applied on a conditional MFN basis and ad hoc liberalization of specific barriers to trade and investment in goods and services;

- Comprehensive coverage of service industries, with time-limited reservations for problem industries;

- Prohibition of a list of trade-related investment measures, including local-content, export performance, and trade-balancing requirements; and

- Elaboration of new standards and enforcement mechanisms for protection of intellectual property in such areas as biotechnology, software, and pharmaceuticals.

With regard to dispute settlement procedures and other institutional issues, the reforms should include:

- Provision for the expeditious formation of panels on any GATT–related issue, and for the binding acceptance of panel rulings, subject to review by an appellate tribunal;

- Provision for automatic right to retaliate if the offending country does not comply with panel rulings within the time period prescribed by that ruling;

- Acceptance of cross-retaliation that allows countries to impose sanctions against the goods or services of a country in violation of its obligations;

- Establishment of a permanent and stronger trade policy review mechanism; and

- A commitment to expand talks among the Bretton Woods institutions to ensure the consistency and compatibility of their efforts on trade, monetary, and development issues.

Agreement on such a big package of reforms will require acceptance by the major trading nations of three important trade-offs. A precondition for each of these trade-offs is US–EC agreement on substantive agricultural reforms. In brief, the trade-offs involve:

- Reforms in agriculture and textiles by the developed countries in return for agreement on new rules and liberalization in services, investment, and intellectual property by the developing countries;

☐ Limited provision for selective actions under Article XIX and the prohibition of gray-area measures in return for tighter criteria for the calculation of antidumping and countervailing duties, and constraints by developing countries on the use of Article XVIII measures for balance of payments purposes; and

☐ Acceptance of cross-retaliation in the new issue areas in return for acceptance of more effective and expeditious GATT dispute settlement procedures that will reduce the need to resort to unilateral measures.

All countries will gain from the new trading opportunities that a big package would create, and from the security of improved dispute settlement procedures and other institutional reforms. These results should more than justify the long years of effort to launch and conclude the round.

For the United States, which needs to expand exports to reduce its large trade deficit and to bolster economic growth, a big package would create significant new trading opportunities for both traditional and sunrise industries. Trading rules in the new areas would benefit competitive US service industries and US investors in foreign markets, and would protect holders of intellectual property rights from counterfeiting and the misappropriation of technology. At the same time, however, these reciprocal agreements will likely spur foreign pressure to reduce US barriers, such as the Glass-Steagall and McFadden acts that inhibit banking activity in the US market.

However, a big package would not deal with the "Japan problem." Despite prospective Japanese concessions on rice and government procurement, the Uruguay Round package would have only a marginal effect on the bilateral US–Japan trade balance. Both countries will need to continue to deal bilaterally to resolve key areas of dispute that were not subject to trade negotiations, perhaps expanding the scope of the Structural Impediments Initiative.

For the European Community and Japan, a big package of agreements would provide access to, and protection for, their firms in foreign markets through new multilateral discipline on services, investment, and intellectual property. More importantly, it would strengthen the multilateral trading system in which they will play an increasingly important leadership role, and enable the GATT to better mediate trade disputes so that they do not spill over and adversely affect political relations among the major trading nations.

Developing countries have the most to lose from the drift away from multilateralism by the United States and the European Community, which will accelerate if the Uruguay Round does not produce substantial reforms to reinvigorate the GATT. However, the developing countries are in a difficult position: they need to push hard for a big package of agreements that is strongly weighted in their favor, and therefore they need to insist on linkages between the acceptance of new rules in services, investment, and intellectual property and the liberalization of agriculture and textiles; yet they cannot demand these linkages too stridently lest they lead the developed countries to settle for conditional MFN codes among themselves alone and forgo reform of the Multi-Fiber Arrangement.

Among the developing countries, the newly industrializing countries (NICs) have the most to gain from a stronger GATT system, because it would help to protect the access to developed-country markets on which their growing prosperity has been largely based. Unlike in past rounds, the NICs should therefore contribute substantially toward Uruguay Round reforms, both by participation in the codes covering the new issues and by liberalization of barriers to their markets (including in textiles and agriculture).

In particular, the NICs could undertake two specific reforms to help dispel the charge that they are free riders. The first would link reforms on safeguards by developed countries (including gray-area measures) with reform of balance of payments safeguards rules used by developing countries (the Article XVIII-XIX issue). The second would be textile liberalization by the developing countries, which would complement the broader reform of the existing quota system by the developed countries, and participation by some NICs (e.g., Korea) in the agricultural reforms.

In sum, the task of completing the Uruguay Round is too important for it not to succeed. The GATT negotiators have laid the foundation for the conclusion of a comprehensive set of agreements; following the prescriptions of this study, they can finish the job, and significantly liberalize trade and strengthen and modernize the multilateral trading system.

References

Bergsten, C. Fred. 1990. "From Cold War to Trade War?" *International Economic Insights*, vol 1, no. 1, (July/August).

Bergsten, C. Fred, Kimberly Ann Elliott, Jeffrey J. Schott, and Wendy E. Takacs. 1987. *Auction Quotas and United States Trade Policy.* POLICY ANALYSES IN INTERNATIONAL ECONOMICS 19. Washington: Institute for International Economics, September.

Bergsten, C. Fred, and John Williamson. 1983. "Exchange Rates and Trade Policy." In William R. Cline, ed., *Trade Policy in the 1980s.* Washington: Institute for International Economics, 99–120.

Bhagwati, Jagdish N. 1989. "United States Trade Policy at the Crossroads." *The World Economy,* vol. 12, no. 4 (December).

Cline, William R. 1990. *The Future of World Trade in Textiles and Apparel,* rev. ed. Washington: Institute for International Economics.

Diebold, William Jr. 1952. "The End of the I.T.O." Essays in International Finance 16. Princeton: International Finance Section, Princeton University. October.

GATT. 1986. "Launching of Uruguay Round." *GATT Focus.* no. 41, October.

GATT. 1989. *News of the Uruguay Round.* no. 27, April 24.

Graham, Edward M., and Paul R. Krugman. 1989. *Foreign Direct Investment in the United States.* Washington: Institute for International Economics.

Hathaway, Dale. 1987. *Agriculture and the GATT: Rewriting the Rules.* POLICY ANALYSES IN INTERNATIONAL ECONOMICS 20. Washington: Institute for International Economics, September.

Hudec, Robert E. 1989. "Thinking about the New Section 301: Beyond Good and Evil." Paper presented to a conference on "Super 301 and the World Trading System" at Columbia University, 1–2 December.

Hufbauer, Gary Clyde, Diane T. Berliner, and Kimberly Ann Elliott. 1986. *Trade Protection in the United States: 31 Case Studies.* Washington: Institute for International Economics.

Hufbauer, Gary Clyde, and Jeffrey J. Schott. 1985. *Trading for Growth: The Next Round of Trade Negotiations.* POLICY ANALYSES IN INTERNATIONAL ECONOMICS 11. Washington: Institute for International Economics, September.

Jackson, John. 1990. *Restructuring the GATT System.* New York: Council on Foreign Relations; and London: Pinter for the Royal Institute of International Affairs.

Krause, Lawrence B. 1990. "Trade Policy in the 1990s: Good-bye bipolarity, hello regions." *The World Today,* 46, no. 5, 83–84.

Leutwiler, Fritz, et al. 1985. *Trade Policies for a Better Future: Proposals for Action,* Geneva: GATT Independent Study Group, March.

Organization for Cooperation and Development. 1990. *Agricultural Policies, Markets, and Trade: Monitoring and Outlook 1990.* Paris: OECD.

Roningen, Vernon O., and Praveen M. Dixit. 1989. "How Level is the Playing Field? An Economic Analysis of Agricultural Policy Reforms in Industrial Market Economies." Foreign Agricultural Economic Report Number 239, Economic Research Service, US Department of Agriculture, December.

Schott, Jeffrey J., ed. 1989. *Free Trade Areas and U.S. Trade Policy*. Washington: Institute for International Economics.

Schott, Jeffrey J. 1990a. "Is the World Devolving into Regional Trading Blocs?" *The World Economy,* vol. 13, no. 3 (forthcoming).

Schott, Jeffrey J. 1990b. "US Policies toward the GATT: Past, Present, Prospective." In Reinhard Rode, ed. *GATT and Conflict Management*. Boulder, CO: Westview Press (forthcoming).

2

Agriculture

Dale E. Hathaway

To observers of past GATT rounds it is all too familiar. The multilateral talks begin with a resounding declaration of the intent to reform agriculture; improvement in agricultural trade is stated as a priority, especially by the United States; the negotiation quickly deteriorates into a contest of wills between the United States and the European Community, with the former insisting on reform of the Common Agricultural Policy (CAP) and the Community refusing; a deadlock develops, which is finally broken by the United States abandoning its demands for reform; finally, the prospects for major reform in agricultural trade policies are regretfully put aside for the next round. Meanwhile protected and supported farm commodity producers in the rich countries relax and return to their normal activity of lobbying their governments for higher supports and greater protection from market forces.

This has been the story of most multilateral trade negotiations to date, and thus far the Uruguay Round is right on track. We are now at the point in the script where the United States usually begins to accommodate the Community's reluctance to reform, and the question is whether the remaining portion of the traditional scenario will be played out. It would be reckless to predict that the outcome of the

Dale E. Hathaway is a partner in the Consultants International Group, and former US Under Secretary of Agriculture for International Affairs and Commodity Programs.

51

Uruguay Round will follow this pattern, yet at the same time it would be foolish to predict that the traditional outcome will be avoided. My view, as this volume goes to press, is that a repetition of the past can only be avoided by creating a major political crisis, which could backfire and wreck the Uruguay Round and sacrifice desired agreements in other areas. We can look at the likely outcomes in agriculture, and then judge whether agricultural reform is worth the gamble.

The Issues

In one regard the negotiations on agriculture in the Uruguay Round are unique: they are focused on the right issues. Talks on agriculture in the last two rounds foundered over attempts to negotiate agreements to control world prices of agricultural commodities, ignoring the fact that agricultural exemptions and national agricultural policies that escape GATT disciplines are a major destabilizing force in world markets and make a mockery out of trade rules in agriculture. The Uruguay Round began with a goal to reduce or eliminate trade distortions in agriculture by doing something about the national agricultural polices that distort production, consumption, and trade.

From the outset this negotiation has been a struggle between the proponents of reform and the proponents of restraint. Reform implies removing the agricultural exceptions from current GATT Articles XI and XVI; phasing out all gray-area practices, grandfather clauses, exceptions, and waivers; and eventually prohibiting domestic subsidies that produce trade distortions. Proponents of restraint oppose changes in GATT rules that would remove the present agricultural exemptions or prohibit any national policies. Instead, they suggest that national policies be allowed to continue but that the levels of protection and support granted under them be restrained.

The reform group has been led by the United States and the Cairns Group,[1] which have similar but not identical goals and have offered similar proposals. The group advocating restraint has been led by the

---

1. The Cairns Group consists of 14 countries that are exporters of agricultural products: Argentina, Australia, Brazil, Canada, Chile, Colombia, Fiji, Hungary, Indonesia, Malaysia, New Zealand, the Philippines, Thailand, and Uruguay.

European Community, joined in philosophy if not in detail by Japan, the Nordic group (Sweden, Norway, and Finland), Switzerland, and Austria. Given these lineups, it is not surprising that the negotiation has become a US–EC confrontation, an all-too-familiar situation in agricultural trade negotiations.

The jousting between reform and restraint has been going on for three and one-half years. It led to a deadlock at the midterm review in Montreal in December 1988, where the Cairns Group refused to approve the reports of the other 14 negotiating groups in the absence of an agricultural framework. A compromise framework for agriculture was agreed to in April 1989. Yet virtually no progress has occurred in the agricultural negotiations since then, as the various participants have repeated their basic positions without substantial change in detailed proposals and elaborations.

Finally, at an informal GATT ministerial meeting in Puerto Vallarta, Mexico, in April 1990, the lack of progress in certain sectors prompted two actions. The meeting of the Trade Negotiations Committee (TNC) in late July was set as a deadline for all 15 negotiating groups to submit a draft text of an agreement. The final agreements were then to be negotiated in time for the final ministerial meeting in December 1990. To arrive at a draft text in agriculture, it was proposed that four working groups be formed in the Negotiating Group on Agriculture, on market access, domestic supports, export competition, and sanitary and phytosanitary regulations.

MARKET ACCESS

The policies at stake in the area of market access are some of the most politically sensitive policies in agriculture. They include the EC variable levy; the US Section 22 waiver, which is used to protect dairy products, sugar, cotton, and peanuts; the Japanese prohibition against rice imports; Canada's import quotas on dairy, poultry, and egg products; all voluntary export restraints, including those periodically negotiated on beef exported to the United States and currently on manioc to the European Community; and a host of other tariff and nontariff barriers around the world (for a fuller description of these practices see Hathaway 1987). These policies have two common features: they help maintain internal prices above world prices, and they isolate producers in the countries using them both from competition and from changes in world markets.

The meaning of reform in this area is easy. It means getting rid of this plethora of import barriers and replacing them with transparent protection in the form of tariffs. In the version of reform proposed by the United States, all import restraints would be converted to tariffs, which would then be cut to zero over 10 years. The United States has also proposed tariff rate quotas to provide access until tariffs are completely removed. However, reform does not have to extend to complete elimination of tariffs. Indeed, complete elimination would only be possible if there were a complete phaseout of all support programs, which is not going to happen.

Restraint in the area of market access would mean allowing all of the present import policies to be continued, but the difference between the world price of a commodity and its internal price would be limited and perhaps reduced over time. These levels would be tied to the level of internal support, which would be the only term to be negotiated. The current GATT Article XI:2(c) exception allowing agricultural import quotas (when domestic production controls exist) would be clarified and continued.

Negotiations on market access are further complicated by the special and separate demands of the European Community and Japan. An important EC demand stems from the Community's desire for border protection on oilseeds. In the Dillon Round, the Community agreed to bind its duties on oilseeds and oilseed products and certain grain feed substitutes such as manioc, corn gluten feed, citrus pulp, and mill by-product feeds at zero. As the EC variable levy on grains has risen to protect the rising levels of support, there has been a huge incentive to increase the use of imported lower-cost oilseed meal and grain substitutes in animal feeds. This, of course, has reduced the use of EC grains for feed within the Community and has exacerbated the EC grain surpluses, increased the use of export subsidies, and raised the cost of the grain supports.

To counter this effect, the European Community implemented an oilseed policy that encouraged the production and domestic use of EC oilseeds via the payment of subsidies to EC oilseed processors who purchased domestic seeds at a high target price and crushed the seeds for domestic use. In the course of a decade this program brought a fivefold expansion of EC oilseed production. In 1989 the United States won its case—the biggest GATT case ever filed in terms of trade value—against the EC oilseed policy. The panel hearing the dispute ruled that the processor payments discriminated against imports, and that the program was an impairment of the EC tariff binding on soybeans and soy products. The Community accepted the panel decision and must change its oilseed policy as a result.

As a way of solving its oilseed problems, the Community has said it might consider tariffication of its variable levies under certain conditions: first, the resulting tariffs would have to have a variable component to adjust for exchange rate changes and at least some of the changes in world market prices; second, nations (i.e., the members of the Community) would be allowed to convert deficiency payments to tariffs; and third, the Community would be allowed to rebalance the final tariffs by raising those it considers too low while lowering those on some highly protected products. The last two points are generally called "rebalancing" and are said to be the Community's make-or-break issue in agriculture.

The special demands made by Japan in the area of market access relate to the insistence of the Japanese that they must have the right to maintain complete self-sufficiency in rice to ensure their food security. They want a special category of import controls established for this purpose, and they oppose both the conversion of quotas to tariffs and guaranteed minimum access.

Even this brief and oversimplified summary of the access issues in agriculture makes clear that there are immense differences between the reform and the restraint positions. Moreover, it is hard to see how one could split the difference and take two proposals from column A and two from column B. This is almost certainly a case in which either everybody reforms or no one does.

INTERNAL SUPPORTS

The Montreal midterm agreement called for a "substantial progressive reduction" in support and protection. The European Community immediately declared a victory for restraint, saying that this ended the

US and Cairns Group demands for complete elimination of all trade-distorting domestic policies. The US delegates insisted that substantial reductions still meant reducing to zero, but their heart has not been in it, and US officials privately admit that the Uruguay Round will not achieve agreement on the phase-out of all trade-distorting subsidies.

Now the arguments are about how the reductions are to be implemented, monitored, and enforced. The negotiators have not even gotten to the really difficult political issue of to what degree internal supports should be reduced and which specific policies and commodities should be subject to reductions. The United States and the Cairns Group have been pushing for policy-specific reductions and limitations across all commodities. The European Community and Japan are calling for reductions to be measured and monitored by an aggregate measure of support on a limited number of commodities. As yet there is no agreement on which subsidies will be subjected to reductions, what the commodity coverage will be, and whether the exercise should involve a common percentage reduction or a reduction to a common level of subsidy.

From the beginning, the quest for a complete prohibition against trade-distorting domestic subsidies in agriculture did not appear realistic. Such a prohibition would liberalize agricultural trade to a point well beyond where other sectors are, and that seems unlikely. This issue strikes at national sovereignty and is as likely to be as unpopular with the US Congress as with the EC Council of Ministers.

Even if the idea of reform of domestic policies is set aside, how the cuts in domestic supports are to be made and how deeply they are to be made are important questions. This issue is as sensitive as the access issue in many countries where farmers are heavily dependent upon supports and protection.

EXPORT COMPETITION

It is in the area of export competition that the difference between reform and restraint is most pronounced and the political confrontation most stark. The special exemption of agriculture from the general prohibition against export subsidies in Article XVI of the GATT has been a major source of disputes in international agricultural trade for decades, a major source of distrust and contempt for the GATT dispute settlement process, and a major sticking point of US–EC negotiations in the last few rounds of trade negotiations.

There is little question about what reform of policies relating to export competition would imply. It would mean phasing out and henceforth prohibiting all export subsidies for either raw or processed agricultural products. Restraint in this area, on the other hand, would involve some additional refinement of Article XVI:3, which has been a source of constant tension and immense dissatisfaction since the inception of the GATT. At best, restraint would involve defining what constitutes an "equitable share" of the world market and the base period to be used as a yardstick. At worst it could involve some market-sharing formula of one type or another.

If rebalancing is the make-or-break demand for the Community, reform of the rules on export subsidies is the make-or-break political issue in the agricultural negotiations for both the United States and the Cairns Group. Effective control over EC export subsidies is a must for any agricultural package that the US Congress would judge credible. To satisfy the Cairns Group, it will also be necessary to get the United States to give up its own highly popular export subsidy programs—the Export Enhancement Program and the Targeted Export Assistance Program—created under the 1985 farm bill. Getting rid of both the EC and the US export subsidies is the main focus of the Cairns Group's demands.

On the other side of the table, the export restitution policy of the Community is an integral and increasingly key part of the CAP. As the Community has moved from net importer to net exporter status in product after product, export subsidies have allowed the maintenance of internal price levels at well above world prices. Thus far, the Community has proposed that export subsidy levels should be related to internal support levels, that they should not exceed import levy levels, and that modest revisions in Article XVI:3 might be in order. The EC delegation has refused to discuss a separate commitment on export subsidies.

It was this impasse on the issue of specific negotiations on export subsidies that prevented agreement on a statement dealing with the Uruguay Round agricultural negotiations at the OECD ministerial meeting at the end of May 1990; it was also the sticking point at the

Houston economic summit in July 1990 and at the TNC meeting later that month, and it will likely remain so to the end of the negotiation.

Even if there were agreement to reform the GATT's rules on export competition, there would be some very difficult issues left. One is the question of what constitutes an export subsidy. The usual definition of a bounty or payment for exporting a product would of course apply. But what about the US deficiency payments on products that are exported, especially payments made under the marketing loan programs for cotton and rice, which compensate producers for any difference between a fixed target price and the world price? The European Community argues that these payments are as disruptive to world markets as the EC export restitutions, and the Cairns Group tends to agree. Not surprisingly, the United States does not.

Another point of contention is whether producer-financed export subsidy programs would be allowed under a general prohibition on export subsidies. This issue has not yet been confronted because there have been no negotiations on export subsidies. The prospect for US compromise on this issue would appear limited because most US groups are convinced that mere restraint will not work, at least as being proposed. Congress is likely to be highly skeptical of any restraints in this area and to insist on either reform or nothing. Thus, for the United States and the Cairns Group, some kind of real and effective limits on export subsidies in the short run and a phase-out of such subsidies in the long run together constitute a minimum requirement for a successful agricultural negotiation.

HEALTH AND SANITARY STANDARDS

The fourth set of issues under negotiation in the agricultural portion of the Uruguay Round involves a major effort to reduce the adverse trade effects of national health and sanitary standards for food and agricultural products. This effort arises from a belief that these standards have been and will increasingly become a major nontariff barrier.

The objectives of this part of the negotiations are to harmonize national standards so as to reduce their negative impact on trade; to develop an effective dispute settlement mechanism within the GATT on such issues; and to bring scientific evidence and judgment to bear in the dispute settlement process. On the surface, these appear to be issues upon which significant agreement could be reached in a way that would substantially benefit trade, but it is useful to remember that the US–EC dispute over the use of hormones in beef production has defied resolution for several years. In addition, there are fundamental differences in the approaches the two sides have adopted on certain key issues. Meanwhile these issues have taken on a new political dimension as consumers in rich countries have become increasingly sensitive to real or perceived health hazards. The complexity of the issues and the rapidly changing political conditions suggest that the real gains in this area will be modest in this negotiating round.

Where Do We Go From Here and How Do We Get There?

As I see it, there are three possible outcomes of the agricultural negotiations in the Uruguay Round. I would label them the minimum outcome, the maximum outcome, and no outcome.

The minimum outcome would be close to but not identical with the current EC position. It would concentrate on modest cuts in support and protection using an aggregate measure of support. It would involve some product-specific minimum access commitments. It would not, however, involve rebalancing. It would not require any specific policies to be phased out. It would require tinkering with Article XI:2(c) and XVI:3, with some cosmetic constraints on export subsidies. Essentially, this solution would leave agricultural trade where it has been for the last 40 years, but with some additional commitments to reduce protection and support.

The maximum agreement would be in the direction of the US and the Cairns Group positions but would fall well short of the reforms they have proposed. It would involve the conversion of all import restraints to tariffs and some cuts (or limits) in the level of those tariffs. It would also involve tariff rate quotas and safeguards provisions.

The maximum agreement would settle for restraint rather than reform where domestic subsidies are concerned. That restraint is likely to be in the form of some aggregate measure, but one that is perhaps applied to specific policies and commodities as well as to broad groups. It would provide broad coverage in terms of commodities. It would involve modest (less than 25 percent) cuts in support from a mid-1980s base.

The maximum agreement would place limits on direct export subsidies in terms of either quantities or expenditures, with these limits to be reduced over time, but it would allow producer-financed export payments.

The possibility of no agreement emerging in agriculture is real, because of the major political shifts that will be required to reach either the minimum or the maximum agreement. The minimum agreement would require that the United States and the Cairns Group abandon their goals for reform in agriculture, something they might be unwilling or unable to do. Conversely, the maximum agreement I have sketched out, or anything close to it, would require a major political shift by the European Community and Japan.

The Chairman of the Negotiating Group on Agriculture, Aart de Zeeuw of the Netherlands, produced a draft text of a negotiating framework in late June. In essence it outlined a compromise that would lead toward what I have defined as a maximum agreement. It calls for reform on access barriers (through tariffication), reform of export subsidies (in the form of effective and declining limits), and restraint (using an aggregate measure) on domestic subsidies.

The chairman's text was immediately embraced by the United States and the Cairns Group, but the Community refused to accept the idea of negotiating separate and binding limits on export subsidies. They refused it as well at the Houston summit and at the TNC meeting in Geneva. Thus, there was no agreement on a negotiating text for agriculture, and discussions continue on the same issues that have divided the two camps from the beginning.

The question is whether the political crisis created by the lack of an agricultural framework in July will be enough to force a change in political position by one or more of the key participants. My judgment is that it will not; thus, in all likelihood, the December 1990 ministerial meeting in Brussels will begin with major agricultural issues unresolved.

Therefore, it appears that no significant results in agriculture is a possible outcome. The question that then arises is whether a significant number of countries will believe it is worth torpedoing the entire Uruguay Round for lack of progress on agriculture. The answer probably depends upon several factors, including what else has been achieved in the round and especially what else is in the package for those countries that have pushed for agricultural reform. A major crisis is likely to erupt in Brussels in December because of the absence of an agricultural agreement. However, the ultimate political decision whether to compromise on agriculture or abandon the round will not be made by the trade ministers, and therefore the political decisions on the agricultural portion of the round are unlikely before early 1991.

Looking Beyond the Uruguay Round

What would each of the three outcomes I have outlined mean for future trade relations in agriculture and for the GATT in general?

A failure in agriculture, if it is not allowed to destroy the entire round, would mean that the world would go on much as it has for nearly half a century: agricultural trade would continue to be a constant irritant, or worse, especially for smaller, low-cost exporters. The major powers would find ad hoc bilateral arrangements to avoid all-out trade wars just as they have in the past. There would continue to be significant resource misallocations and trade distortions, but they primarily occur in rich countries, which can afford them. The main losers would be the low-cost agricultural producers in developing countries, which would be prevented from using their advantages in world markets.

Oddly enough, the achievement of a minimum deal in agriculture might raise rather than lower tension over agriculture in the GATT. A minimum deal would not significantly improve world resource alloca- tion, nor would it significantly reduce trade distortions, but it would introduce new areas of ambiguity into the GATT, which would require dispute settlement. Thus, restraints on domestic subsidy levels would be added to the ongoing issues over access and export subsidies, which are already areas of contention.

The maximum agreement I have outlined could lay the foundation for truly bringing agriculture into the GATT, but it would not neces- sarily reduce tensions. It would require complex calculations that would have to be agreed to, described, written down, and executed for a large number of countries and commodities. It would require a GATT commitment of a different type, and monitoring and dispute settlement procedures of a type never before tried on issues never before subjected to dispute settlement in the GATT.

In the event there is agreement to convert access barriers to tariffs, the complexity of the task will be multiplied. There are endless possibilities for disagreement in these issues.

Most interesting to watch will be the dispute settlement process. If the United States violates a commitment on the target price for wheat, for example, who will be allowed to complain, who will be designated the injured party, and how will compensation be calculated and provided? An entirely new era of international policy battles will be opened. Extreme patience and flexibility will be required in the early years of this new era, if it should come to pass. Yet patience and flexibility have never been hallmarks of international trade policy in agriculture or of the political actions of agricultural groups around the world. Thus, even if the Uruguay Round is successful in agriculture, we will have guaranteed ourselves a long period of agricultural disputes in the GATT, and the new dispute settlement process also being negotiated in the Uruguay Round will quickly be put to a test.

Reference

Hathaway, Dale E. 1987. *Agriculture and the GATT: Rewriting the Rules.* POLICY ANALYSES IN INTERNATIONAL ECONOMICS 20. Washington: Institute for International Economics, September.

3

Textiles and Apparel

William R. Cline

The Uruguay Round seeks to extend GATT rules for international trade into new areas, including services, intellectual property, and investment. It also seeks to improve trading rules on nontariff barriers negotiated in the previous Tokyo Round, and in particular to incorporate countries that did not sign these codes. In these and other areas, firms in industrial countries consider adherence of the developing countries to be of prime importance, as these countries have had among the most closed trading practices. However, developing countries are unlikely to subscribe to the Uruguay Round results unless they consider its new obligations warranted by its new opportunities. Improved access to industrial-country markets in textiles and apparel is perhaps the single most important area for expanded export opportunity for the developing countries.

The Uruguay Round offers a historic chance to move textile and apparel trade back from the regime of bilateral quotas under the Multi-Fiber Arrangement (MFA) to the discipline of the GATT. Special protection in these products has now lasted for more than a quarter century, through the Short- and Long-term Arrangements on Cotton Textiles of the mid-1960s and the MFA, first negotiated in 1974. This

William R. Cline is a Senior Fellow at the Institute for International Economics. This chapter summarizes the updated analysis of textile liberalization proposals in the revised edition of his book The Future of World Trade in Textiles and Apparel, *published by the Institute in June 1990.*

chapter evaluates the principal proposals for textile and apparel trade liberalization that have been submitted in the Uruguay Round negotiations.

The Proposals

The United States has proposed that special protection in textiles and apparel be phased out over a period of 10 years, by 2001 (United States 1990). The two main approaches to the transition in the US position are global quotas and global tariff rate quotas. In addition, the US position acknowledges that expansion of current MFA quotas may be an alternative approach.

Japan has proposed that the sector be liberalized by 1999. During the transition period, there would be a regime of relatively strict objective conditions required for imposition of any quotas. Essentially there would be injury-type tests, subject to approval by an international body. Switzerland has proposed that each country could choose its own transitional modality, once a target date for reintegration of textiles and apparel into GATT practices has been agreed.

In contrast, the European Community has insisted that there be only one "modality" for reintegration of textiles into the GATT. It has proposed an "MFA-based modality," taking existing restrictions as the starting point and thereby avoiding introduction of new restrictions by product or country (European Communities 1990). The Community's transition mechanism assumes "strengthened" GATT rules and disciplines, presumably including selective safeguards as favored by the Community in the Uruguay Round negotiations. Management of quotas would remain in the hands of the exporting countries. The time period for reintegration would be negotiated late in the Uruguay Round, apparently as a means of offering an incentive to developing countries to be forthcoming in other areas of the negotiations. A list of products immediately subject to GATT rules would be negotiated. The transition period would be divided into stages, with specified targets for elimination of quotas (by volume of trade covered) in each period. Quotas would be phased out by fiber, product, country, or combinations thereof. Remaining quotas at any given point would be subject to higher growth rates than in the past. Products liberalized during the transition would be subject to a special safeguards mechanism with multilaterally agreed tests for market disruption.

GLOBAL QUOTAS

The US proposal for global quotas contains a key element that US textile and apparel producers have long sought: closure of the MFA loophole that has permitted increased imports from countries not currently covered by the MFA. For each category, a global total ceiling would be set, based on actual trade of the past three years and a growth factor. A minimum growth rate of x percent would be set for the most sensitive categories. Quotas would grow at x percent for the first three years, $x + 1$ percent for the next three, $x + 2$ percent for the next two years, and $x + 3$ percent for the final two years of transition. Thereafter all quotas would be eliminated. The schedule of annual growth rates would be 1 percent higher for products of intermediate sensitivity and 2 percent higher for products of lesser sensitivity.

In the past, industrial countries (with the partial exception of Japan) have been exempted from MFA restrictions by a gentlemen's agreement. The global quota would control industrial-country suppliers for the first time—a feature that has led to sharp criticism of the US proposal by the European Community, which has a positive trade balance with the United States in textiles and especially apparel. More generally, global quotas would run the risk of increasing protection by controlling formerly noncontrolled countries (including many developing countries). They would only be liberalizing if their growth were set at sufficiently high rates that overall imports expanded faster than under the existing MFA restrictions, particularly those on the major suppliers.

The global quota would, however, increase efficiency of international resource allocation by directing textile and apparel production to low-cost countries rather than those previously exempt or in possession of historical quotas. This reallocation would occur through the redistribution of one-tenth of existing country quotas to a global pool each year, as well as allocation of annual quota growth to the global pool.

In practice, the most important issue for the global quota is the rate at which quotas would grow over time. If the rate were set low, the intensity of protection would actually increase over the next several years, and the commitment to go "cold turkey" by eliminating quotas at the end of the decade would be highly suspect—as the gap between quota-free and actual import levels at that time would be so great. If the rate is set high, intense opposition may be expected from the textile and apparel producers in industrial countries.

A mechanism would be required for allocation of quotas in the global pool (country-specific quotas would presumably be distributed among firms as in the past). The logical choice would be an auction by the importing-country government. Assignment to importers by historical market share would confer a windfall rent on these firms. Retailers have emphasized that an auction system would disrupt their supply networks and be subject to monopolization by a few actors with "deep pockets." Gradual phase-in of auctioned quotas could help minimize disruption for all parties, however (for an analysis of auctioned quotas, see Bergsten et al. 1987).

GLOBAL TARIFF RATE QUOTAS

The tariff rate quota would replace absolute, physical quotas with corresponding thresholds at which a punitive tariff surcharge would be added to the basic tariff. The intent would be to replicate the effect of the initial quota. Use of the surcharge rather than absolute prohibition of marginal imports would provide greater flexibility and thus avoid potentially extreme consumer costs. A crucial feature of the tariff rate quota would be its convenient means for gradual liberalization: scheduled phasedown and elimination of the surcharge. A complementary element of the liberalization transition would be growth in the threshold at which the surcharge applies.

Identification of the appropriate level for the tariff surcharge is one challenge of the tariff rate quota option. Past estimates of tariff-equivalents of quotas suggest that on average a surcharge of 25 percent would replicate the existing protective effect of apparel quotas. However, producers might fear that higher surcharges would be required to ensure effective restraint. In principle, empirical surveys could determine appropriate surcharges from tariff-equivalents of present quotas. However, it would also be possible to apply a presumptive surcharge rate based on the "column 2" tariffs still on the US tariff books from the Smoot-Hawley tariff law of the 1930s. The median column 2 tariff in apparel is 70 percent, corresponding to a surcharge of 39 percent applied on top of the basic apparel tariff (22½ percent).

A high surcharge such as this would not jeopardize consumer or importer interests, so long as the threshold at which the surcharge applies is as high as the quota otherwise would be. The alternative, an absolute quota, actually enforces a surcharge of infinity. However, if high initial surcharges were employed, it would be essential to ensure an adequate rate of threshold growth; otherwise, in the early years before phasedown of the surcharge has proceeded very far, protection could increase.

It is also important to recognize that the tariff rate quota is not the same thing as "tariffication" of existing quotas. Under outright conversion of the quota to a tariff ("tariffication"), the resulting tariff applies to the whole amount of imports—not just to imports above and beyond the former quota level. In contrast, under the tariff rate quota only the original, base tariff would be paid on all amounts imported below the threshold ceiling. Adverse reaction of some importers to the tariff rate quota concept appears to stem from failure to distinguish between the tariff rate quota and tariffication.

In other regards the tariff rate quota would have the same features as the global quota in the US proposal—such as reallocation of country-specific quotas (in this case, entitlements to surcharge-free market access) to a global pool over time. In addition, the US proposal provides that special arrangements would have to be made for state-trading nations, to deal with the risk that their supply might not be impeded by the surcharge as their firms do not face the same profit-loss constraints as firms in market systems.

MFA QUOTA GROWTH

A third option, less enthusiastically mentioned by the United States, would be simply to expand the existing MFA quotas at appropriate rates, and to eliminate them at the end of the 10-year transition period.

This approach is relatively close to the EC proposal, especially if primary reliance in that proposal is placed on acceleration in the growth rate of quotas as opposed to immediate or phased elimination of quotas.

Quantitative Evaluation

It is possible to apply the model of production, trade, and employment in textiles and apparel described in Cline (1990) to examine the economic effects of these alternative proposals. First, however, it is appropriate to ask whether the projections of the model in the first edition of that study in 1987 fared well in practice.

Figure 3.1 shows the actual paths of US imports and exports in apparel for the period 1978–89, as indexes with 1986 equal to the base of 100. In addition, the figure shows the levels of trade predicted for 1987 through 1989 in my earlier study. As is evident in the figure, the model did broadly succeed in capturing the sharp changes that were in store for apparel trade at that time. Apparel imports had risen at extremely high rates in the early 1980s, but the model predicted that imports would flatten out in the period 1987–89 as the result of the major real depreciation of the dollar and improvement of US competitiveness compared with the mid-1980s when the dollar was severely overvalued. The same phenomenon was the basis for the model's projections of sharp increases in exports, which indeed came to pass.[1]

CONSUMER COSTS

The performance of the model for 1987–89 suggests that it can serve as a useful basis for examining future trends in trade under alternative policies. The first step for this analysis is identification of the "baseline" under unchanged levels of protection. The US apparel model indicates that after a transitory adjustment period in 1987–91 in

---

1. The slowdown in apparel imports was in part attributable to tighter US bilateral quotas negotiated with such countries as Korea and Taiwan. Note that the model projections for textiles similarly captured the basic trends that actually occurred in 1987–89.

Figure 3.1 Predicted and actual US apparel trade, 1978–89

A: Imports

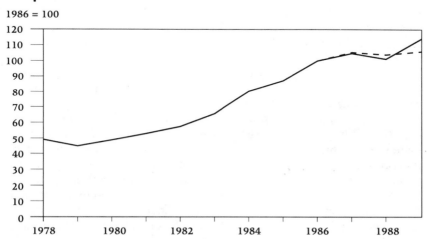

B: Exports

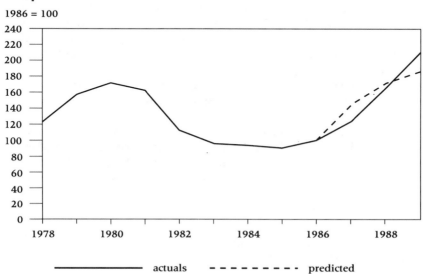

response to exchange rate changes, US imports of apparel should resume annual growth at approximately 7 percent in real terms. The bulk of these imports are from developing countries. The 7 percent rate is composed of a 2 percent trend factor (down from much higher levels in the 1970s) and a 5 percent rate reflecting growth in import demand. The 5 percent component derives from an "income elasticity" of 1.7 as applied to US GNP growth assumed at 3 percent annually. The baseline projections already provide a crucial policy implication: *any rate of global quota growth lower than 7 percent annually would increase the level of apparel protection* rather than progressively reduce it during the transition period.

The projection model provides estimates of US consumer costs resulting from protection. These costs stem from the direct effect of higher prices on imports than would be the case in the absence of protection, and the indirect effect of higher prices charged for domestically produced apparel in the face of constrained import competition. Table 3.1 presents the annual consumer costs estimated by the model. The first column refers to the baseline and includes consumer costs of both the underlying tariff and the impact of quotas (estimated to have an additional, multiplicative effect of raising import prices by another 25 percent). For 1989 (not shown), total US consumer costs from tariff and quota protection in apparel amounted to $22.4 billion (of which tariffs accounted for $12.5 billion and quotas approximately $10 billion). In the baseline projections, with imports growing at approximately 7 percent annually in real terms, the consumer costs rise to $36.6 billion annually by the year 2000 (at 1989 prices) even though protection levels remain unchanged. As the market grows larger, so does the absolute size of the excess cost consumers pay because of protection.[2]

The remaining columns of table 3.1 identify the additional consumer costs (beyond baseline levels) that would result from adoption of each of the alternative negotiating proposals. For each proposal, the estimates show alternative ranges of the key unknown—the growth rate for the quota (or tariff rate quota "threshold"). Each variant has a

---

2. Moreover, the share of imports in the market rises, and the excess cost for imports is proportionately higher than that for domestically produced goods.

Table 3.1 Projected consumer costs of alternative apparel liberalization proposals, 1992–2000
(billions of 1989 dollars)

Year	Baseline consumer costs	Increments above baseline costs by mechanism and growth path											1990 Textile bill[b]
		Global quotas				Global tariff rate quotas				MFA quota expansion			
		1-4[a]	3-6	5-8	7-10	1-4	3-6	5-8	7-10	1-4	3-6	5-8	
1992	26.1	3.7	2.3	1.0	-0.3	3.7	2.3	1.0	-0.3	3.1	2.1	1.1	5.0
1993	27.2	7.7	4.9	2.1	-0.5	7.7	4.9	2.1	-0.5	6.4	4.3	2.2	9.0
1994	28.3	11.9	7.6	3.4	-0.8	7.5	7.5	3.4	-0.8	10.0	6.7	3.5	13.3
1995	29.5	15.8	9.9	4.0	-1.7	4.8	4.8	4.0	-1.7	13.2	8.7	4.2	18.1
1996	30.7	20.1	12.3	4.7	-2.7	1.7	1.7	1.7	-2.7	16.7	10.9	5.1	23.2
1997	32.1	24.6	14.9	5.5	-3.8	-1.8	-1.8	-1.8	-3.8	20.5	13.3	6.0	28.7
1998	33.5	28.7	17.0	5.6	-5.7	-5.8	-5.8	-5.8	-5.8	23.9	15.2	6.4	37.7
1999	35.0	33.2	19.2	5.7	-7.8	-10.4	-10.4	-10.4	-10.4	27.5	17.2	6.8	41.3
2000	36.6	37.1	20.7	4.9	-10.8	-15.6	-15.6	-15.6	-15.6	30.8	18.7	6.6	48.5

a. Each set of numbers in this row represents quota growth rates in the first and last years of the 10-year transition period. For example, a growth path of 1–4 corresponds to quota growth of 1 percent in each of the first three years, 2 percent in the next three, 3 percent in the next two, and 4 percent in the final two years.
b. Quota growth under this proposed legislation would be limited to 1 percent per year.
Source: Cline (1990).

4-percentage-point range (for example, 1–4), referring to the sequence of growth rates in the successive subperiods as discussed above (for example, 1 percent in 1992–94, 2 percent in 1995–97, 3 percent in 1998–99, and 4 percent in 2000–01).

It is apparent from the table that the global quota option could impose extremely high additional consumer costs beyond baseline levels if quota growth were set at low rates. Thus, in the example of a 1 percent rising to 4 percent quota growth path, by 1996 US consumers would pay an additional $20.1 billion annually (for a total of $50.8 billion in protection costs). However, at quota growth rates in excess of the baseline 7 percent, additional consumer costs turn negative, as the level of protection declines. Thus, in the path "7–10," the global quota proposal would reduce annual US consumer costs by $2.7 billion from baseline in 1996, and by $10.8 billion in the year 2000 (leaving consumer costs at $25.8 billion instead of $36.6 billion in that year). These estimates underscore the point stressed initially: in the global quota proposal, the rate selected for quota growth is crucial to determining whether the transitional period increases or reduces protection.

To provide a smooth transition out of protection, global quotas must grow at a rate that not only reduces quota protection but reduces it to minimal levels at the end of the transitional period. The model projections for the global quota show that *a smooth transition out of quotas at the end of the decade would only occur if average quota growth amounted to 9 percent annually or above.*[3] If instead average growth were only 7 percent, or the baseline rate for unchanged protection, at the end of the decade the apparel industry would be just as vulnerable to a sudden adjustment shock from quota removal as it is today. In terms of the US sliding scale of quota growth, an average 9 percent quota growth rate would be achieved with an initial rate of 8 percent for three years, 9 percent for another three, then 10 percent for two years, and then 11 percent for the final two years.

---

3. The specific analysis identifying the 9 percent rate is based on estimating the percentage price increase above baseline required to compress import demand to the quota level under each quota growth path. For a path with average 9 percent growth, this price increase by the year 2001 is −20 percent, or just enough to neutralize the baseline 25 percent tariff-equivalent of quotas (that is, $0.8 \times 1.25 = 1.0$).

Table 3.1 next shows the incremental consumer costs (beyond baseline) for the tariff rate quota approach. The formulation here applies an initial tariff surcharge of 40 percent (essentially the median Smoot-Hawley-based rate). As may be seen, in the initial years consumer costs tend to be the same as under the global quota approach. The reason is that the surcharge is so high that imports are determined by the physical threshold (below which the surcharge does not apply), which grows at the same rates as in the corresponding quota experiments. However, in later years the incremental consumer costs are typically lower in the tariff rate quota approach than under global quotas. The reason is that after a few years the surcharge has fallen by enough that importers and consumers are prepared to pay the surcharge, and it is this price that sets the import level—which exceeds the threshold level.[4]

The broad implication of the comparisons shown in table 3.1 is that, for a given growth rate of quotas or tariff rate quota "thresholds," the tariff rate quota approach is considerably more liberalizing, and has lower incremental consumer costs, than is the global quota approach. The essential reason is that a given threshold growth path can always permit the same amount of imports as the corresponding quota growth path, but in addition the tariff rate quota approach can permit extra imports if the surcharge has been phased down far enough to no longer remain prohibitive.

A corresponding implication of this comparison between the global quota approach and the tariff rate quota approach is that to achieve approximately equivalent liberalization, the global quota strategy would have to set considerably higher quota growth rates than the rates of threshold growth in the tariff rate quota approach. For example, with an initial 40 percent surcharge, the tariff rate quota system would *reduce* consumer costs from baseline by $5.8 billion by the year 1998, even if the threshold growth path were as low as 1–4 percent (table 3.1). To achieve the same liberalization, the global quota approach would have to raise quotas along the 7–10 percent growth path (with a $5.7 billion reduction in consumer costs from baseline). Essentially,

---

4. In general, high threshold growth rates and high surcharges tend to leave the threshold as the factor determining the volume of imports; low threshold growth rates and low surcharges tend to leave the surcharge as the determining factor.

the global quota approach liberalizes primarily by raising quotas; the tariff rate quota approach, by reducing the surcharge.

The next portion of table 3.1 reports the estimates of incremental consumer costs under the "grow the MFA" approach. These estimates are a subset of the global quota approach, with the quotas in question this time limited to countries constrained by the MFA. Consumer costs of the MFA growth approach are smaller than under the global quota approach (but not radically so, because the bulk of apparel imports in the US market come from MFA–controlled sources). For example, if MFA quotas grow at a path of 3 percent rising to 6 percent, incremental consumer costs beyond baseline amount to $10.9 billion in 1996, lower than the $12.3 billion incremental cost under global quotas at the same growth rates.

PROTECTIVE LEGISLATION

Even as the negotiators deliberate in Geneva, supporters of textile and apparel producers have introduced into Congress the Textile, Apparel, and Footwear Act of 1990. This proposed legislation would adopt global quotas and limit annual quota growth to 1 percent.[5] The final column of table 3.1 reports the incremental consumer costs beyond baseline that would result from this proposed legislation. As may be seen, the successively higher levels of protection that would be required to compress imports further and further below their 7 percent baseline growth path would bring consumer costs to extremely high levels. By the year 2000, a 1 percent quota growth path would place incremental consumer costs at $48 billion annually, and total consumer costs at $85 billion annually.

EMPLOYMENT AND REVENUE EFFECTS

The choice of a restrictive transition using low global quota growth rates, or a liberal transition applying high rates, would have considerable impact on employment. In the baseline projections at unchanged

---

5. On 17 July 1990 the Senate version of the bill passed by a vote of 68 to 32.

protection, the number of jobs in US apparel production would decline from 1.09 million today to 927,000 in the year 2000. If a restrictive transition such as the path with global quota growth of 1 percent rising to 4 percent were adopted, an additional 190,000 jobs would remain in apparel by the year 2000. However, "cold turkey" termination of quotas in the year 2001 would throw these workers and more out of jobs overnight—the main reason that fulfillment of the quota elimination pledge would be highly suspect at low rates of quota growth during the transition period.

Moreover, the extra sectoral employment through the year 2000 would be purchased at an additional consumer cost of $195,000 per job, in the example just cited. The 1990 textile bill would create 252,000 apparel jobs beyond baseline employment by 1990, at an annual consumer cost of $192,000 per job. The high consumer cost per job created strongly suggests the merit of a consumer-worker bargain whereby more liberal import growth paths are accepted, but consumers accept a modest levy to fund adjustment assistance. The calculations here suggest that a fee of ⅔ percent on apparel imports would be sufficient to finance two years of $10,000 in adjustment assistance support for each worker potentially displaced by rising imports (Cline 1990, 32).

Additional calculations for the global quota approach also show that there could be substantial revenue from quota auctions. With the progressive allocation of quotas to the global pool subject to auction, and with low global quota growth rates, quota revenue could rise to as high as $18 billion annually by the year 2000 (Cline 1990, 322). In this case, it would be the fiscal accounts that would face going cold turkey in 2001.

Textiles Subsector

The analyses here refer to the apparel sector. For the sector of textiles, industrial countries should generally be in a better position to liberalize. Investment in capital-intensive methods has increased the competitiveness of industrial countries in textiles, whereas in apparel it has proven more difficult to mechanize. The OECD industrial countries have approximately balanced trade in textiles, with imports and exports both equal to about $50 billion annually (Organization for Economic Cooperation and Development 1989, vol. I, 215; vol. II, 192). The United States had a trade surplus in textiles in 1980 before the dollar became overvalued, and in 1989 textile exports were back up to 61 percent of the value of imports (versus a ratio of only 8 percent in apparel). Protection and consumer costs have also tended to be lower in textiles than apparel.[6]

Whatever transitional mechanism toward elimination of special protection is chosen in apparel, the approach applied in textiles should be at least as liberalizing. In my model for textiles, the baseline growth rate of US imports at unchanged protection is 3.8 percent annually. Nonetheless, the 7 percent benchmark suggested above as the minimum growth rate for quotas during the decade of transition toward liberalization for apparel would be appropriate for textiles as well (indeed, an even higher quota growth rate might be warranted). In view of the greater competitiveness of textiles, it would be inappropriate to impose slower quota growth than for apparel.

Developing-Country Proposal

The International Textiles and Clothing Bureau, representing developing countries, has recently proposed an alternative liberalization plan (Indonesia 1990). The MFA would be abolished upon expiration of its current term (mid–1991). Quotas would be phased out over six years, with quota growth of at least 6 percent in the first year, 8 percent in the second, 11 percent in the third, 15 percent in the fourth, 20 percent in the fifth, and 25 percent in the sixth year. Some current categories of restrictions (e.g., products of vegetable fibers) would be eliminated immediately. Exceptions from the transitional quota growth rates would be permitted under safeguards procedures but only with strict disciplines (e.g., injury tests).

The developing-country proposal amounts to an "MFA growth" option with a short transitional period. That is, transitional quotas

---

6. In 1986, annual consumer costs of protection amounted to an estimated $2.8 billion in textiles, compared with $17.6 billion in apparel (Cline 1990, 191).

would be based solely on existing MFA quotas (there would be no new global quotas), even though the MFA itself would disappear. The likelihood is, however, that import growth rates of even 9 percent, the rate identified above as required for smooth transition out of special protection in apparel over a decade, will meet stiff resistance from producers in the United States and other industrial countries. Rates escalating rapidly to 25 percent would seem unlikely to meet the test of political feasibility.

Policy Implications

At the broadest level, the most significant aspect of textile negotiations in the Uruguay Round is not the choice among specific liberalization modalities, but the fact that the major parties are considering a program of liberalization at all. The past history of protection under the MFA has tended instead toward successive tightening (even though the various loopholes in the MFA have meant that the actual rates of import growth in the United States have been in the range of 8 percent annually over the past two decades). The seeming consensus on the need to phase out MFA restrictions marks an important breakthrough.

My own preference for the specific means of liberalizing remain as set forth in my 1987 study: what may be called the "historically based tariff rate quota." Instead of new global quotas or tariff rate quotas, there would be no new protection. Existing quotas would be converted to tariff rate quotas, with the surcharge phased out over a decade.

Among the US proposals in the Uruguay Round, either the global tariff rate quota or the MFA-growth approach would appear to be the most desirable. MFA-growth would have the advantage of avoiding imposition of protection on suppliers currently uncontrolled. However, a global tariff rate quota approach could actually liberalize faster unless high growth rates were set for quotas in the MFA-growth approach (table 3.1). The global quota approach would seem likely to be more protective than either the global tariff rate quota approach or the MFA-growth approach.

If either the global quota or the global tariff rate quota is adopted, it would be highly desirable to exempt industrial countries and the least developed countries. In apparel, these two groups supply less than one-sixth of US imports in any event, and exclusion would facilitate achievement of Uruguay Round agreements with Europe on the one hand and with the developing countries on the other.

To reiterate, if the global quota approach is selected, it will be imperative to apply quota growth rates of at least 7 percent annually on average. Otherwise, protection will intensify rather than decrease over the transitional decade, and political pressures are likely to become overwhelming to postpone liberalization indefinitely rather than meet the commitment to eliminate quotas at the end of the decade. Similarly, if the MFA-growth approach is selected, the minimum growth rate for quotas should be set at 7 percent to ensure that the severity of protection does not increase.

The EC proposal could be implemented in a way that places it toward the liberal end of the spectrum for the MFA-expansion option. However, if the negotiated transitional phase is long (e.g., 15 years), if there is little meaningful discipline on floor growth rates for quotas, and if few products were initially liberalized, the approach could yield a more protective outcome than those recommended here. For its part, the Japanese proposal could prove difficult to implement because of likely debate about measurement and concepts for injury criteria, and resistance to injury determination by an international body.

References

Bergsten, C. Fred, Kimberly Ann Elliott, Jeffrey J. Schott, and Wendy E. Takacs. *Auction Quotas and United States Trade Policy*. POLICY ANALYSES IN INTERNATIONAL ECONOMICS 19. Washington: Institute for International Economics, September.

Cline, William R. 1990. *The Future of World Trade in Textiles and Apparel*, rev. ed. Washington: Institute for International Economics.

European Communities. 1990. "Communication from the European Communities." GATT Negotiating Group on Textiles and Clothing, Geneva, 12 June.

Indonesia. 1990. "Communication from Indonesia." GATT Negotiating Group on Textiles and Clothing, Geneva, 5 June.

Organization for Economic Cooperation and Development. 1989. *Foreign Trade by Commodities*, Series C, 1987. Paris: OECD.

United States. 1990. "Communication from the United States." GATT Negotiating Group on Textiles and Clothing, Geneva, 5 February and 5 March.

4

Safeguards

Colleen Hamilton and John Whalley

The status of GATT negotiations on safeguards is little changed today from what it was in the Tokyo Round; indeed the issues and debate remain much as they were 15 years ago. Surprisingly, while all parties seem to agree that the Safeguards Negotiating Group has the potential to play a crucial role in the round, new proposals are relatively scarce, and activity is at a low level, at least as measured by the space devoted to the group in recent issues of *GATT Focus* and *News of the Uruguay Round*.

The main area of controversy in the negotiations remains selectivity—whether to allow the discriminatory application of safeguards measures against certain exporters perceived to be causing injury and not others. Other issues actively under consideration include retaliation and compensation, multilateral surveillance, degressivity (the principle that protection should decline over time), and the linkage of structural adjustment measures for import-competing industries to the application of safeguards measures. The resolution of these issues will likely require the negotiation of trade-offs involving other areas of the Uruguay Round talks. The intricacy of these potential trade-offs

Colleen Hamilton is Research Analyst at the Centre for the Study of International Economic Relations, University of Western Ontario. John Whalley is William G. Davis Professor of International Trade and Director of the Centre for the Study of International Economic Relations, University of Western Ontario.

complicates the negotiating process and helps account for the relative inactivity and confusion in the talks on this issue so far.

The Problem with Existing Safeguards

The GATT safeguards clause embodied in Article XIX allows countries to erect trade barriers temporarily to protect against imports causing or threatening to cause serious injury to a domestic industry. The purpose of safeguards is to provide insurance for import-competing industries by permitting them to escape from their obligations to liberalize trade if the resulting imports prove too disruptive.

Safeguards provisions pose something of a paradox. Although they allow the imposition of trade restrictions, safeguards also make it possible to arrive at agreements to liberalize trade that otherwise could not have been achieved. The stronger the limits placed on safeguards, however, the weaker the insurance they provide, and hence the less willing import-competing groups are likely to be to go along with new liberalization.

The insurance value of present GATT safeguards arrangements is open to question, however. They are seemingly difficult for importing countries to apply: there are tight criteria for eligibility, and they require compensatory liberalization of other imports (or else the exporting country is allowed to retaliate). Jackson (1989, 155) summarizes the GATT restrictions on the use of safeguards measures:

1. To apply Article XIX safeguards measures under the GATT, it must be shown that imports of a product are increasing either absolutely or relatively, and such increase must be a causal result of (a) unforeseen developments, and (b) GATT obligations.

2. It must also be shown that domestic producers of competitive products are seriously injured or threatened with serious injury, and that this injury or threat is caused by the increased imports.

3. If 1 and 2 are shown, then an importing nation is entitled to suspend "such" GATT obligations in respect of such product for such time as necessary to prevent or remedy the injury.

4. The importing nation must consult with the Contracting Parties (CPs) having a substantial interest as exporters. If an agreement is not reached, exporting CPs have the right to suspend "substantially equivalent concessions."

The tests that have to be met, together with the requirement for compensation or retaliation, are widely believed to constitute rigid criteria for the implementation of safeguards measures.[1]

The present safeguards arrangements are also imprecise as far as their translation into concrete action is concerned. As Jackson (1989) indicates, they have been the source of both confusion and debate since their first appearance in the GATT. Many of the key terms (such as "competitive," "injured," "seriously injured," and "unforeseen") are not clearly defined.[2] It is also unclear whether the measures permitted under a country's suspension of obligations are limited to tariffs, in which case the most-favored-nation (MFN) principle prohibits applying safeguards in a discriminatory manner, or whether quotas may also be imposed.[3] This question has been at the heart of the debate over whether the application of Article XIX measures can or cannot be selective by country.

Largely for these reasons, in the last two decades the use of Article XIX safeguards measures, even in the larger trading areas, has declined as industries have increasingly resorted to other import relief measures as their first avenue of protection. As table 4.1 shows, the declining use of Article XIX safeguards has been paralleled by a rise in

---

1. According to Tumlir (1974, 262), Article XIX is both "too exacting and too lenient": too exacting in that the country invoking it risks retaliation (and thus having to pay too much for what it feels is a legitimate measure), and too lenient in that what was intended as emergency protection may become permanent.

2. For a detailed discussion of the difficulties caused by the ambiguity of the language in Article XIX, see Jackson (1989, 160–65).

3. Even in the literature, there is no agreement on the interpretation of Article XIX. Sampson (1987, 143) argues that "Article XIX does not state that actions should be non-discriminatory," whereas Petersmann (1988, 25) states that ". . . the system of GATT law and the subsequent practice of GATT Contracting Parties make it clear that safeguards measures under Article XIX against 'fair' import competition must be applied transparently and without discrimination to imports from all Contracting Parties." See also Jackson (1989) and Nicolaides (1990).

Table 4.1   Cases of administered protection by type of action and country, 1980–86 (number of cases)

Type of action	1980	1981	1982	1983	1984	1985	1986	Total, 1980–86
Safeguards								
United States	2	6	4	2	6	3	5	28
Australia	1	0	1	2	0	0	0	4
Canada	0	1	2	0	0	1	0	4
European Community	3	1	1	1	1	0	2	9
Countervailing duties								
United States	8	10	123	21	51	39	30	282
Australia	0	0	2	7	6	3	3	21
Canada	3	0	1	3	2	3	4	16
European Community	0	1	3	2	1	0	0	7
Antidumping								
United States	22	14	61	47	71	65	71	351
Australia	62	50	78	87	56	60	63	456
Canada	25	19	72	36	31	36	74	293
European Community	25	47	55	36	49	42	40	294
Other unfair trade practices								
(United States only)	28	19	73	39	33	39	28	259
All categories								
United States	60	49	261	109	161	146	134	920
Australia	63	50	81	96	62	63	66	481
Canada	28	20	75	39	33	40	78	313
European Community	28	49	59	39	51	42	42	310
Total	179	168	476	283	307	291	320	2,024

Reprinted with permission from Finger, J. Michael. 1990. "Subsidies and Countervailing Duties." In H.E. English, ed., *Pacific Initiatives in Global Trade*. Halifax, Nova Scotia: Institute for Research on Public Policy, 87–100.

the number of antidumping and countervailing duty actions, which are also subject to GATT disciplines under the Antidumping and Subsidies codes. The provisions in these codes were designed to defend importers only against these specific unfair trade practices; as such, the requirements for invoking antidumping and countervailing duty actions are meant to be easier to meet than those for Article XIX safeguards that apply to goods that are fairly traded. However, the language of the code provisions is sufficiently vague that code signatories (particularly the United States and the European Community) have been able to interpret them unilaterally in quite broad fashion. Exporters, on the other hand, claim that, as a result, antidumping and countervailing duties are being used in an overzealous manner (i.e., to augment protection as well as to offset foreign unfair trade practices).[4]

Also increasing in frequency at the expense of GATT safeguards has been the use of so-called gray-area measures, which fall entirely outside the discipline of present GATT rules. Voluntary export restraints (VERs) are the most conspicuous example of this form of trade restriction. VERs are agreements in which a (typically small) exporting country undertakes to limit its exports of certain goods to a (typically large) importing country. A recent GATT study lists 146 such agreements in place in September 1989; this total excludes arrangements in textiles and clothing and those covering farm products. If those sectors are included (with the exception of bilateral agreements under the Multi-Fiber Arrangement), the number rises to 249 (GATT 1990, appendix table 2).

Exporting countries typically agree to VERs when faced with the threat of an alternative measure should they refuse to negotiate. The alternative measure is often a safeguards action, but increasingly it has taken the form of an antidumping or countervailing duty investigation, or even unilateral action by the importing country, such as under US Section 301. Importing countries prefer to use gray-area measures because they are free of the restrictions placed on classic safeguards actions: there are no issues of nondiscrimination and compensation, and injury determination is not linked to GATT obligations. Exporters

---

4. See the discussion of these measures in the chapters in this volume by Hufbauer and Messerlin.

prefer them because they believe they can usually negotiate a better deal than under the alternative measures: the relative attraction to the importing country of gray-area restrictions gives the exporting country some degree of bargaining leverage.[5]

Safeguards in the Tokyo and Uruguay Rounds

A major objective set forth in the 1973 declaration that launched the Tokyo Round was to develop a new safeguards code, which, it was hoped, would somehow put an end to the circumvention of present Article XIX safeguards.

In the Tokyo Round, the European Community proposed to move away from the principle of nondiscrimination and allow a degree of selectivity in the application of safeguards measures.[6] This would be accomplished by adding a system of selective measures that could be applied without compensation; Article XIX itself would be left intact. Also called for in the proposal were commitments to adjustment measures by countries invoking safeguards, as well as multilateral surveillance of the use of safeguards measures.[7] The EC proposal was driven by the idea that if some element of selectivity were allowed under Article XIX, a portion of existing gray-area measures could be brought back within the GATT system. Selective safeguards could thus lessen the need to resort to gray-area measures in the future.

The counterargument to the EC proposal, pressed strongly in the Tokyo Round by the smaller and mid-sized developing countries, and by the United States, stressed the importance of the nondiscrimination principle as the central pillar of the GATT. For smaller countries, it is the key element of the trading system that, in principle, prevents them from being picked off one by one under pressure from larger powers (for example, to negotiate VERs). These countries argued that the way to deal with gray-area measures is directly, through notification to the

---

5. See Tumlir (1985) for a discussion of the difficulties VERs present.

6. See the discussion of selectivity in Wolff (1983, 380–86).

7. See Merciai (1981, 55–57) for a discussion of the positions of the main participants in the Tokyo Round; see also Robertson (1977, 47–53) and Wolff (1983).

GATT, surveillance, and ultimately agreement to restrict or ban them, not indirectly through a weakening of safeguards disciplines.

The attempt to negotiate a new safeguards code in the Tokyo Round failed mainly over the issue of selectivity, although there was also disagreement over the issues of surveillance, retaliation, adjustment, and determination of injury, not to mention over what to do about existing VERs and preferential treatment for the developing countries. Safeguards thus remained one of the key elements of unfinished business from the Tokyo Round, figuring prominently in the 1982 ministerial and later in the 1986 launch of the Uruguay Round.[8]

In the early stages of the Uruguay Round, several papers and proposals were put on the table before the Safeguards Group, both by the large trading countries and from groups of countries such as the "Pacific Five" (Hong Kong, Australia, New Zealand, Singapore, and Korea), which offered joint proposals. These proposals stressed the need to maintain nondiscrimination.

More recently, negotiations have centered on a draft text of a comprehensive agreement prepared by the group chairman, Brazilian ambassador George A. Maciel. This draft is summarized in table 4.2. It envisages degressive, nondiscriminatory measures to be overseen by a multilateral surveillance body, with adjustment assistance required as a condition for allowing time extensions to safeguards measures, and with exemption from safeguards arrangements for the least developed countries. The draft also raises the possibility of selective measures being used in special cases; this matter is left as an issue to be negotiated.

If there has been a change from the Tokyo Round, it is in the alignment of countries on the selectivity issue. In the Tokyo Round, the United States joined the smaller and mid-sized countries (including all of the developing countries and Japan) in strongly opposing the European Community's limited-selectivity approach. In the Uruguay Round, the EC position remains much the same, but the US position is far less firm. The United States has described as "interesting" the latest EC proposals to allow selective safeguards in carefully pre-

---

8. See Sampson (1987) and Petersmann (1988) on the evolution of safeguards discussion since the Tokyo Round. See also Kleen (1989).

Table 4.2   Key proposals and positions in the GATT safeguards negotiations

Group Chairman's draft of comprehensive agreement, June 1989[a]

- Time limits for safeguards measures; extensions to require justification and accompanying adjustment measures for protected industries. Overall maximum period of applications, to be followed by a period in which no safeguards measures can be applied.
- Measures to be MFN, but working group to examine possibilities for selectivity in special situations, in which case tighter disciplines and surveillance will apply.
- Measures to be in tariff form, but use of quantitative restrictions to be discussed.
- During initial period of application, compensation and retaliation need not apply. Retaliation and compensation will apply for extension beyond initial deadline.
- No safeguards measures to apply to products of least developed countries or of less developed countries with minimal market shares.
- All safeguards measures inconsistent with the provisions of the agreement to be phased out or brought into conformity.
- Surveillance to take place through surveillance committee.

United States[b]

- Criteria to be agreed for determination of justification of safeguards measures at the national level. Tariff increases could be allowed up to 50 percent over existing rates, while any quantitative restrictions must reflect imports over most recent representative period.
- Two options possible on MFN:

  Safeguards measures are to be MFN only, recognizing that countries may resort to gray-area measures, or
  Selectivity with varying disincentives.
- Measures can remain in place for up to eight years and should be degressive.
- Safeguards to be subject to compensation or retaliation and overseen by a safeguards committee.

European Community

- Safeguards measures could consist of MFN tariffs or global quotas and would not normally be open to countermeasures.
- Two-track procedure:

  Short-term safeguards to be applied through border measures alone and for a short period (e.g., 3 years)
  Longer-term measures to be accompanied by an adjustment process.
- Call for examination of circumstances where selective safeguards and stricter disciplines might be applied; for example, when a sudden surge of imports from a limited number of suppliers is sufficient to cause serious injury.

Source: GATT Focus, and *News of the Uruguay Round,* various issues (1989, 1990).
a. There have since been two revisions based on discussions within the safeguards group, but the main points remain the same.
b. The US position is not yet firm, and negotiators remain willing to discuss various ideas.

scribed circumstances (GATT 1990b), and has indicated a willingness to discuss the selective use of safeguard actions.

The US approach also focuses on eligibility criteria for the use of safeguards measures, accepting that some limited form of selectivity is an option, and stressing degressivity. The European Community has offered a short- versus long-term distinction, with adjustment facilitation a prerequisite in the longer term but not in the short, and has called for discussion of circumstances where selectivity may be used.

The small and mid-sized countries meanwhile remain strongly opposed to any form of selectivity. These countries are fearful of an EC–led and US–accepted move toward selectivity in the Safeguards Group.[9] Such a development would undermine the already fragile developing-country commitment to the round, yet any accommodation of the strong developing-country position on nondiscrimination would seem to make a new safeguards code less likely to emerge.

Prospects for an Agreement

Given the previous experience with safeguards negotiations, and given further that the major change thus far is the US shift toward accepting a limited form of selectivity, one might question whether there is enough movement to generate an agreement, or whether developments in other groups will be needed to make the difference.

We would suggest that the question should be put the other way around. Our sense of the situation in Geneva is that the Safeguards Group is viewed as one that is crucial to the success of the round, and that progress in a number of other key groups is now tied to what occurs in safeguards. Something may have to happen in safeguards before progress can occur elsewhere. What needs to be done is not entirely clear, but because the negotiations on safeguards were a failure in the last round, there is a lot of pressure to succeed this time.

The outcome in safeguards may also prove critical to progress in the textiles area. In the Negotiating Group on Textiles and Clothing,

---

9. See Hindley (1987) for a discussion of developing-country interests in the reform of safeguards and control over VERs.

proposals have been put forward to return trade in this area to GATT disciplines from its present regime under the Multi-Fiber Arrangement (MFA).[10] The European Community has argued, however, that if MFA quotas are eventually to be eliminated, more-flexible safeguards arrangements will be needed to guard EC producers against potential import surges. Such special safeguards procedures would be available during the transitional period, after which regular Article XIX procedures would be followed. Developing-country exports of textiles are now restricted by import quotas under the MFA, and these countries have long held that even more stringent rules are needed to prevent new Article XIX restrictions from perpetuating textile protection after the elimination of MFA quotas.

In the Negotiating Group on Non-Tariff Measures, conflicting arguments are also heard. On the one hand, exporting countries argue that firmer disciplines on the use of safeguards are needed to reduce the threat of Article XIX measures, and thus mitigate the pressures that force exporters into a VER negotiation. On the other hand, lax discipline on safeguards (such as the sanctioning of limited selectivity) would allow some of the present gray-area measures to continue.[11]

Safeguard issues have also arisen in the GATT Articles Group, where there was talk early in the round of a possible arrangement between developing and developed countries involving reform of Article XVIII:B[12] (which allows trade restrictions to be used for balance of payments reasons) and Article XIX. Article XIX disciplines might be extended to gray-area measures (used primarily by developed countries) in return for some tighter application of criteria for the imposition of Article XVIII measures. Here again the primary objective for the developing countries is a firm commitment to nondiscrimination. They would also like to see a commitment by the developed countries to enact structural adjustment measures before restricting

---

10. For a description and economic analysis of the various proposals to return textiles and apparel trade to GATT disciplines, see the chapter by Cline in this volume and Cline (1990).

11. Hindley (1987, 704) points out that a relaxation of the conditions governing the use of Article XIX could make it easier to substitute other VER measures. See also the discussion in Tumlir (1974), Nicolaides (1990), and Zietz (1989).

12. See Sociedad Editora Latinoamericana (1988) and Eglin (1987) for more details.

imports. Also of concern are how like-product, injury, and causation are to be defined.

Other GATT articles potentially affected by changes in safeguards include Article XIII (on nondiscriminatory administration of quantitative restrictions) and Article XXVIII (on modification of schedules).

The Most Desirable Outcome

An agreement in safeguards cannot be achieved in isolation from the negotiations going on elsewhere in the GATT. The best approach would seem to be a comprehensive one that takes a broader view of safeguards measures than those provided for in Article XIX of the GATT.

We would argue that relaxing disciplines on Article XIX safeguards, as in the EC proposal, is not the way to go, since it would allow the level of discipline in this area to decline to that in other areas. Instead, we believe that the most sensible approach would be to maintain high levels of discipline on Article XIX safeguards (regarding nondiscrimination and time limits, for example), and tighten disciplines elsewhere. VERs should be attacked directly rather than indirectly, with a commitment to eliminate these GATT–incompatible measures; in the interim a notification requirement and a surveillance mechanism should be established.

One should go further, however, to address weaknesses in the other elements of what Jeffrey Schott has called the "safeguards complex," namely, antidumping and countervailing duties. As we have seen, use of these measures is also growing. As these measures are already subject to GATT disciplines, tighter controls could be achieved by changes in the Antidumping Code and the Subsidies Code (which governs countervailing duty actions). Some of these changes would be technical, others merely procedural.

Beyond this, we would suggest concentrating on those elements of a new safeguards arrangement that would, in the medium to longer term, reduce adjustment pressures and hence reduce protectionist pressures.[13] Such an approach would tie adjustment assistance measures to the use of safeguards measures, as has already been proposed in the Safeguards Group. There are a variety of ways to do this. For example, the assistance measures could be made a mandatory part of any renewal of a safeguards measure, after an initial, time-limited application under MFN rules. Or they could be made available as an option linked to limited selectivity (say, for one year only), as an alternative to a time-limited MFN measure. Or, finally, they could be tied immediately to the use of any MFN safeguards measure sanctioned by the GATT.

There are some thorny issues to be resolved with the adjustment assistance programs themselves. What limits should be set on the size of such programs, and at what level should they be administered? Should the payments go to workers or to firms? How are trade-impacted workers to be identified? How are funds to be used so that they accelerate rather than retard adjustment? Many permutations, combinations, and levels of discipline are possible, and issues of program design remain, but the direction that should be taken is clear.

We suggest that a new safeguards code that places significant emphasis on adjustment assistance for industries or firms seeking protection, combined with tightened rules on the use of antidumping and countervailing duties, would generate relatively more use of Article XIX measures. It would also, importantly, facilitate adjustment out of affected industries, which in turn would reduce protectionist pressures over time.

Summary and Conclusion

The Safeguards Group is one in which the issues and debate remain much as they have been for 15 years. The central issue remains

---

13. Further suggestions for safeguards reform can be found in Robertson (1977), Tumlir (1974), Sampson (1987), Bergsten et al. (1987), Hufbauer and Schott (1985), and Petersmann (1988). There are themes to each suggestion, including the need for transparency so that individuals and countries can be made aware of the nature of protection for the industry and its cost; well-defined time limits; and structural adjustment measures.

selectivity; supporting issues include structural adjustment, compensation and retaliation, and multilateral surveillance. Group activities have continued to focus, as they have for a year, on discussion of a draft text submitted by the chairman, which hints at possible limited selectivity.

Progress will be required in safeguards before progress in other groups, including textiles and apparel, nontariff measures, and the GATT Articles group, can be made, but there are conflicting pressures for change from different participants and groups in the negotiation. A successful outcome in the Safeguards Group is less likely to occur from a balancing of interests within the group than from a comprehensive deal involving offsetting trades in other areas. Time is short, and how this bargaining works itself out in the remainder of the negotiation remains to be seen.

We stress in our description of a desirable outcome that safeguards arrangements cannot be evaluated in isolation from the rest of the trading system. To break the present impasse, we argue for an approach to safeguards based on tightening GATT disciplines on other import relief measures (gray-area measures, antidumping, and countervailing duties), rather than relaxing safeguards disciplines (such as through a move to limited selectivity). We also stress the need to link the use of safeguards actions to adjustment assistance to help defuse pressures for similar trade-restricting measures in the future.

References

Bergsten, C. Fred, Kimberly Ann Elliott, Jeffrey J. Schott, and Wendy E. Takacs. 1987. *Auction Quotas and United States Trade Policy.* POLICY ANALYSES IN INTERNATIONAL ECONOMICS 19. Washington: Institute for International Economics, September.

Cline, William R. 1990. *The Future of World Trade in Textiles and Apparel,* rev. ed. Washington: Institute for International Economics.

Eglin, Richard. 1987. "Surveillance of Balance of Payments Measures in the GATT." *The World Economy* 10, no. 1:1–26.

Finger, J. Michael. 1990. "Subsidies and Countervailing Duties." In H. E. English, ed., *Pacific Initiatives in Global Trade.* Halifax: Institute for Research on Public Policy, 87–100.

GATT. 1989. *Review of Developments in the Trading System. September 1988–February 1989.* Geneva: GATT.

GATT. 1990a. *The International Trading Environment.* Report by the Director-General. Geneva: GATT.

GATT. 1990b. *News of the Uruguay Round,* no. 34, p. 4.

Hindley, Brian. 1987. "GATT Safeguards and Voluntary Export Restraints: What are the Interests of Developing Countries?" *The World Bank Economic Review* 1, no. 4:689–706.

Hufbauer, Gary Clyde, and Jeffrey J. Schott. 1985. *Trading for Growth: The Next Round of Trade Negotiations.* POLICY ANALYSES IN INTERNATIONAL ECONOMICS 11. Washington: Institute for International Economics, September.

Jackson, John H. 1989. *The World Trading System: Law and Policy of International Economic Relations.* Cambridge, MA: MIT Press.

Kleen, Peter. 1989. "The Safeguard Issue in the Uruguay Round. A Comprehensive Approach." *Journal of World Trade* 23, no. 5:73–92.

Merciai, P. 1981. "Safeguard Measures in GATT." *Journal of World Trade Law* 15, no. 1:41–66.

Nicolaides, Phedon. 1990. "Safeguards and the Problem of VERs." *Intereconomics* (January/February):18–24.

Petersmann, Ernst-Ulrich. 1988. "Grey Area Trade Policy and the Rule of Law." *Journal of World Trade* 22, no. 2:23–44.

Robertson, David. 1977. *Fail Safe Systems for Trade Liberalization.* London: Trade Policy Research Centre.

Sampson, Gary. 1987. "Safeguards." In M. Finger and A. Olechowski, eds., *The Uruguay Round: A Handbook on the Multilateral Trade Negotiations.* Washington: World Bank, 143–52.

Sociedad Editora Latinoamericana. 1988. "Reform of Articles XII and XVIII-B (Balance of Payments Restrictions)." Technical Paper on the Uruguay Round No. 15. Caracas: SELA.

Tumlir, Jan. 1974. "Emergency Protection Against Sharp Increases in Imports." In H. Corbet and R. Jackson, eds., *In Search of a New World Economic Order.* London: Croom Helm Ltd., 260–85.

————. 1985. *Protectionism. Trade Policy in Democratic Societies.* Washington: American Enterprise Institute for Public Policy Research.

Wolff, Alan W. 1983. "Need for New GATT Rules to Govern Safeguard Actions." In William R. Cline, ed., *Trade Policy in the 1980s.* Washington: Institute for International Economics, 363–91.

Zietz, Joachim. 1989. "Negotiations on GATT Reform and Political Incentives." *The World Economy* 12, no. 1:39–52.

5

Subsidies

Gary Clyde Hufbauer

Trading nations have long recognized that government subsidies to industry must be disciplined as part of the broader quest for free trade. Otherwise each nation will be reluctant to lower its own trade barriers. Indeed, it can be argued that the elimination of tariffs and quotas, without comparable discipline on subsidies and other behind-the-border barriers, will simply promote the growth of these more opaque forms of protection. The maritime industry illustrates this sort of plague.[1]

In the 1970s and early 1980s, government subsidies proliferated in response to hard times in agriculture and declining industries. This trend has been reversed. In most industrial countries subsidies are stable or declining, and in certain developing countries they are being slashed. The subsidy climate changed dramatically in the late 1980s for several reasons:

---

1. For a general treatment and a summary of the international rules on subsidies established in the Tokyo Round of multilateral trade negotiations, see Hufbauer and Erb (1984).

Gary Clyde Hufbauer is a Visiting Fellow at the Institute for International Economics, and Marcus Wallenberg Professor of International Financial Diplomacy at Georgetown University.

☐ Budget stringency, as the claims of health, education, the elderly, and the environment pressed upon resources in nearly all the industrial countries;

☐ Growing public skepticism that industrial policy can revive sunset industries (even though sunrise industries remain the object of public affection); and

☐ Fiscal bankruptcy in many Latin American countries, which brought to a halt the long-standing practice of allowing their industrialists to feast on a rich menu of public subsidies.

Yet despite the present adverse climate for public subsidies, many delegations to the GATT Negotiating Group on Subsidies and Countervailing Measures are less than anxious to see their future freedom to subsidize curbed by an international code. Why the hesitation to adopt strict rules just when the climate for discipline is so favorable?

To begin with, many delegations in Geneva see as their principal task the negotiation of new restraints on the US law on countervailing duties (CVDs), not the design of new limits on subsidy practices. The imposition of CVDs is still a one-sided proposition, with the United States accounting for some 90 percent of the CVD cases launched worldwide between 1980 and 1986. In the 1990s, the European Community may face subsidized trade from Turkey and North Africa, and may step up its use of CVDs, but that danger lies in the future. For its part, however, the United States has no flexibility to change its CVD law unless significant new disciplines are agreed on domestic subsidies.

Also contributing to the difficult negotiating climate is the fact that the delegates in Geneva are often disconnected from the home ministries that control the dispensation of public subsidies. This is clearest in the case of the European Community: Directorate-General 1 (DG-1) handles external trade negotiations, DG-4 handles competition policy (including member-state aids to industry), and DG-6 handles agriculture. (To be sure, agriculture is not part of the subsidies negotiation, but DG-6 fears that the Subsidies Committee could set a "bad example.") In a situation where trade ministers have little control over industry ministers, many trade negotiators come to see their duty as preserving maximum freedom of action for their ministerial colleagues.

Finally, the US business community seems more anxious, on balance, to retain unfettered access to the US CVD law than to acquire new international discipline over foreign subsidies. Unlike the situation with antidumping duties (ADD), US firms have not yet experienced the harassing impact of foreign CVD actions. Yet many in the US business community fail to appreciate the consequences of the extensive overlap between the CVD and the ADD statutes. Many unfair trade cases can be (and are) filed as both CVD and ADD complaints. If the rules on the use of ADD law are tightened in the Uruguay Round, these cases will spill over to the CVD law, unless comparable disciplines are agreed to in the subsidies negotiations. This potential spillover is not attractive to the GATT Committee on Anti-Dumping Practices and could limit reforms in that negotiating group.

The Cartland Draft

In early May 1990 Michael D. Cartland of Hong Kong, the chairman of the Subsidies Negotiating Group, tabled a draft text that reflects elements from prior submissions offered by Canada, the European Community, Switzerland, the United States, and others, together with the chairman's own innovative ideas.[1] The Cartland draft is still incomplete: still to be written are the revised list of prohibited subsidies; provisions for special and differential treatment for developing countries (although the chairman has offered some tentative ideas on this subject); dispute settlement provisions; provisions for notification and surveillance; details on the functioning of the code committee and auxiliary bodies; and miscellaneous final provisions.

It deserves mention that, outside the GATT subsidies talks, subsidy discipline is also being negotiated in several other fora concerned with sectoral issues: steel (where the talks are principally between the United States and the European Community), the Airbus consortium (also primarily a US–EC issue), export credits (in the OECD), ship-building (in the OECD), and agriculture (also in the Uruguay Round).

---

2. The active participants in the negotiating group include the countries mentioned, plus Australia, Brazil, Mexico, Argentina, and Singapore.

Presumably the results of these talks will be folded into the GATT Subsidies Code, perhaps by cross-reference or detailed annexes. Of course the subsidy issues in agriculture are almost a make-or-break matter for the entire Uruguay Round (see the chapter by Hathaway in this volume); however, some of the other sectoral talks may well continue after the conclusion of the round.

The Cartland draft follows the familiar "traffic light" approach, in which subsidies are categorized under "red," "yellow," and "green" headings. Subsidies in the red category are prohibited outright; subsidies in the yellow category (actionable subsidies) may be challenged if they exert an adverse trade impact on another code signatory; subsidies in the green category are generally permitted, but even they can be challenged if they have a severe or prolonged adverse trade impact.

PROHIBITED SUBSIDIES

Part I of the Cartland draft defines the prohibited subsidies by enumerating three subcategories:

☐ The subsidies enumerated in the Illustrative List of Export Subsidies, with amendments (yet to be drafted);

☐ Subsidies contingent on export performance, even if they have other purposes; and

☐ Subsidies contingent on the use of domestic rather than imported goods as inputs.

The common thread running through this enumeration is the intentional encouragement of exports or discouragement of imports, either through fiscal subventions or through measures that have a comparable impact (e.g., tax holidays, loan guarantees, and bargain prices for goods or services supplied by public agencies).

The connection between the work on local content requirements in the Subsidies Negotiating Group and that on Trade Related Investment Measures (TRIMs) deserves mention. The TRIMs group has agreed to prohibit the use of local-content requirements (which mandate that certain of a firm's inputs be purchased from local suppliers) as an entry condition for the establishment of production facilities by foreign firms (see the chapter on TRIMs by Graham and Krugman in this volume). Still at issue is the use of local-content requirements as a condition for receiving public subsidies—for example, a tax holiday. The ASEAN countries, in particular, are fighting any prohibition of such practices. Thus, it is notable that the Cartland draft lists, as a prohibited practice, "subsidies contingent, whether solely or as one of several other conditions, upon use of domestic over imported goods." If this language survives in the Subsidies Code, it would knock out the use of subsidies as a means of implementing local-content requirements, at least among code signatories.

Under the Cartland draft, if a code signatory discovers that another signatory is granting a prohibited subsidy, it has two remedies: its first resort must be to consult with the offending signatory; if that fails, the country can complain to the Subsidies Committee. In turn, the committee may call upon a Permanent Group of Experts to judge whether the subsidy belongs to the prohibited category. The conclusions of the permanent group are presumptively accepted, unless disapproved by the committee.

The committee must make its recommendations within 120 days of receiving a complaint. If the decision goes against the subsidizing country, other signatories (not just the complainant) may take countermeasures. Countermeasures by the United States could take the form of a Section 301 reprisal for the loss of markets in the subsidizing country or in third countries.

ACTIONABLE SUBSIDIES

Part II of the Cartland text enumerates in broad terms the subsidies in the actionable category. Types of actionable subsidies include direct (from the government itself) and indirect (e.g., through parastatal organizations) subventions and loan guarantees, tax holidays, bargain provision of goods or services, and income or price supports. The limiting condition is that a financial contribution leading to an actionable benefit must be conferred on "certain enterprises" only and not be generally available throughout the economy. In addition to GATT discipline, actionable subsidies are subject to national CVD remedies.

Signatories would agree not to use actionable subsidies to cause "adverse effects" to the interests of other signatories. In the Cartland draft, adverse effects are defined to include:

□ Injury to the domestic industry of another signatory;

□ Nullification or impairment of benefits under the GATT, in particular tariff concessions (e.g., the use of a subsidy to undermine a bound tariff); and

□ "Serious prejudice" to the interests of another signatory.

The new feature in the Cartland draft is the content given to the term "serious prejudice," drawn from GATT Article XVI. Cartland establishes a rebuttable presumption that serious prejudice exists if:

□ The overall rate of subsidization exceeds x percent of the value of the product (the value of x is to be negotiated); or

□ The subsidy is contingent on trade performance (i.e., a required net trade surplus); or

□ The subsidy is granted to firms that sell x percent or more of their production for export.

In addition, serious prejudice may arise if the complaining signatory can establish that:

□ The subsidy displaces imports that otherwise would have been bought by consumers in the subsidizing country; or

□ The subsidy displaces exports of another signatory into a third-country market; or

□ The subsidy leads to price undercutting; or

□ The subsidy enables the subsidizing country to increase its share of the world market.

Under the Cartland draft, a mere investment incentive by itself does not constitute an actionable subsidy; the flow of commerce must be affected before a complaint can be lodged. This means, for example, that if an investment incentive attracts a foreign firm in

1990, but the firm produces nothing from that investment before 1992, and no displacement effects are felt for another year after that, the complaining signatory cannot bring a GATT case before 1993. The scope for mischievous maneuver created by this time disjuncture is apparent.

As with prohibited subsidies, the first remedy against actionable subsidies is consultation. If this proves ineffective, the signatory can then bring a complaint to the Subsidies Committee, which has 120 days to confirm that adverse effects exist (bearing in mind the presumptions as to serious prejudice). If adverse effects are found, and the subsidizing country does not either eliminate those effects or withdraw the subsidy, then countermeasures may be authorized.

NONACTIONABLE SUBSIDIES

Part III of the Cartland draft enumerates nonactionable subsidies. There are two subcategories: first, generally available subsidies, and second, subsidies that meet all of the following four distinct criteria:

☐ The subsidy is for the purpose of regional development, precompetitive research and development (R&D), environmental protection, or worker adjustment assistance;

☐ The subsidy is granted for a strictly defined period, not exceeding x years, and is degressive (i.e., gradually declining in force) within this period;

☐ Notification of the granting of the subsidy is given in advance; and

☐ No code signatory can demonstrate adverse effects.

Furthermore, if a nonactionable subsidy in the second subcategory causes "serious" or "long-lasting" adverse effects during its implementation, the affected signatory can resort to the remedy procedures already described. In other words, high-trade-impact tests are the safeguard against the abusive use of nonactionable subsidies.

COUNTERVAILING DUTIES

Part IV of the Cartland text outlines the standards for national application of CVDs. National authorities may proceed with CVD cases whether or not a complaint is launched with the GATT. No election or sequence of remedies is spelled out. This two-track approach represents a continuation of present practice. However, there are four points on which part IV of the Cartland text would significantly alter the present application of the US CVD law.

First, there is the open question of how nonactionable subsidies are to be dealt with under national CVD proceedings. The Cartland text does not spell out, although it clearly suggests, that the sole redress for the abusive use of nonactionable subsidies would be GATT–sanctioned countervailing measures. These measures would require a higher trade impact than the material injury test for national CVDs. Likewise, if nonactionable subsidies exert their trade impact in the home market of the subsidizing country, or in third-country markets, the Cartland text would seem to preclude unilateral action by the affected signatory (such as under US Section 301). Again, first recourse should be to the GATT Subsidies Committee.

Second, the Cartland draft would require that a CVD case be dismissed against a signatory if imports from that signatory are less than x percent of the importing country's domestic market (unless imports from several signatories granting prohibited or actionable subsidies cumulatively account for more than y percent of the market), or if the subsidy is less than x percent of the value of the product. Moreover, cumulation for purposes of making an injury determination is to be discretionary, not mandatory.

Third, the petitioner must demonstrate that, through the effects of the subsidy, the subsidized imports are causing injury; other factors must be explicitly considered and dismissed as the cause of the injury. This requirement would compel the US International Trade Commission to make more rigorous analyses in CVD cases than it has in the past.

Fourth, there is a sunset provision on CVDs. They are to be terminated when the subsidy ceases, or after five years unless "good cause" is shown for their continuation.

As a concession to the United States and the Community, an anticircumvention clause, patterned after drafts circulating in the Anti-dumping Negotiating Group, has been included in the Cartland text. Once a CVD finding has been made, the exporter could not avoid the CVD simply by shipping the component to a third country, assembling it into the final good, and then shipping the end product to the original importing country.

Negotiating Issues

PROHIBITED SUBSIDIES

The central negotiating issue, present at the beginning of the talks and remaining open right at the end, is how to bridge the gulf between the US and the EC views on the scope of prohibited subsidies. The United States is not willing to broaden the green light category of permitted subsidies beyond the "generally available" category already recognized in US jurisprudence, or otherwise "weaken" its CVD law, unless the Community is willing in return to enlarge the red light category of prohibited subsidies. The core issue for the United States is the lack of symmetry in the present treatment of green and red subsidies, with a *per se* test used for the former and a trade impact test for the latter. The United States will not be content with updating the Illustrative List to catch a few minor export subsidies that slipped through in the Tokyo Round. Nor will the United States be satisfied with Cartland's establishment of a rebuttable presumption of serious prejudice based on quantitative tests; instead the United States wants those practices that meet the tests to be prohibited outright.

The Community, on the other hand, argues that the Cartland text goes much too far; the Europeans are adamantly opposed to rebuttable presumptions of serious prejudice based on the quantitative scope of actionable subsidies. Moreover, within the Community, Germany has shifted from its historical "subsidy-discipline" stance and is now aligning itself with the "subsidy-tolerance" thinking prevailing in southern Europe. Germany is worried about the consequences of a rebuttable presumption of serious prejudice both for Airbus and for the contemplated revitalization of East Germany. The divergence between US and EC views on this critical issue threatens to scuttle the entire exercise.

One bright note is that the United States and the Community agree by and large on the need to update the Illustrative List of prohibited export subsidies.

INDUSTRIAL TARGETING

The main concern of Japan in the area of subsidies is the definition of industrial targeting: what practices, or combination of practices, amount to targeting an industry for global success? This issue is not addressed in the present Cartland text, but it is high on the US agenda. The United States would define targeting as an actionable subsidy if it involves a financial contribution coupled with a specific industrial policy, and backed up with collateral measures such as a high level of domestic protection, R&D support, relaxation of competition laws, or export credits. The Japanese are trying to ensure that the definition of targeting does not catch present Japanese practices. Likewise the European Community wants to avoid an encompassing definition.

WHEN IS A SUBSIDY SPECIFIC?

In determining whether a subsidy is specific or generally available, the key question is whether the test for specificity is *de jure* or *de facto*. Is a subsidy generally available if it is legally open to a wide range of enterprises? Or must the subsidy also be widely distributed in practice? In the Cartland text, both legal and factual tests must be met for a subsidy to be deemed generally available. Many countries, however, argue that legal availability alone should suffice. They fear that their programs will be compared against a standard of thinly spread jam: if any lumps are found, *de facto* specificity will be claimed, even where there was no intent to favor certain enterprises.

PERMITTED SUBSIDIES

Progress has been made on one issue: R&D support. Both the United States and the Community want to limit permitted R&D subsidies to "precompetitive" support, where the results of the research can be published and used "without restriction." However, it is not clear whether this phrase in the Cartland text includes the charging of uniform royalties to all users of the results. Detailed definitions of precompetitive support remain to be proposed.

Agreement has not been so easy to reach on other permitted subsidies. A big debate surrounds the scope of permitted regional subsidies, and there has been some shifting of positions. Canada, which historically has wanted maximum freedom to extend regional subsidies, now wants a strict geographic demarcation test and a general availability test for regional subsidies. Meanwhile, the Community has embraced the historical Canadian position, seeking maximum freedom to provide selective industrial assistance in depressed regions. Partly this position reflects the Community's commitment to Spain, Portugal, and Greece. But East Germany has added a new twist. While the West German government is currently talking in terms of rebuilding the infrastructure and cleaning up the environment in the East, it also wants freedom to subsidize the revival of the East German industrial apparatus.

Another innovative and contentious position put forward in the Cartland text is the idea that adjustment for declining industries should be limited to degressive worker assistance. This idea is most welcome to Canada, the United States, and some other delegations. But some parties—notably the Community, with a view to the problems facing automobiles and textiles in the 1990s—want the freedom to help sunset capitalists as much as sunset workers. Other countries, notably Japan, want to retain the freedom to honor their social contract of lifetime employment.

DEVELOPING COUNTRIES

One of the stranger twists in the subsidy negotiations is the newfound enthusiasm for subsidy discipline on the part of certain developing countries. Severe financial pressure has prompted many developing nations to push their industrialists off the public payroll. Enthusiasm for discipline at home has translated into a willingness to discuss international limits in Geneva. Argentina, Brazil, Mexico, Bolivia, and Chile are at least considering the merits of an international code that would back up their internal discipline.

By contrast, most East Asian nations simply want more discipline on countervailing measures, especially the United States' CVDs. Despite its free-market orientation, Singapore has been particularly prickly both in resisting new disciplines on subsidy practices and in attacking the American CVD process.

CVD REFORM

The most articulate exponent of changing the US CVD laws is Canada. In addition to the reforms spelled out in the Cartland text, the Canadian agenda includes three main elements:

☐ It would rely on specified factors to determine whether material injury is present; for example, if subsidized imports lead to lower prices or lost sales, then material injury would exist, otherwise not.

☐ It would give legal standing to industrial consumers and public representatives to testify at CVD hearings.

☐ It would measure actionable subsidies on a "net-net" basis, subtracting any offsetting charges imposed by the exporting country, as well as any subsidies paid to its own industry by the importing country.

Although the United States is not adamantly opposed to modifying its CVD law, substantial new discipline on subsidies will be required to sell a reform package to the US business community and to Congress.

The Ideal Finish Line

The Cartland text contains much that is admirable. How could I say otherwise? I endorsed many of its innovations in a paper I gave at the

Graduate Institute of International Studies in Geneva in November 1989 (Hufbauer 1989).

The basic question is whether unilateral flexibility to apply CVD and (in the case of the United States) Section 301 remedies will be traded for multilateral discipline on subsidies. The ideal outcome would be a maximum-maximum code: maximum discipline on subsidies together with maximum reform of CVD proceedings. This implies building on the Cartland text, not watering it down.

Maximum subsidy discipline is an essential ingredient of the broader movement toward free trade among GATT members. Without binding restraints on government subvention, it will be difficult to lower border barriers and even harder to dismantle behind-the-border restraints. Suspected subsidization by one government will breed emulation by others.

Maximum discipline on subsidies requires at least four modifications to the Cartland text. First, subfederal and parastatal subsidies must be made subject to code disciplines. At the very least, federal governments should be obligated to notify other signatories of all subsidies provided by subfederal and parastatal organizations. Otherwise foreign governments will be left in the dark, able only to apply *ex post* remedies when they discover an offensive practice. If a federal government cannot, for political or constitutional reasons, bind its subfederal or parastatal organizations to the disciplines agreed in Geneva, subsidies granted by those organizations should be subject to countermeasures without the benefit of any trade impact test.

Second, the types of subsidies that, in the Cartland text, give rise to a presumption of serious prejudice should be shifted to the prohibited category. This is no more ambitious than the discipline that the European Community and many other countries are trying to achieve internally.

Third, outside the agricultural field, the most offensive export subsidy is the widespread use of mixed credits (official credits extended on commercial terms but linked to soft loans or outright grants). Unless the OECD Export Credit Group makes significant progress in limiting this practice, it should be treated as a prohibited export subsidy in the revised Illustrative List.

Fourth, it should be possible for a signatory to bring an action against investment subsidies at an early stage, when plant location is being decided. If the complainant must wait to bring an action until the plant is installed and operating, the injury may by then have already been done.

Maximum reform of the CVD process entails at least three things beyond the Cartland text. First, all subsidy cases should be brought to the GATT Subsidies Committee, not only when third-country and subsidizing-country markets are at stake, but also when the impact is felt in the importing country. In other words, GATT proceedings should be initiated prior to, or parallel with, national CVD proceedings. In this way, a consistent international jurisprudence as to the classification of subsidies (red, yellow, or green), measurement of their amount, assessment of their trade impact, and permissible countermeasures would gradually evolve.

Second, greater restraint should be placed on the use of price undertakings (agreements between exporters and an importing government to set minimum prices) in lieu of CVDs. Price undertakings, especially those resulting from antidumping proceedings, have become a breeding ground for "soft" international cartels. As presently written, the price undertakings clause can mean that the worst punishment coming out of an ADD or CVD proceeding is that the offender is told to raise his prices—hardly an effective deterrent.

Third, some of the reforms urged by Canada belong in a maximum package. In particular, the Canadian emphasis on a few dispositive indicators of material injury and on public interest representation in CVD proceedings, is well placed.

After the Round

If the negotiations on subsidies succeed in yielding an outcome along the lines of a maximum-maximum package, two major tasks will remain for the post–Uruguay Round years.

First, of course, there will be a great deal of implementation work: surveillance, dispute resolution, and rule refinement. This will require substantial GATT Secretariat resources and periodic meetings of the Subsidies Committee.

Second is the whole complex of environmental issues. How long and to what extent will subsidies be permitted for such worthy purposes as new technologies to replace chlorofluorocarbons or to cut back on greenhouse gas emissions? How quickly must countries implement the ''polluter pays'' principle?

On the other hand, if the negotiations fail, much of the post–Uruguay Round work will involve picking up the pieces. Some may be picked up on a sectoral basis, but it may take the threat of unilateral countermeasures to get any work at all started in the dismal aftermath of failed negotiations.

References

Hufbauer, Gary Clyde. 1989. ''Discipline on Subsidies: The Uruguay Round and Beyond.'' Paper presented at the Graduate Institute of International Studies, Geneva, 29 November.

Hufbauer, Gary Clyde, and Joanna Shelton Erb. 1984. *Subsidies in International Trade.* Washington: Institute for International Economics.

6

Antidumping

Patrick A. Messerlin

The stakes of the Uruguay Round negotiations on antidumping are considerable. During the 1980s antidumping has emerged as the dominant mode of protection in manufacturing trade. As table 6.1 shows, import-competing firms have increasingly resorted to antidumping actions rather than to countervailing duty actions, escape clause actions, and Section 301 cases; more than 2,000 antidumping cases have been filed in the past decade alone. As a result, three core principles of the GATT are coming increasingly under stress:

☐ The principle of tariff binding is eroded by average antidumping duties four times higher than the corresponding tariffs on goods from countries enjoying most-favored-nation status;

☐ The principle of nondiscrimination is battered by the fact that, on average, an antidumping action leads to four different duty rates where previously there was one tariff; and

☐ The principle of tariff protection is evaded by use of antidumping actions, or the threat thereof, as leverage to obtain exporters' acceptance of nontariff barriers. Two-thirds of the voluntary export restraints imposed by the European Community and the United

Patrick A. Messerlin is Professor of Economics at the Institut d'Etudes Politiques in Paris. He wishes to thank Tom Bayard, Mike Finger, David Palmeter, and Jeffrey Schott for their useful comments on earlier drafts.

States between 1980 and 1987 have been negotiated in the context of antidumping actions.

Moreover, many antidumping actions have been terminated by agreements to fix minimum prices and quantitative restrictions on the product in question; antidumping enforcement has thus emerged as a powerful force for price collusion and cartelization in domestic markets. As a result, entire industries—steel and chemicals in the United States, both of these plus electronics in the European Community—are increasingly molded by this protectionist and anticompetitive instrument.

The Uruguay Round negotiations consecrate this dominance of antidumping actions over other modes of protection. Discussions on GATT Article XIX safeguards and on Article VI countervailing measures are meaningless as long as the disciplines governing antidumping procedures are less binding than the rules on safeguard actions and on countervailing duties. As disciplines on countervailing duties are traded for rules on subsidies, antidumping has an indirect influence over the latter. Likewise, discussions on the rules of origin for traded goods and on local-content requirements have emerged from obscurity precisely because they are closely connected with the controversy over firms' use of assembly plants in third countries to circumvent antidumping measures. Finally, discussions on Article XVIII:B, which provides for safeguards for balance of payments reasons, have led to the idea that increased discipline in the use of this safeguard by the developing countries could only be achieved if, among other concessions, increased discipline was imposed on antidumping by the industrial countries.

The protective effects of antidumping are powerful enough to threaten the trade liberalization envisaged in the Uruguay Round. In textiles, the gains from progressive dismantlement of the Multi-Fiber Arrangement will prove illusory if the more ''effective'' antidumping rules now being proposed are also adopted; the recent and increasing number of antidumping cases in this industry indicates the risk. In the negotiations on trade-related investment measures, the distortions introduced by the proposed anticircumvention procedure would endanger the benefits from liberalization of barriers in this area (see the chapter by Graham and Krugman in this volume). Finally, in the

Table 6.1   Import relief measures initiated, by type and country, 1979–88

Type of action	1979	1980	1981	1982
World		*Percent of total*		
Antidumping	59.0	89.3	77.0	61.8
Countervailing duty	33.3	9.4	13.2	35.4
GATT safeguard	0.0	0.0	0.6	0.5
Escape clause[a]	3.4	1.3	3.4	0.7
Other[b]	4.3	0.0	5.7	1.6
World		*Number of actions*		
All actions	117	149	174	432
United States				
Antidumping	16	24	15	63
Countervailing duty	37	11	22	145
GATT safeguard	0	0	0	0
Escape clause	4	2	6	1
Other	5		10	7
European Community				
Antidumping	53	26	47	55
Countervailing duty	2	0	1	4
GATT safeguard	0	0	0	1
Escape clause	0	0	0	2
Other	0	0	0	0
Australia				
Antidumping	n.a.	58	49	77
Countervailing duty	n.a.	0	0	3
GATT safeguard	n.a.	0	0	0
Canada				
Antidumping	n.a.	25	23	72
Countervailing duty	n.a.	3	0	1
GATT safeguard	n.a.	0	1	1
Developing countries[c]				
Antidumping	0	0	0	0
Countervailing duty	0	0	0	0
GATT safeguard	0	0	0	0

n.a. = not available.

a. The numbers in the table represent the proportion of each proposal (as measured by number of lines) that deals with the article in question.

b. Japan, Hong Kong, Korea, and the Nordic countries. Singapore is not included because its presentation differs from that adopted by the other proposals.

c. These changes would involve the creation of new articles.

Source: Country proposals.

1983	1984	1985	1986	1987	1988	Total, 1979–88
			Percent of total			
78.9	74.0	78.0	84.9	84.1	89.9	76.9
13.4	22.3	16.9	11.1	6.3	6.9	18.0
1.1	0.4	0.4	0.7	0.5	0.0	0.5
3.8	2.6	4.3	2.3	6.3	0.9	2.7
2.7	0.7	0.4	1.0	2.9	2.3	1.9
			Number of actions			
261	273	255	298	207	218	2,384
47	73	65	70	14	40	427
22	52	38	26	5	13	371
2	0	0	0	0	0	2
5	6	3	3	2	2	34
7	2	1	3	4	5	44
43	42	35	31	34	40	406
3	1	0	0	2	0	13
0	1	1	2	1	0	6
5	1	8	4	11	0	31
0	0	0	0	2	0	2
80	56	63	62	17	16	478
7	6	3	3	0	0	22
1	0	0	0	0	0	1
36	31	36	85	86	53	447
3	2	2	4	6	2	23
0	0	0	0	0	0	2
0	0	0	5	23	47	75
0	0	0	0	0	0	0
0	0	0	0	0	0	0

context of the proposed multilateral framework in services, the introduction of antidumping rules would work against the competition rules being offered to address the complex issue of national treatment through an "effective market access" clause.

The Current State of Play

As summarized in table 6.2, the negotiations on antidumping center on two very different topics: the enforcement of "classic" antidumping rules—those embodied in the Antidumping Code negotiated in the Tokyo Round—and the introduction of "new" antidumping issues not covered by the code. The talks involve a dozen active participants: the four main users (the European Community, the United States, and, to a lesser extent, Australia and Canada) of the present code; five countries and country groups (Hong Kong, Japan, Korea, the Nordic countries, and Singapore) often named as defendants in the antidumping cases initiated during the 1980s; and a few developing countries that have recently adopted or are about to adopt antidumping laws (Mexico, Morocco, Pakistan, and Turkey).

Since January 1990, the discussions have followed an informal procedure that allows a GATT deputy director to participate in the negotiating group; this change is itself a recognition of difficult times to come. The proposals on the table indeed show the polarization of objectives among the participants. All of the countries, except the European Community and the United States, would like to impose new limits on classic antidumping enforcement and are reluctant to consider the new issues. In contrast to this "liberal" camp, the European Community and the United States are resisting stricter disciplines on classic antidumping and advocate the introduction of the new issues. Their proposals mirror strong domestic forces lobbying for a still more "effective" protective instrument.

ENFORCEMENT OF CLASSIC ANTIDUMPING RULES

The proposed modifications to the classic antidumping rules can be classified according to the usual trilogy: establishment of the existence

Table 6.2 Extent of proposed changes in the GATT Antidumping Code, by article (percentages)a

Article	New issues		Classic antidumping							
	US	EC	US	EC	Japan	Korea	Hong Kong	Nordics	Liberal group^b	All countries
Preamble	3.5	17.9	0	0	0	0	5.8	3.0	2.2	1.5
1 Principles	0	0	0	0	0	0	5.8	3.0	2.2	1.5
2 Determination of dumping	3.5	0	0	13.6	53.2	59.3	24.2	46.4	45.8	32.8
3 Determination of injury	4.4	0	15.5	12.7	10.3	14.1	8.6	10.1	10.8	11.9
4 Definition of industry	32.7	0	8.7	8.2	5.7	1.6	4.3	3.0	3.7	5.3
5 Initiation and investigation	0	0	1.9	17.3	4.6	4.9	17.9	15.3	10.7	10.3
6 Evidence and investigation	0	0	45.7	12.7	4.0	1.1	14.0	0	4.8	12.9
7 Price undertakings	3.5	0	1.9	3.6	0	1.6	2.9	0	1.1	1.7
8 Imposition of antidumping duties	18.6	0	11.7	0.9	6.8	6.6	10.2	11.1	8.7	7.9
9 Duration of antidumping duties	3.5	0	3.9	15.5	7.5	10.9	1.0	4.0	5.9	7.1
10 Provisional measures	7.1	0	2.9	8.2	0	0	0	0	0	1.8
11 Retroactivity	23.0	0	7.8	4.5	0	0	0	0	0	2.1
12 Antidumping on behalf	0	0	0	0	0	0	0	0	0	0
13 Developing countries	0	0	0	2.7	0	0	0	0	0	0.5
14 Committee on antidumping practices	0	0	0	0	0	0	0	0	0	0
15 Dispute settlement	0	0	0	0	8.0	0	5.3	4.0	4.3	2.9
16 Final provisions	0	7.7	0	0	0	0	0	0	0	0
New issues^c	0	74.4	0	0	0	0	0	0	0	0

a. The numbers in the table represent the proportion of each proposal (as measured by number of lines) that deals with the article in question.
b. Japan, Hong Kong, Korea, and the Nordic countries. Singapore is not included because its presentation differs from that adopted by the other proposals.
c. These changes would involve the creation of new articles.
Source: Country proposals.

of dumping, demonstration of injury, and proof of a causal relationship between the two.

The approach of the liberal camp could be called one of "soft containment" because it does not openly address the basic question: is there any rationale for a code on antidumping when minimum standards for its enforcement by national agencies are not secured? In other words, does negotiation over the rules hold the prospect of gaining anything of value that the users of antidumping actions will give up with certainty for the next decade? That written general rules are sufficient was a tenable assumption for the Tokyo Round, where the participants were largely unaware of how easily antidumping procedures could become a mere protectionist instrument (this despite early warnings from the GATT working group; see Jackson 1969). That is not the case in the Uruguay Round, which inherits the legacy of a decade of protectionist drift (Finger 1990a, Hindley 1988, Messerlin 1989, Norall 1986, Palmeter 1989).

The liberal camp instead addresses the basic question indirectly, by underlining the absence of any economic rationale for dumping, and therefore for antidumping actions. Singapore and Hong Kong cite the principle that antidumping should not limit comparative advantage, whereas the Nordics assert the domestic competition principle: antidumping actions should not be aroused by "normal business practices." Corresponding changes in the preamble and Article I of the code have been put on the table.

The indirect approach has two weaknesses. First, it does not address the problem of the strong political rationale for antidumping, that is, the fact that "fair" general rules can be implemented in such a way that they lead to "unfair" outcomes; the US Congress or the EC Council is left with an impression of fairness, while pressure groups get the degree of freedom necessary to obtain most of the protection they want (Palmeter 1987, Cass 1989).

The second flaw is that the indirect approach, in negotiations lasting several years, runs the risk of being eroded, particularly when such statements of principle are followed by proposals that descend into the usual business of tinkering with the present Tokyo code articles. The impression that results is that dumping is "unquestionably" likely to occur, that stopping it makes economic sense, and that enforcement of antidumping rules by national agencies can be trusted to follow the rules set out in the code. Indeed, the erosion is well advanced: those who question the rationale of the code already risk being labeled "ideologues." Advocacy of stronger positions is often met with the objection that the negotiators have to be "realistic." This objection assumes that negotiators have no power—a debatable assumption in complex economies where opposing lobbies of equal strength may leave substantial room for maneuver to negotiators with firmly held views and clear-cut goals.

The soft containment approach is also illustrated by the relative weight the liberal countries give to the various Tokyo code articles in the reforms they have proposed. As table 6.2 shows, the provision most often targeted for revision is Article 2, which deals with the determination of whether dumping has occurred, and in particular with the methods for constructing "values" as proxies for prices in the overseas markets of foreign exporters. The proposals range from imposing a preference for third-country prices over constructed values (proposed by Korea, Hong Kong, and the Nordics), to holding that sales at a loss, even over an extended period of time, should be deemed to be in the ordinary course of trade if they result from reasonable market assessments (suggested by the Nordics), to stating that constructed values should include actual production costs and the commercially accepted profit margin in the exporting country (a proposal of Japan, Hong Kong, the Nordics, and Singapore), and to eliminating the possibility of "asymmetric" deductions and unfair comparisons (proposed by Japan and Singapore).[1] This focus on Article 2 is an implicit recognition of the absence of any serious hope of disciplining the two other parts of the trilogy.

The combative approach of the European Community and the United States regarding the enforcement of classic antidumping contrasts with the soft containment attitude. Their evaluation of antidumping enforcement during the past decade ignores the systematic and strong protectionist biases of national laws based on the Tokyo code. Indeed, most of the few stricter disciplines suggested by the European

---

1. Antidumping agencies have progressively introduced asymmetries in cost deductions when computing and comparing overseas prices and export prices.

Community and the United States concern antidumping laws adopted by developing countries.

Moreover, both the European Community and the United States have suggested new rules that if adopted would considerably reduce investigation costs in important situations for government agencies charged with enforcing antidumping laws.[2] For instance, the allegedly "unduly" restrictive condition of market isolation that must be fulfilled in regional dumping cases would be replaced by much looser conditions of import and production concentrations in the region concerned (an EC proposal).[3] The Community would also encourage the use of sampling in investigations involving many interested parties or products. Both the Community and the United States would extend the period of validity of provisional measures to six or nine months from the present four. The definition of industry would be stretched to cover agricultural goods processed in a single continuous line of production (a proposal of the United States and Canada). Last but not least, existing efforts of a domestic industry to develop and produce "derivative or more advanced versions" of the like product would be considered in the determination of injury (a US proposal),[4] and the mere coincidence of an import surge with declining sales for domestic producers, or of changes in the prices of dumped goods with changes in domestic prices, would be considered sufficient to establish causality (under a proposal put forward by the Community).

The European Community and the United States are in an awkward situation in which they no longer care to defend some of their own past provisions and positions on antidumping—this is an illustration of the drift in their enforcement. For instance, the Community has carefully

---

2. In the area of classic rules, the Community has taken the lead, whereas the US proposal mainly addresses matters of form rather than substance (including requests for more information and notification). Conversely, on the new issues it is the United States that has taken the lead.

3. A third condition is the existence of serious injury. This proposal would be a potential substitute for Article 115 of the Treaty of Rome governing EC member state protection.

4. This US proposal implicitly suggests that firms may need a long period for marketing new products. However, the United States refuses to consider that sales below cost may be necessary for a long period of time, as has been suggested in some liberal camp proposals.

avoided the introduction of a public interest clause, an embarrassing remnant in its own law that provides for representation by consumers and other interested parties. The United States for its part has succeeded in defining "other interested parties" by listing producers under four different headings (manufacturers, producers, wholesalers, and labor unions), while ignoring users and consumers.

THE NEW ISSUES

Both the United States and the European Community have proposed extending the Antidumping Code to cover so-called new issues. Their proposals conceive relief from dumping as a paramount right and openly aim at making antidumping actions more "effective." This extension of the code would be a massive one, as is best illustrated by the proposed US changes in 9 out of the 16 articles of the code to introduce the new concepts of "recurrent injurious dumping" and "repeated corporate dumping."

Recurrent injurious dumping would occur when a foreign exporter of a product already restricted under a previous antidumping measure undertakes changes in its production to avoid application of the antidumping measure.[5] Two types of recurrent injurious dumping are considered. They roughly correspond to the concept of "circumvention" the Community has developed in its own proposal.

The first type comprises situations where the changes are "so minor" that a *de novo* investigation of dumping and injury is deemed unnecessary. If circumvention is found to exist, the antidumping duty would be applied from the time the inquiry is instituted. The second type involves more "significant" changes in production. "Significance" for these purposes is defined in terms of five situations. For instance, in one situation the original exporter exports parts for assembly by a related party in the importing country, and the value of the parts is less than a certain percentage (to be fixed by the code) of

---

5. Strangely enough, the wording of the US proposal does not make any reference to the prerequisite of "change" mentioned in the explanations accompanying the legal text. In other words, plants owned by a foreign dumper at the date of the termination of the case could be covered under the legal wording of the provision.

the total value of the finished product. In a second situation, a third-country producer related to a previously investigated firm exports the product covered by the original dumping finding. Cases of "significant" change in production would require full investigations, but with more expeditious rules and procedures because of the related prior dumping.

Repeated corporate dumping would occur when a single corporate entity engages in repeated dumping in a single national market across the same general category of merchandise. Again the imposition of duties would start from the initiation of the investigation.

The Most Desirable Outcome

The most desirable of all outcomes would be the renunciation of antidumping actions, the most conspicuous survivor of the trade warfare of the 1920s and 1930s; this would imply elimination of the provisions relating to antidumping in Article VI of the GATT. The small fringe of dumping cases that do call for some form of counter-measure—mainly cases of predatory pricing—could be handled well by existing rules to promote competition. Yet the clear message of the last three years is that the lobbies and institutions involved in antidumping in the European Community and the United States will not surrender graciously.

What, then, would be the Uruguay Round's most desirable *achievable* outcome? That outcome can be summarized as follows: the introduction of no new issues and, in the domain of classic antidumping, the establishment of a few better rules combined with the introduction of some counterbalancing forces.

THE NEW ISSUES: PROTECTING PROTECTION

The proposals covering new issues are offered by their proponents as a way to update the Tokyo code to reflect commercial reality. In fact, they are designed to update the code in order to cope with the consequences of past antidumping measures. They are a way of "protecting protection."

Whether "recidivist" dumping will occur is determined by the type of antidumping measures taken. It is unprofitable for any dumper to dump again if the cost imposed by the antidumping measure is greater than the benefit it receives from its price discrimination. This is not the case if the matter is resolved through a price undertaking (a negotiated fixing of a minimum price), where the gains (the rent associated with the price increase) may be higher than what the dumper hoped to get from the price discrimination. Price undertakings are frequent in EC practice, and the way in which the United States enforces duties leads to a kind of *de facto* price undertaking.[6] Existing antidumping measures thus induce foreign exporters to dump again. It is amusing to note in passing that the concept of "recidivist antidumper" has never been suggested. However, evidence suggests it would be worth examining the point. Some complainants are more regular clients of the antidumping laws than other complainants or defendants. For instance, the Italian conglomerate Montedison was a party to 37 percent of all the EC chemical cases initiated between 1980 and 1985; the respective figures are 32 and 24 percent for ENI (another giant Italian firm) and Hoechst, and 22 percent for a non–EC firm, Alusuisse.

Similarly, high antidumping duties trigger circumvention, just as high taxes trigger tax fraud. Anticircumvention cases are a sign that domestic lobbies have been so successful in obtaining high duties—and so unsuccessful in producing competitive products—that the construction of foreign-owned assembly plants in the importing countries has become the most viable solution. The best illustration is the antidumping duties imposed by the European Community, which are as high (on average) as 15 percent to 20 percent on Japanese electronic goods.

Economic arguments aside, its defenders argue that this "protection of protection" merely reinforces legally made decisions and is therefore itself legitimate. The validity of this argument depends crucially on one question: was the initial protection granted under unbiased rules? Detailed studies of antidumping cases (Messerlin 1990) give an unambiguous answer, which is confirmed by many practitioners: the initial protection was granted under rules that have been captured by vested

---

6. David Palmeter has pointed out to me that it is debatable how often these *de facto* price undertakings occur in the United States.

interests to such an extent that any legitimacy they may have had has been lost. To address these new issues in the code would be to legitimize the biases and distortions that have arisen in the original measures.

CLASSIC ANTIDUMPING: TURNING BACK THE TIDE

The GATT is based on an uneasy paradox: it achieves freer trade by appealing to the mercantilist interests of nations, for whom the access they gain to foreign markets is worth more than the access to their own markets they give up. The price of adopting this approach is that the GATT is good at liberalizing trade, but weak at maintaining an open trade regime. Whatever rules the GATT adopts, mercantilist states in the end do what they want. Indeed, the European Community and the United States have already put into practice some of the ideas they are now offering as amendments to the Tokyo code. The best example of this is the anticircumvention provision adopted in the EC antidumping regulation in 1987, which the Community has applied in seven cases. Similarly, since 1988, the US Commerce Department has included parts and components in "classic" antidumping cases, for example in cellular mobile phones, and in that year the United States also amended its antidumping law to include an anticircumvention ("corporate strategy") provision; it has since initiated one case under the new provision.[7]

The GATT approach has another flaw. Its rules, including those governing antidumping, are subject to capture because they are static, fixed for a decade and exposed to abuse by import-competing firms with the motive, money, and time to find and exploit their loopholes. As with political constitutions, what counts is less the rules themselves than the balance established between institutions of relatively equal power but driven by different motives. There is no balance in the current GATT antidumping rules: firms are the driving force of the mechanism; the public authorities are merely its enforcers.

---

7. In 1989, the US Commerce Department announced that it would no longer include parts and components in cases dealing with finished products (Vermulst 1990).

These observations suggest two sets of proposals that might begin to turn back the tide in the area of classic antidumping. First are a few changes that would help to reduce the virulence of antidumping enforcement in the short run. It must be recognized that the computation of "constructed values" is an impossible task in a world dominated by flexible multinational firms. Therefore, agencies charged with enforcing antidumping rules should only consider observed prices. Moreover, calculations of dumping margins should include *all* transactions—those where overseas prices are higher than export prices as well as those where the opposite is true. Finally, a sunset clause providing for automatic expiration of antidumping measures after three years, and a public interest clause to involve users and consumers in assessing the costs and benefits of antidumping measures, should be adopted.

Second, and much more important, the only way in the long run to address the main issue—the capture of static rules by dynamic import-competing firms—is to introduce dynamic counterforces. These would take the form of institutions driven by different motives and rules than those motivating the antidumping enforcement agencies. One such type of institution would be "trade review" institutions at the national level. These would not be involved in antidumping enforcement on a day-to-day basis, but instead would provide annual reports on the way antidumping rules have been enforced and the impact of that enforcement on trade policy overall and on the country's welfare.

Another useful type of institution would be concerned with antitrust, or the promotion of competition more generally. These agencies would impose their guidelines on the definitions of products and markets and assess the impact of antidumping measures on the level of competition in domestic markets.[8] As is shown below, antidumping activity is highly correlated with the extent of price collusion and cartelization, and therefore authorities charged with promoting competition would be a natural counterforce to the antidumping authorities.

Two objections are usually made to the introduction of such institutions. The first is that countries are already free to introduce them if

8. Few GATT negotiators or observers have realized that working out such definitions in Geneva is equivalent to generating another set of competition laws, which is largely in conflict with the existing competition laws.

they want to, and therefore there is no need to include provisions in the code for this purpose. The second is that these institutions, where they exist, are less strong in some countries than in others—the Japanese Fair Trade Commission is often mentioned in this regard. These two arguments are mutually inconsistent: the best way to reinforce weak institutions is to enhance their legitimacy through international support.

If a choice has to be made, it is clear that these counterforce institutions are the more important reform, as the pitiful capture of the public interest clause of the EC regulations suggests. The desired outcome is not only fewer antidumping actions (a target that presumably the first set of suggestions would help to achieve, at least in the short run), but more competition, including competition from abroad. A shift from antidumping actions to safeguards or quantitative restrictions would be the likely—and undesirable—outcome of much stricter antidumping rules unaccompanied by institutions devoted to the promotion of competition.

HOW LIKELY IS THE MOST DESIRABLE OUTCOME?

Many would argue that the desirable outcome I have described is not likely to become reality. Yet it could be realized if three conditions could be met.

First, the liberal camp must be willing to resist any "linkage" between the introduction of the new issues and increased disciplines on classic antidumping. Such resistance will require determination, since the EC and the US negotiators are insisting on a balance between the two, and because the working document prepared for the July 1990 meeting of the Trade Negotiations Committee left the door open to such a linkage. Such a balance assumes the absence of actual links between the classic rules and the new issues, since if there are such links a bargain makes no sense. Yet there are indeed links between the two: rules affecting the new issues, if adopted, would reinforce the impact of classic antidumping rules. For instance, they blur even more the already vague definition of "like-product," so that foreign exporters could expect that an antidumping action against one product will more quickly spill over to others.

The second condition is that antidumping be included as one of the few elements in the final trade-off of the round, along with agriculture, intellectual property, textiles, and services. This condition is related to the first one. The "balanced" package between the two aspects of antidumping advocated by the EC and the US negotiators intends to withdraw the antidumping issue from the final trade-offs. If antidumping were included as part of the final bargain of the round, each major player could reach a satisfactory compromise with a common denominator: a more economically sound antidumping code. Although such a trade-off is likely, its possibility is still being denied by some negotiators. In any case, its likelihood and extent will depend less upon the negotiators than upon the relative strength of the domestic lobbies in the last months of 1990: pharmaceuticals and telecommunications services versus steel and textiles in the United States, banks versus electronics and textiles in the European Community, services versus manufacturing in Japan.

The last condition is that Japan must take a more aggressive stance on this issue. That it has not yet done so is intriguing, since Japan is one of the countries most hurt by the enforcement of EC and US antidumping rules in the late 1980s. It may be that Japan has been waiting for the outcome of the panel studying the Community's proposed anticircumvention procedure before taking action.[9] Or it may consider the political costs of leading a coalition on these matters excessive. Yet three other reasons—more interesting because more permanent—may explain Japan's attitude.

First, Japan may perceive that fighting over rules is useless, that what counts is rule enforcement—and Japan is not keen about winning Pyrrhic victories. Therefore, Japan may be saving its bargaining power for the frequent dispute panels expected in the future. This approach offers two additional advantages: Japan looks more convincing as a victim using international law to enforce its rights and reverse the "unfair" stance, and it keeps open for Japanese protectionist lobbies the possibility that they themselves may initiate antidumping actions in

9. The unilateral introduction of anticircumvention provisions by the Community and the United States induced their main target, Japan, to request a GATT panel in 1988. In March 1990, the panel concluded that the Community had violated certain GATT rules (*Inside US Trade,* 30 March 1990).

the future. Second, the past two decades have taught the Japanese that, in the long run, protection by the United States and the Community hurts those countries more than it hurts Japan, so that it does not pay Japan to fight it. Finally, Japanese interests themselves may be split. Those Japanese firms that paid the full price of EC and US antidumping rules by investing earlier and more heavily in those economies may see their rules as now protecting them against the entry of their strongest competitors, namely, other firms from Japan and the newly industrializing countries (Wolf 1989). Ironically, these firms may see EC and US enforcement of antidumping as a profitable extraterritorial version of Japan's own alleged anticompetitive stance.

Meeting these conditions will be helped by looking at some of the consequences of the new concepts introduced. For instance, the United States has suggested the possibility of imposing retroactive antidumping duties when sporadic dumping—defined as massive dumping of a product in a relatively short time—is accompanied by a history of dumping based upon findings by the authorities of the importing country—or a third country. Such a definition would allow the authorities of the developing countries to implement "cheap" antidumping actions based on cases investigated in the European Community or in the United States. EC and US exporters are increasingly aware of these dangers.

After the Round

The most desirable outcome described above would be a crucial first step toward gaining control over antidumping enforcement. It would be particularly useful for avoiding the dissemination of antidumping laws among the developing countries and the kind of "cold trade war" situations it may favor. It is worth remembering that 60 percent of the antidumping actions initiated by Brazil, Korea, and Mexico between 1986 and 1988 concerned goods that were also subject to EC and US antidumping actions.

However, even the preferred outcome cannot solve the more basic and increasingly frequent conflicts between antidumping and procompetition policy. Antidumping enforcement has become a cartel-favoring policy at the domestic level, and it is antidumping actions, not dumping itself, that tend to favor predatory behavior as part of a corporate strategy at the international level. As a result, the next decade will see countries having to choose between enforcement of antidumping and promotion of competition.

ANTIDUMPING ENFORCEMENT AS A CARTEL-FAVORING POLICY

Antidumping is often presented as a form of protection against foreign cartel-like behavior. Yet the evidence from the antidumping cases lodged since 1980 shows that quite the opposite is true: far from limiting unfair foreign competition, antidumping enforcement favors "fair domestic noncompetition." A significant number of cases involve only a single domestic producer. Many others are lodged by firms that find themselves in a situation where collusion or cartelization would bring advantages, but the firms are too weak to impose such collusion by their own means. Publicly enforced antidumping measures such as the establishment of minimum prices through price undertakings are an invaluable substitute for the lack of private discipline.

Detailed evidence on the true nature of antidumping has emerged only recently, because anticartel cases typically require long investigations. EC policy to promote competition has begun to reveal the existence of "twin" antidumping and anticartel cases. Two anticartel cases in the petrochemical industry, which is responsible for 40 percent of all EC antidumping cases, contain enough information about the intent, timing, and ways and means of the EC firms that originated the complaints to establish a crucial role of antidumping measures in the cartelization of EC markets between at least 1983 and 1986 for the two products concerned. Roughly speaking, one-fourth of the antidumping cases initiated during the 1980s can be related to one-fourth of competition cases in the Community.

There is little doubt that such twinning exists in the United States and in the other countries that make use of antidumping actions. US practitioners often suggest such a link when examining the inconsistencies between US antitrust and antidumping laws (for example, see Applebaum 1988, Palmeter 1989, and Wood 1989; on EC links see Bourgeois 1989). And the manner in which antidumping duties are enforced in the United States is likely to be a strong inducement to US firms to stick to prices determined by the minimum prices implicitly imposed on foreign exporters.

The oblique language adopted in the GATT and in the Antidumping Code obfuscates the cartel-favoring nature of antidumping actions. The use of price undertakings as a substitute for price collusion disciplines is the best example, but many other GATT concepts have similar potential. For instance, the practice of cumulation, whereby foreign exporters are aggregated into a single case even if they have minute market shares, is the mirror image of a weak cartel's need to eliminate mavericks. The mavericks' small market shares are not what matter; what is really at stake is the fact that even tiny mavericks can ruin tentatively agreed-upon price disciplines among cartel members. Similar arguments could apply to the definition of an industry or the right to demand hearings, and even to the ways in which sunset clauses are granted.

ANTIDUMPING AS PREDATORY BEHAVIOR

Dumping is often described as a form of predatory behavior, yet the evidence from actual antidumping cases suggests a very different reality. Predatory behavior simply cannot explain the almost 56 percent of EC antidumping cases in which no foreign country—much less any individual firm—has more than 5 percent of the EC domestic market. It seems highly unlikely that it can explain the almost 90 percent of cases in which foreign countries have less than 25 percent of the market (the figures for US cases are likely to be similar). On the contrary, antidumping enforcement can *favor* predatory behavior in corporate strategies because it offers import-competing firms a powerful instrument for raising their rivals' costs.

Anticircumvention rules provide a good example. If adopted, these rules would force efficient foreign firms to invest in countries that have no initial comparative advantage. The ultimate consequence would be that foreign firms would be induced to forgo any possibility of arbitrage in the future among the markets supplied by their various plants; in other words, the result would be to create trade barriers for the lifetime of the plants.

Another strategic use of antidumping enforcement involves plants specializing in export sales. The profitability of such plants can be hurt by antidumping measures restricting their exports. If there is no way to divert the plant's output without incurring large losses, the plant's value—and possibly that of the exporting firm's assets generally—will be artificially reduced; this opens the door for the original complainant to buy the plant at an artificially low price and then restore the plant to profitability by securing the removal of the antidumping measures.

From this perspective, it is amusing to listen to the emotional accusations of "unfair" competition—which are a good marketing device to sell the "us against them" argument in the political arena—and then observe who the complainants actually turn out to be. For instance, in the United States, the antidumping case in specialty steel against the Swedish firm Sandvik was mainly lodged by A.L. Tech Specialty Steel Corp., now a subsidiary of a Korean firm, the Sammi Group (Finger 1990b). In the 1987 EC synthetic fiber case, BASF–USA and Celanese–USA were not subjected to antidumping duties. Both are subsidiaries of EC firms—BASF and Hoechst, respectively—which happened to be complainants in the case (along with Du Pont). Indeed, Celanese had the *highest* margin of dumping (23 percent) among all US exporters in this industry. In contrast, all but one US exporter were subject to antidumping duties, a measure likely to give the EC (US) producers a dominant position in EC–US trade in these products. In Mexico, a 1987 case involving graphite electrodes for furnaces pitted Union Carbide against the French firm Péchiney. Examples of this kind abound.

ANTIDUMPING VERSUS COMPETITION: WHICH WILL DOMINATE?

The current state of the antidumping issue leaves no other recourse than to turn to procompetition policy. In the United States one hears many arguments against such policy. Despite their pertinence, they do not take into account one crucial point: the United States already has a "competition" policy, namely, antidumping enforcement.

Conflicts between antidumping policy and competition-promoting policy are likely to increase in number and extent, as the situation in the United States best illustrates. For instance, a bill recently approved by the US House of Representatives that intends to relax antitrust laws for joint ventures in manufacturing is likely to generate price discrimination behavior, and as a result trigger foreign antidumping actions against the joint ventures. This likelihood is probably increased by the fact that the bill concerns joint ventures in which foreign interests hold less than a 30 percent share—that is, ventures that may enjoy a more monopolistic situation in the United States than in world markets. Another potential source of conflict is the proposed extension of antitrust laws to strike at US subsidiaries of foreign firms that are found to engage in price fixing or other noncompetitive practices in their home markets. Under this law, antitrust lawsuits could be filed against foreign-owned firms for the damage their collusion might cause to American concerns operating abroad. In other words, this extension aims at fighting collusion or cartelization that previous antidumping cases may have created or reinforced.

Finally, combined conflicts between antidumping and competition policy in both the European Community and the United States may create worldwide disputes, as is best shown by the EC antidumping case involving the soda ash industry. This case witnessed an explosive combination of US firms acting under the Webb-Pomerene Act and EC antidumping and anticartel cases. Solvay, the Belgian firm that is a major complainant in the EC antidumping case and a firm under investigation in the EC anticartel case, has announced that if antidumping duties on soda ash are lifted, it will sue US soda ash producers in EC courts for infringement of competition, since the US exporter is a joint subsidiary of the six US producers.

Will antidumping policy capture procompetition policy, or vice versa? The Uruguay Round will not provide the definitive answer, but it will definitely prepare the ground on which the battle will be waged.

References

Applebaum, Harvey M. 1988. "The Coexistence of Antitrust Law and Trade Law with Antitrust Policy." *Cardozo Law Review* 9, no. 4 (March): 1169–73.

Bourgeois, Jacques H.J. 1989. "Antitrust and Trade Policy: A Peaceful Coexistence? A European Community Perspective." *International Business Lawyer* 17, nos. 2 and 3 (February and March): 58–67, 115–21.

Cass, Ronald A. 1989. *Economics in the Administration of US International Trade Law.* Toronto: Ontario Center for International Business, University of Toronto.

Finger, J. Michael. 1990a. "The Meaning of 'Unfair' in US Import Policy." Washington: World Bank, Country Economics Department, 27 February (mimeographed).

Finger, J. Michael. 1990b. "American Trade Policy toward Sweden: Bad Law Becomes Embarrassing Diplomacy." Paper presented at the Stockholm School of Economics, 21 May 1990.

Hindley, Brian. 1988. "Dumping and the Far East Trade of the European Community." *The World Economy* 11, no. 4 (December): 445–64.

Jackson, John H. 1969. *World Trade and the Law of the GATT.* Indianapolis: Bobbs-Merrill.

Messerlin, Patrick A. 1989. "The Uruguay Negotiations on Antidumping Enforcement: Some Basic Issues." In P.K. Matthew Tharakan, ed., *Policy Implications of Antidumping Measures.* Amsterdam: North Holland.

Messerlin, Patrick A. 1990. "Antidumping Regulations or Procartel Law? The EC Chemical Cases." *World Bank Working Paper Series* 397. Washington: World Bank.

Norall, Christopher. 1986. "New Trends in Antidumping Practices in Brussels." *The World Economy* 9, no. 1 (March): 97–111.

Palmeter, N. David. 1987. "Dumping Margins and Material Injury: The USITC is Free to Choose." *Journal of World Trade* 21, no. 4 (August): 173–75.

Palmeter, N. David. 1989. "The Capture of the Antidumping Law, A Review Essay." *Yale Journal of International Law* 14, no. 1 (Winter): 182–98.

Vermulst, Edwin. 1990. "The Reform of the GATT Antidumping Code: Circumvention." Paper presented at a conference on "The Reform of the GATT Anti-Dumping Code" sponsored by the Université Libre de Bruxelles, Brussels, 16–17 March.

Wolf, Martin. 1989. "Why Voluntary Export Restraints? An Historical Analysis." *The World Economy* 12, no. 3 (September): 273–91.

Wood, Diane P. 1989. "Unfair Trade Injury: A Competition-Based Approach." *Stanford Law Review* 41, no. 5 (May): 1153–99.

7

Services

Brian Hindley

Unless the whole Uruguay Round unravels, I believe that there will be a General Agreement on Trade in Services (GATS). The content of the agreement is still far from clear, however, and the number of signatories, especially among the developing countries, is still uncertain. A draft framework agreement constructed by the GATT Secretariat on the basis of the Montreal Declaration of April 1989 and the stated views of participants in the negotiation in the following months (GATT Secretariat 1989) gives some indication of the state of agreement in the Group on Negotiations on Services (GNS). On my count, the draft contains 178 bracketed passages, each indicating a point of disagreement. Of course, not all of these brackets are independent of one another, so that 2^{178} overestimates the number of possible variants contained in the draft. Even so, 2^{178} is a very large number (roughly 10^{54}). A number that 10^{54} overestimates may still be very large. The GNS has much work still to do. It may not be possible to complete the negotiation before the December 1990 deadline.

Special Characteristics of Services Trade

The underlying difficulties of any negotiation about trade in services, compared with a negotiation about trade in goods, stem from two principal differences between goods and services. They are that:

Brian Hindley is a Senior Lecturer at the London School of Economics.

130

☐ International transactions in services more often entail some form of international factor movement, and the establishment of operations by the provider in the country of the receiver, than do transactions in goods; and that

☐ Government regulation of service industries often assumes an intensity and a form that is rarely found in goods industries.

INTERNATIONAL FACTOR MOVEMENT AND ESTABLISHMENT

Goods are tangible. With more or less trouble or cost, they can be transported from their place of manufacture to the place where they are consumed. Thus, goods can be traded across borders without the provider or the recipient leaving their own countries. Some services can also be traded across borders. If I can conduct business with my bank across town by computer terminal, so can a customer in another country. Any service transaction that takes place within a country entirely by mail, facsimile (fax), or phone, without direct personal contact, can also be traded internationally. Such services, called "tradeable services," or "long-distance services" in the terminology of Bhagwati (1984), do not, strictly speaking, involve the "movement" of the service from place to place in the way that goods move. Instead the outcome of the service (the person or thing changed by the service) or the signifier of property rights generated by the service (for example, a bank statement or an insurance policy) is transported, either within a country or across international borders, without relocation of either the provider or the receiver of the service.

Other services require only a brief period of relocation rather than permanent residence: an architect or consulting engineer, for example, may need to make only a few brief visits to a site or project. Such services are also traded internationally with relative ease.

Transactions in many services, on the other hand, require the geographical proximity of the service provider and the service receiver. International transactions in these services are much more likely to require some form of international factor movement than are international transactions in goods or in tradeable services. This does not necessarily mean that the factors of production needed to provide the service will have to move to the country of the receiver (Sampson and Snape 1985)—movement may occur in the opposite direction instead, as in the case of tourism—but that is what it will often mean in practice.

Imports of most services are not easily detected by customs officers at international frontiers. Hence, domestic providers of these services cannot be protected from foreign competition by border measures such as tariffs and quotas. Instead, laws, administrative actions, or regulations that bear on foreign service providers with a particularly heavy weight become the primary means of protection. Services that require the presence or the establishment of operations by foreign firms in a country's domestic market are particularly vulnerable. Restrictions on foreign presence or establishment in fact constitute one of the most effective barriers to international transactions and competition in the service sector.

For this reason, a central issue in the services negotiations in Geneva is whether a General Agreement on Trade in Services (GATS) will apply only to cross-border trade in services—services that can be supplied by a provider in country A to a receiver in country B without relocation by either—or will also include transactions that require the movement of factors of production. If the latter, two further questions arise, both of which touch upon major political sensitivities. The first is whether the GATS will extend to the right of firms to establish operations in foreign countries. The second is whether and to what extent the GATS should apply to international movements of labor for the purpose of providing a service. The answers to these questions will play a large role in determining the scope of the GATS. A GATS that applied only to cross-border trade could be useful: the potential for such trade is growing rapidly. But relative to the service sector as a whole, its scope would be quite limited.

REGULATION

The second relevant characteristic of service industries is the prevalence and extent of regulation and the different form that regulation often takes in services as opposed to goods trade. Services are typically customized. A lawyer or a doctor advises one person on one problem and one set of circumstances, and another person on another problem and set of circumstances. This one-of-a-kind character of many services makes regulation of the *output* of service industries difficult. It is less costly for governments to regulate instead the quality of *inputs* into the provision of services.

Regulation of inputs, however, easily becomes a barrier to the entry of new competitors, including foreign competitors, and thus a barrier to trade or inward investment. From this point of view, regulation is a form of nontariff barrier (NTB), and its use for protective purposes in services is analogous to the use of health and safety regulations to impede trade in goods. In fact, health and safety regulation of traded goods also sometimes takes the form of regulation of inputs; among these cases are some classic examples of stiff protection amounting to an effective ban on imports.[1] In both goods and services industries, regulation is widely regarded as a justified measure of public policy and as essential to the efficient supply of the regulated good or service. And in both, identification of the point at which legitimate action ends, and protection against foreign competition begins, is difficult.

If domestic service industries are to be protected, the protection typically must be by NTBs, and hence to a large extent by regulation—there is often no tariff alternative. Thus, regulatory NTBs impeding trade in services may be even less tractable than NTBs that affect trade in goods, for which tariffication provides a possible liberalizing option on the way to open trade. The difficulty is further increased by the broad discretionary power of many regulatory authorities. Regulations on paper are one thing; the actions of regulatory authorities may be quite another.

The prevalence of regulation in service industries creates yet another problem—one not so usefully thought of as an NTB. It is that when there is cross-border trade in services, differences in the form or the level of regulation between national jurisdictions lead to competition among national regulatory systems. Regulation affects the costs incurred by the producers of a service. Hence, when producers subject to the

---

1. An extreme example is that of British heat-treated (long-life) milk imports. In this case, the British authorities required on-site inspection of all dairy facilities producing for the UK market, but no funds were made available for the inspectors to travel to facilities located abroad. The result was that no imports were allowed to enter.

regulations of country A are free to sell services in country B without being subject to country B's regulatory system, and vice versa, there is not only competition between producers in the two countries. There is also competition between the national regulatory systems of country A and country B.

When compliance with the regulations of country A is more costly than compliance with those of country B, free cross-border trade threatens the ability of the country A regulatory authorities to apply what they regard as proper and legitimate regulation. Proposals for free cross-border trade in regulated services are therefore likely to rouse powerful opposition. Mere differences in regulation, in other words, can be the foundation of major difficulties to the negotiation of free trade in services.

An obvious solution is to harmonize regulations across countries. The difficulty, however, is to choose the harmonized regulations. If countries A and B have different regulatory structures, which each nevertheless regards as the best way to do the job, how can a compromise be struck between them?

The European Commission spent years trying to find such a compromise and failed. If the Commission, backed by the Treaty of Rome, could not negotiate harmonized regulations within a group of countries that is much more homogeneous than the membership of the GATT, that route is not likely to be a useful one for the GATT negotiations to follow.

The European experience illustrates all of the problems touched upon here. The Treaty of Rome mandates free intra-Community trade in both goods (Articles 30 to 36) and services (Articles 59 to 66). Progress in liberalizing trade in goods was rapid—removing tariffs and quotas is technically easy, whatever its political difficulties. By contrast, liberalization of intra-Community trade in services had hardly started before the 1992 initiative was launched. That failure was due to the prior existence of different levels of national regulation, which the member states with the heaviest regulation stubbornly defended (Hindley 1987b).

The Commission's approach to services in the 1992 program involves mutual recognition of regulatory standards, so that in principle (although not yet in practice) a British insurer can sell insurance in Germany subject only to the approval of the British regulatory authorities. Some elements of that solution might be transferable to a GATS. As practiced in the European Community, however, mutual recognition calls for negotiation of minimum standards of regulation. That is an easier negotiating target than harmonization, but it still raises major problems, and would surely raise greater problems in the GATT than in the European Community.

The establishment problem and the regulation problem are not independent of one another. Another solution to the problems raised by national regulatory systems would be to combine a right of establishment with an agreement that the national regulations of the host country shall apply to establishments within that country. That solution avoids, or begs, the question of appropriate regulatory structure, but it runs into the hostility, especially marked among developing countries but not confined to them, to rights of establishment enforced through the GATT. It would, however, allow competition between service providers of different nationalities within given regulatory structures. That would be a considerable advance on the current situation, in which, in many services and countries, there is neither competition among regulatory systems nor competition between domestic and foreign suppliers (and indeed sometimes little competition among domestic suppliers).

What Would Constitute a GATS of Economic Substance?

A *sine qua non* of a GATS of genuine economic substance is a solution to either or both of the regulatory problem and the establishment problem. There exist services in which international transactions are not heavily affected by national regulations and regulators. And there certainly are services that can be traded across borders without the need for establishment. But there are few services in which international transactions neither are subject to regulation nor require establishment—and trade in services in that fortunate state is typically rather free in any case. A GATS of substance is possible with a solution to only one of the two problems. It is difficult to see that a worthwhile agreement can emerge if neither is solved.[2]

"Solved" does not necessarily mean a cut-and-dried solution in the Uruguay Round itself. Instead "solved" might mean, and almost certainly in practice must mean, acceptance of some set of principles, and some legal or political process for implementing them, that continues well beyond the end of the Uruguay Round but that nevertheless holds the promise of expanding rights of establishment and commercial presence, or of reducing the restrictive effects of national regulations, or both. A bad agreement, on the other hand, would be one that actually made the future solution of these problems more difficult.

What Sort of Agreement is Likely?

The GNS has received draft framework agreements from the United States (United States 1989); from a group of developing countries including Brazil, Chile, Colombia, Cuba, Honduras, Jamaica, Nicaragua, Mexico, Peru, Trinidad and Tobago, and Uruguay (Brazil et al. 1990); from a second group of developing countries including Cameroon, China, Egypt, India, Kenya, Nigeria, and Tanzania (Cameroon et al. 1990); and from the European Community (European Communities 1990). There is a clear separation on the approach to establishment and national regulation between the draft frameworks of the United States and the European Community, on the one hand, and those of Brazil et al. and Cameroon et al. on the other. There are also differences between the US and the EC drafts,[3] but these differences pale into

---

2. Of course, if international transactions in a service are not now impeded, an agreement would be quite useful if it increased the probability of that state persisting. But that can hardly be described as "liberalization."

3. Some important differences are that the EC draft provides for antidumping action (Article VIII), whereas the US draft does not; that the EC draft provides for emergency safeguard action (Article XI), whereas the US draft does not; and that the EC draft provides for action against restrictive business practices (Article X), whereas the US does not. Also, the EC draft permits (Article XXI) a party ". . . to withhold, in whole or in part, the resulting benefits from another party when it considers that the level of commitment of the other party is not in keeping with the characteristics of that party's

insignificance when those drafts are compared with the other pair. Some relevant sections of the US draft are the following:

Article 4: Establishment

4.1 With respect to provision of any covered service, each Party within its territory shall permit persons of any other Party to establish or expand a commercial presence for the provision of a covered service (including, *inter alia,* acquisition of an existing company, establishment of a new company, or joint venture or affiliation with an existing company) on a basis no less favorable than that accorded in like circumstances to its persons. . . .

Article 5: Cross-Border Provision of Services

No party shall establish or maintain any measure that prohibits or restricts the provision of a covered service to persons within its territory on the basis that the service or service provider is located partially or wholly within the territory of another Party. . . .

Article 8: National Treatment

8.1 Whenever market access has been achieved by a service provider of another party with respect to the provision of a service, each Party shall accord national treatment to that service provider with respect to the provision of that service. . . .

8.1.2 For the purposes of paragraph 8.1, a service provider shall be deemed to have achieved market access with respect to a Party, whenever it has entered that Party's market, either through establishment, cross-border transactions, or use of the service of the public telecommunications transport network. . . .

Article 11: Domestic Regulation

11.1 The parties recognize the right of each Party to regulate within its territories the provision of covered services, including the right of Parties to introduce new measures consistent with the Agreement. Parties shall ensure that such measures are not prepared, adopted or applied, the intent or effect of which is to nullify or impair the obligations of this Agreement. . . .

11.3 Each party shall provide procedures for the prompt hearing and reviewing of complaints arising in connection with the regulation of covered services and for the prompt correction of administrative action, where justified. . . .

---

market and its degree of liberalization. . . . '' Thus, the EC draft opens the possibility of discrimination between parties within particular sectors—a possibility that the US draft does not raise.

The US draft clearly supplies the basis for a substantial agreement. Even so, its immediate impact might not be great in practice. Article 22.1, for example, provides that "Reservations to some or all of the provisions of Chapter III ["Market Access," which includes Article 4,] Article 8 and Article 13 ["Government Aid"] of this agreement may be entered with respect to specific services, or specific aspects of existing legislation. . . ."

Even were the US draft to be adopted as it stands, therefore, reservations by individual signatories might dilute its immediate impact. That is an observation, not a criticism. A framework that is strong and clear, even with a separate (and perhaps long) list of national reservations is preferable to a framework that is weakened and distorted by efforts to accommodate national interests within itself.

The US draft does have some notable omissions, however. The only safeguards mentioned are those for balance of payments reasons (Article 15).[4] The strong establishment provision is not matched by any parallel provision for movement of labor for the purpose of providing a service. Finally, except for the language in the preamble, there are no special provisions for developing countries (although special treatment could be achieved informally through the reservations that such countries are allowed to make).

These omissions are fully remedied in the drafts of Brazil et al. and Cameroon et al. Large parts of both these drafts address the issue of special and differential treatment for developing countries. Developing countries in the GNS do not like the term "special and differential," perhaps because of the unfavorable connotations that term has acquired

---

4. The joint effect of Articles 8.4 and 13 is unclear, and the draft may be interpreted as allowing for safeguards to preserve, for example, a partly indigenous banking system. Article 8.4 says that "The provisions of this Article shall not prevent any Party from bestowing government aid exclusively on service providers of that Party." Article 13, on the other hand, rules that "No party may grant, directly or indirectly, government aid for the provision of covered services within its own territory, or within or into the territory of any other country, if such aid causes injury to the interest of another party." (Article 17 [General Definitions] does not define "service providers of that Party" but does define its converse, "service providers of another Party": that definition is in terms of the nationality of the owners or controllers of the service provider.) Does Article 8.4 allow a government to aid banks owned or controlled by its own nationals when they are in direct competition on its territory with banks of another party?

elsewhere in the GATT. Nevertheless, their proposals are in fact proposals for special and differential treatment in that they do not flow from any sound logic connecting development with liberalization of trade in services (Hindley 1988). The economic arguments for special and differential treatment are weak (Hindley 1987a). The case for it is essentially political and turns upon the extent to which developed countries are willing to empty the GATS (or the GATT generally) of content, at least so far as it applies to developing countries, in order to obtain those countries as signatories. The issue should be separated from the primary issues involved in constructing a GATS.

With respect to establishment, Brazil et al. (1990, Article 2) and Cameroon et al. (1990, Article 1) adopt essentially the same formula, which is quite different from that in the US and the EC drafts. The Brazil et al. draft states:

> International trade in services is defined to cover transactions involving:
> a. cross-border movement of the service
> b. cross-border movement of consumers
> c. cross-border movement of factors of production under conditions of specificity of purpose, discreetness of transactions and limited duration. (Brazil et al. 1990, Article 2).

But Cameroon et al. drive the point home with the express addition that:

> 2. Trade in services shall not extend to establishment, or foreign direct investment, or international immigration.
> 3. Factors of production shall be treated symmetrically in the Framework and in market access negotiations. . . .

A similar "symmetry condition" appears as Article 1(10) of the Brazil et al. draft.

On regulation, Article 1(6) of the Brazil et al. draft provides that "The policy objectives of national laws and regulations applying to trade in services shall be respected." And Article 7(1) allows "Parties [to] adopt and enforce such laws and regulations as may be necessary to prevent service suppliers of any origin from engaging in unfair trade, creating market distortions, acquiring undue market domination or otherwise obstructing competition, or frustrating the attainment of the objectives of the Framework. . . . "

Article 11 of the Cameroon et al. draft says that "Parties to the Framework shall have a right to regulate the provision of services within their territories, *inter alia,* through the grant of exclusive rights in certain sectors, in order to implement national policy objectives. . . . The Parties recognize that developing country Parties may have a particular need to exercise this right. . . . "

The drafts of Brazil et al. and Cameroon et al. both contain elaborate safeguard provisions. In addition to balance of payments measures, both would allow safeguard measures to ". . . be applied to avoid or remedy unforeseen injury arising from increased supply of services resulting from liberalization commitments." Article 9(4) of the Cameroon et al. draft would also allow "safeguard" measures to be:

. . . applied by developing country Parties when there is a need to:

a. promote the creation of certain service sectors, sub-sectors or activities, [or]

b. correct structural problems such as those related to technological changes and capital formation in a sector, sub-sector and/or activity, when they have an important bearing on the trade balance.

Moreover, Article 9(5) of the Cameroon et al. draft allows ". . . safeguard measures to be applied in order to deal with adverse trade effects caused by situations of concentration of ownership, market domination and restrictive business practices."

Clearly, there is a very wide gulf between the US position and that of these developing countries. The United States proposes that a right of establishment be included in the agreement, whereas Brazil et al. and Cameroon et al. would exclude it. The United States would exclude the movement of labor for the purpose of supplying a service; the sponsors of the developing-country drafts want labor and capital to be treated symmetrically.

With respect to regulation, the US draft suggests clear rules that would facilitate legal process. The requirement that "Parties shall ensure that such measures are not prepared, adopted or applied, the intent or effect of which is to nullify or impair the obligations of this Agreement" (Article 11.1) would at minimum allow argument as to alternative means of achieving the stated objectives of a regulation. The language of the EC draft is even more direct (as might be expected of a party with direct internal experience of the problems created by regulation): Article V(1)(d) says that "Rules, standards and qualifications required shall not be more burdensome than necessary for the attainment of the public policy consideration envisaged. . . ''

In contrast, the statement in the Brazil et al. draft that ''The policy objectives of national laws and regulations applying to trade in services shall be respected'' is likely to be interpreted to mean that the objectives of a particular government regulation need not be stated. That would effectively block any argument about alternatives.

Moreover, Brazil et al. and Cameroon et al. offer many roles for regulation, and many grounds for the application of safeguards—holes for protectionist rabbits. A framework that enshrines protectionist practice would be worse than no framework at all. No one interested in liberalizing international transactions in services could accept the drafts of Brazil et al. and Cameroon et al. in preference to that of the United States.

This is not to say that the US draft is beyond criticism. The United States is pressing (as is the European Community) for a right of establishment but seeks to exclude a similar right for the international movement of labor. Yet the economic arguments are the same for both. A full range of banking services cannot be offered without establishment, nor can an airport be constructed in a developing country and shipped elsewhere. Countries would gain by permitting establishment of banks, but they would also gain by permitting the least-cost supplier to bring in its workers to build their airports. The political difficulties associated with international movements of labor are easy to understand. But these are essentially the difficulties associated with a right of establishment in developing countries.[5]

Moreover, would it not be sensible to provide (as the EC draft does) explicit safeguards for domestic industries that are threatened with extinction? The United States itself has displayed sensitivity about nationality of ownership of a number of service-providing industries (for example, broadcasting and maritime and air transport). Explicit provisions to allow protection of an indigenous core of an industry, for example, probably would facilitate acceptance of an otherwise stronger framework.

---

5. These issues are discussed in more detail in Hindley (1990).

To become functional, any framework that is agreed upon will require at least two additional sets of documents. The first will consist of sectoral annotations—notes on how particular articles of the framework will or will not apply to specific service industries. In the second, each signatory will list those of its own industries, and/or its policies toward them, to which the framework will or will not apply. Whether these lists will be in positive form (specifying the policies, practices, and industries to which each country is willing to apply the framework, with all others excluded from coverage) or in negative form (specifying only the excluded policies, practices, and industries, with all those not mentioned covered by the framework) is still not agreed.

That whole industries might be excluded creates dangers. It is widely believed that the United States, for example, will exclude maritime transport (more accurately, it is believed that that industry will be able to muster enough political muscle to force its own exclusion, just as it managed to exclude itself from the US–Canada free trade agreement, despite the use of fast-track procedures for congressional ratification). If that happens, and if other major participants use the precedent as a basis for attempts to exclude sensitive industries of their own, the outcome of the negotiations will be thrown into doubt.

Moreover, the United States has not decided its position on the treatment of financial services in the GATS framework. Two propositions seem to lie behind this hesitation. One is that the regulatory needs of financial services are so great and so different from those of other services that the problems cannot be met merely with sectoral annotations to a general services framework. The other is that an agreement on financial services should be stronger than any agreement that is likely to be achieved in a general framework. These propositions are potentially contradictory, but in the US view both lead to the same conclusion, which is that financial services may require an agreement that is quite different in key respects from the general framework.

Some crucial and potentially contentious issues have hardly been broached in the negotiations. Dispute settlement is one. Discussion of that issue is likely to entail discussion of whether remedies for breaches of the GATS rules will be restricted to the service sector involved or may be extended to other service sectors, or even to trade in goods. Influential voices in the United States are urging that cross-retaliation between goods and services should be permitted.

Overall, my guess (and hope) is that the final agreement will resemble the US draft more than those offered by the developing countries. But if it does, that immediately raises the question of how many signatories the agreement will initially have. Perhaps it will not have many. A widely mooted possibility is that the signatories will be the OECD members plus a handful of developing countries, mostly from East Asia. However, with the date for formal completion of the round fast approaching, there is room for serious doubt that the services negotiations can be completed in time. The question therefore arises whether some part of the negotiations can be allowed to continue past December 1990. Self-standing blocks can be discerned within the negotiating program. If the framework and its sectoral annotations could be negotiated by December, for example, exchanges of "concessions," in the form of items to be included (or excluded) from the lists of application (or nonapplication) of the framework, could in principle be completed after that date.[6]

Such an extension would remove the pressure of the December deadline from the business of exchanging concessions, and as a result that part of the negotiation might lag and slide. However, the world economy has survived for a long time without multilateral exchanges of concessions in the services sector; it can probably carry on in that state for a few years more. From an economic or legal standpoint (although perhaps not from a political one), assessment of a GATS calls for a much longer perspective than a couple of years. This negotiation, after all, is about setting the legal framework for international transactions in services for the foreseeable future. Getting that framework right is much more important than the content of the initial exchange of concessions.

---

6. A problem is that from a national negotiating standpoint the framework, the sectoral annotations, and "concessions" are not distinct from one another. A government can achieve a particular policy objective either by appropriate wording in the framework, or by a suitable sectoral annotation, or by an explicit inclusion in (or omission from) the national list. The framework will have a general application, so that there is a clear case for keeping it as free as possible from parochial or local concerns, for treating the sectoral annotations as purely technical matters, and for placing all exclusions in the national lists. However, that may not be possible in practice.

Desirable Outcomes

One way of summarizing this discussion is to say that the services negotiation has so far failed to establish constraints for itself. The participants have moved some distance across the gulf that separated them at the start of the negotiation (Bhagwati 1987). The mere fact that India and Brazil are associated with draft frameworks testifies to that fact. But the remaining gulf is still very wide indeed.

In the vicinity of Geneva it is possible to detect the preliminary tremors of argument about what "success" in the negotiations might mean. That implies the possibility that "success" might mean something less than a comprehensive, far-reaching accord—an alarming and dispiriting state of affairs for some purists outside the negotiating process.

The diplomat's criterion holds that *any* agreement on services with sufficient signatories should be judged a success. A case can be made for that criterion: that a services agreement would emerge from the negotiations is not an outcome that could have been predicted with confidence two or three years ago.

A second criterion is provided by the congressional hurdle: a good agreement is one that can be sold to the US Congress. That is almost certainly a harder test than the diplomat's, but its force is blurred by a number of factors. An important factor is that Congress will be looking at the Uruguay Round package as a whole, not merely at the services component of it.

A still more stringent criterion, and the one I have adopted here, is the criterion of economic substance: will the agreement merely express right sentiments, or will it actually change official policies toward international services transactions in ways that are economically desirable?

Nevertheless, I believe that the negotiation will succeed in fashioning a GATS. What is in doubt is its content. I shall therefore conclude with six principles that seem to me to be essential to a services agreement of genuine economic substance. All of them are implied by arguments made above. They are:

□ The most important function of the services negotiation is to put in place a clear and litigable framework agreement. Proper fulfillment of that function overshadows any immediate exchange of concessions.

□ The framework itself should be as close as possible to a statement of the legal conditions for complete liberalization of international service transactions. Current national objections to that state of affairs, or current national difficulties in putting it into effect, are appropriate subject matter for national lists of exclusions or inclusions.

□ It follows from the preceding proposition that the framework should provide a right of establishment, even if many signatories do not wish to grant such a right at the outset. It also follows that the framework should provide for a temporary right of abode of persons for the purpose of providing a service, even if many signatories do not wish to grant such a right at the outset.

□ Signatories should be required to state the aims of a regulation when parties who believe themselves to be adversely affected request such an explanation. The purpose of such a provision is not to question the aims of a regulation as such. Rather, it is to facilitate discussion of alternative means of achieving those aims that may be less burdensome to international transactions in services.

□ The decisions of regulators and administrators must be open to challenge when those decisions affect competition between domestic and foreign providers of a service.

□ It is much more important that a strong and well-founded agreement be made available for developing countries to join when they are ready to do so than that many of them now join a weak agreement—even if it is weak only for them. No effort should be made to attract developing countries to accept a services agreement by offering special and differential treatment when such treatment would damage their long-run economic interests (even though it might be in the short-run political interest of those countries' governments). Special treatment that does not harm the actual economic interests of developing countries (such as technical assistance or special information facilities) could be dealt with in a special protocol outside the framework itself.

References

Bhagwati, Jagdish. 1984. "Splintering and Disembodiment of Services and Developing Nations." *The World Economy* 7:133–44.

Bhagwati, Jagdish. 1987. "Trade in Services and the Multilateral Trade Negotiations." *World Bank Economic Review* 1, no. 4 (September):549–69.

Brazil et al. 1990. *Structure of a Multilateral Framework for Trade in Services.* (MTN.GNS/W/95) 26 February.

Cameroon et al. 1990. *Multilateral Framework of Principles and Rules for Trade in Services.* (MTN.GNS/W/101) 4 May.

European Communities. 1990. *Draft General Agreement on Trade in Services.* (MTN.GNS/W/105) 18 June.

GATT Secretariat. 1989. *Elements for a Draft Which Would Permit Negotiations to Take Place for the Completion of All Parts of the Multilateral Framework.* (MTN.GNS/28) 18 December. Geneva: GATT.

Hindley, Brian. 1987a. "Different and More Favorable Treatment [of Developing Countries]—and Graduation." In J. Michael Finger and Andrej Olechowski, eds., *The Uruguay Round—A Handbook on the Multilateral Trade Negotiations.* Washington: World Bank, 67–74.

Hindley, Brian. 1987b. "Trade in Services Within the European Community." In Herbert Giersch, ed., *Free Trade in the World Economy.* Tübingen: J.C.B. Mohr.

Hindley, Brian. 1988. "Service Sector Protection: Considerations for Developing Countries." *World Bank Economic Review* 2, no. 2 (May): 205–24.

Hindley, Brian. 1990. "Principles in Factor-related Trade in Services." In Patrick A. Messerlin and Karl P. Sauvant, eds., *The Uruguay Round: Services in the World Economy.* Washington: World Bank and United Nations Center on Transnational Corporations.

Sampson, Gary P., and Richard H. Snape. 1985. "Identifying the Issues in Trade in Services." *The World Economy* 8 (June):171–82.

United States. 1989. *Agreement on Trade in Services* (MTN.GNS/W/75) 17 October.

8

Trade-Related Investment Measures

Edward M. Graham and Paul R. Krugman

Many countries either restrict foreign direct investment or provide special incentives to selected foreign investors. Either policy makes the right to establish or operate a subsidiary in the country a privilege, in return for which the government often tries to extract concessions. When these required concessions affect trade flows—when, to take the two most clear-cut examples, either a local-content or an export requirement is imposed—the result is a trade-related investment measure, or TRIM.

The convergence of two main factors has led the United States to make TRIMs a major concern in the Uruguay Round. First, the success of previous GATT rounds in reducing conventional barriers to trade led to a shift in focus to less conventional measures, of which TRIMs are a prominent example. Second, the agitation for a New International Economic Order focused largely on the role of multinational enterprises (MNEs) and elicited a defensive response from the largest home country of multinationals. Ironically, however, events over the past decade have radically altered both the objectives and the perceived interests of most of the major players in the negotiations, so that disputes over TRIMs are today largely and oddly disconnected from

Edward M. Graham is a Research Fellow at the Institute for International Economics and an Associate Professor in the Fuqua School of Business, Duke University. Paul R. Krugman is Professor of Economics at the Massachusetts Institute of Technology.

current policy concerns, and are carried along by the sheer momentum of the process.

The Theory of TRIMS

Neither the welfare economics nor the political economy of TRIMs is notably different from those of more conventional trade policy measures.[1] If there is a difference, it is one of degree: the case for alleging market failure and using it to justify government intervention is marginally stronger for investment-related measures than for the conventional ones.

In the simplest analysis, TRIMs may be viewed as back-door mercantilist policies that evade existing disciplines on such policies. Thus, an export TRIM is much like an export subsidy, a local-content TRIM much like a general local-content requirement (which in turn is essentially a tariff-cum-production subsidy). The standard case for free trade may then be used to argue that TRIMs, like other trade-distorting policies, reduce world welfare, and ordinarily the welfare of the country that imposes them as well.

It is by now a familiar point, however, that certain market failures can provide second-best rationales for interventionist trade policies. Arguably these rationales are somewhat stronger for TRIMs than for other policies. The reason is that the very existence of MNEs in an industry is prima facie evidence of market imperfections. This is particularly true when foreign-based MNEs have sufficient advantages over potential domestic entrants that they can continue to operate profitably despite the imposition of performance requirements. As described below, some developing countries have argued that market failures that give rise to the existence and market power of these firms make TRIMs a valid tool of development strategy.

Yet even though MNEs almost by definition do not operate in perfectly competitive markets, it is difficult to see why TRIMs represent the appropriate policy response, at least from a global point of view. The market failures that give rise to multinational firms are

---

1. On the theory of TRIMs, see Grossman (1981) and Davidson et al. (1985).

presumably similar to those that give rise to large domestic firms. Theorists of the firm, such as Oliver Williamson (1981, 1985) and Oliver Hart (1989), argue that firms are created in order to mitigate the incentive problems that arise when two or more parties must make specific investments that lock them into a state of bilateral monopoly. Because these incentive problems are only mitigated, not eliminated, there is in principle some room for productive government intervention, but it is unlikely to be optimal or even sensible to require firms to buy more of the host country's inputs or sell more output abroad than it would do on its own.

From a nationalistic point of view, however, TRIMs (and other performance requirements) may serve as a way of extracting surplus from MNEs. There normally is some extractable surplus, for two reasons. First, some of these firms do earn excess returns (but surely less than MNE–bashers seem to imagine). Second, almost by definition an MNE exhibits international economies of scope—that is, some of its costs reflect overhead that cannot be attributed to its operations in any one national market. To the extent that an MNE earns excess returns, a country may hope to appropriate some of these, and to the extent that costs are international in scope, the burden imposed by performance requirements may be spread across other countries, rather than assumed by the country imposing them.

The possibility of national gains from TRIMs, despite probable net costs at a world level, raises the sort of prisoners' dilemma scenario that has become familiar in the discussion of so-called strategic trade policies. Each individual country might rationally impose local-content or export rules as an investment requirement, but the net effect of all countries doing so would simply be to distort incentives and reduce everyone's welfare.

In practice, however, it is doubtful that many nations' motivations for imposing TRIMs stem from a keen sense of potential national gain. Instead, the usual mercantilist bias of trade policy appears to be the principal motivation, reinforced perhaps by the sense that foreign investors can in effect be taxed via these measures.

The bottom line seems to be as follows. Although the markets in which MNEs operate are typically imperfect, TRIMs are unlikely to be an appropriate policy response. Countries may nonetheless choose to impose TRIMs either because they perceive a possibility of gaining at other countries' expense, or (more likely) because TRIMs offer a still poorly policed way to serve domestic interest groups. Whatever the motivation, there is a standard GATT–style argument that says that countries should, in the name of the collective interest, deny themselves the right to impose TRIMs. In other words, the usual logic in favor of multilateral agreements to discipline protectionist actions applies with much the same force to TRIMs.

The TRIMs Negotiations

The subject of the trade effects of governmental measures directed toward MNEs was first formally introduced into GATT discussions by the United States at a meeting of the Consultative Group of 18 in 1981. A study completed not long before the meeting, under the auspices of the Joint Development Committee of the World Bank and the International Monetary Fund, had concluded that performance requirements on MNEs could have trade-distorting effects. Drawing on this study, the United States proposed that the GATT Secretariat compile an inventory of investment measures with particular attention to performance requirements. The developing countries represented on the group did not support this proposal, arguing that performance requirements were outside the competence of the GATT. The European Community and Japan indicated support for the US proposal in principle, but suggested that the GATT Secretariat had higher priorities than compiling an inventory of performance requirements.

In 1982, the United States entered into GATT Article XXIII consultations with Canada over legislation enabling Canada's Foreign Investment Review Agency (FIRA) to impose certain types of performance requirements on local subsidiaries of non-Canadian firms. A GATT panel subsequently ruled that FIRA's local-content requirements were inconsistent with GATT Article III:4 (the national treatment provision), on grounds that such requirements had the effect of discriminating against imported goods relative to domestically produced substitutes. The same panel, however, did not support a US contention that export performance requirements were inconsistent with GATT Article XVII:1(c), which prohibits member governments from preventing an enterprise from behaving in a nondiscriminatory manner. The panel also noted that countries could in principle invoke GATT Article XVIII:C (on government assistance to promote economic development) to justify local-content requirements. Developing countries have used this ruling to claim that their local-content requirements are not inconsistent with the GATT panel's findings in the FIRA case.

The United States introduced a widened version of its 1981 proposal at both the preparatory discussions for the 1982 ministerial meeting and the Senior Officials Group meeting of 1985, and again found no support. Still more ambitious proposals were offered in meetings preparatory to the 1986 Punta del Este meeting. At Punta del Este, a last-minute compromise was reached between the United States and other parties under which the Uruguay Round would include an examination of only the trade-related effects of investment measures such as performance requirements. In line with this compromise, the ministerial declaration of the Punta del Este meeting established the following mandate for the TRIMs discussions:

> Following an examination of the operation of GATT articles related to the trade restrictive and distorting effects of investment measures, negotiations should elaborate, as appropriate, further provisions that may be necessary to avoid such adverse effects on trade. (GATT 1986)

The Negotiating Group on Trade-Related Investment Measures was created to examine TRIMs in accordance with this mandate. Almost from the outset, however, questions have been raised as to the competence and jurisdiction of this new negotiating group.

For example, a number of countries have tied performance requirements to the awarding of investment incentives (subsidies and subsidy-like measures intended to draw international investors to the country offering them). The practice has been quite prevalent in certain industrialized nations as well as in many developing nations. The United States felt, therefore, that the TRIMs exercise should encompass investment incentives, but at the Punta del Este meeting other negotiating parties felt that these incentives should fall under the competence of the Negotiating Group on Subsidies and Countervailing Measures rather than the TRIMs Negotiating Group.

Once the Uruguay Round discussions got under way, it became clear that the main issue in the TRIMs discussions would be which investment measures, if any, would be prohibited and which, if any, would be subject to some sort of discipline short of prohibition. As the initiating party for the exercise, the United States proposed 14 measures to be considered for prohibition or other discipline. Other negotiating parties, including the European Community and the Nordic countries, subsequently offered shorter lists.

At present the United States advocates prohibition of eight TRIMs. Japan supports the US position on the first seven of these measures, the European Community on the first six. The TRIMs proposed for prohibition are the following:

□ Local-content requirements

□ Export performance requirements

□ Local manufacturing requirements

□ Trade balance targets

□ Production mandates

□ Foreign-exchange restrictions

□ Mandatory technology transfer

□ Limits on equity participation and on remittances.

There are issues before the TRIMs Negotiating Group other than the identification of what TRIMs should be banned. For example, as suggested above, there is disagreement over whether performance requirements subject to prohibition as a condition of establishment can be imposed as a condition for receipt of subsidies or other investment incentives. The United States, again the hard-liner on this issue, is seeking in both the TRIMs Negotiating Group and the Subsidies Negotiating Group to decouple investment incentives and performance requirements. The US position is that governments should be prohibited from imposing performance requirements as a condition for receipt of these incentives. As noted, there is as yet no agreement even on which of these negotiating groups has competence over the issue.

The TRIMs Negotiating Group must also consider possible conflicts between the goals of the TRIMs exercise and the goals of other negotiating groups, and if so, what to do about them. For example, some governments are concerned about local subsidiaries of MNEs that perform final assembly operations only (so-called screwdriver operations). The concern is that these operations might be used to circumvent antidumping duties that would otherwise be imposed on imports of the final product; by assembling the product locally from imported components, the firm can claim the product to be of local origin rather than an import. One way a government could deal with this would be to apply a local-value-added test to the final product. But would such a test be tantamount to a local-content requirement and hence subject to prohibition under a prospective TRIMs agreement? If so, how exactly is a government to deal with such circumvention? The problems here are both substantive (i.e., how to accomplish the goals of the TRIMs exercise and of antidumping discipline in such a way that they do not conflict with one another) and procedural (i.e., whether the substantive issue should be handled in the TRIMs Negotiating Group, the negotiating group dealing with antidumping, or both).

Shifting Ground

Perhaps the most unusual aspect of the TRIMs negotiations is the way in which rapid change in the world economy has outpaced the negotiating positions of the participants. In particular, the countries that are the strongest advocates and opponents of new restrictions on TRIMs are representing not so much their present concerns as those of a decade ago.

Pressure for limits on TRIMs came initially from the United States, but the United States has experienced a radical shift in its role with respect to MNEs. As recently as the late 1970s, foreign direct investment in the United States was negligible compared with US direct investment abroad; this situation made the United States the natural advocate of the rights of multinationals in their dealings with host countries. This state of affairs had already begun to change when the first US proposal on TRIMs was made in 1981, but few would have foreseen that by 1990 the United States would be a net host country to foreign investment, as it currently is at least in book-value terms. The buildup of foreign investment in the United States has increased the pressures on Congress to enact new measures to regulate foreign ownership. One such measure was introduced into law, the Exon-Florio amendment to the Omnibus Trade and Competitiveness Act of

1988. This amendment gives the President limited power to block foreign acquisitions of US firms when the acquisition is judged to present a threat to national security. In 1990 there was still pressure on Congress to pass additional measures; one of these would amend the 1988 act to give the President explicit authority to impose performance requirements on foreign investors in US firms as a condition for not blocking the acquisition under Exon-Florio authority. US trade policy officials who in 1981 saw GATT discipline on investment measures as something that would apply primarily to other nations were by 1990 espousing such discipline, in part as a means to limit congressional initiatives to regulate foreign direct investment in the United States itself. Clearly, however, the strong US advocacy of restrictions on TRIMs now reflects the history of the negotiating process as much as it does the currently perceived national interest.

The traditional US role as advocate of the rights of MNEs might to some extent logically shift to Japan. In 1981, Japanese firms had limited direct investment abroad, primarily located in natural resource–based industries in Southeast Asia. Japan in 1981 thus seemed little concerned about performance requirements. By the late 1980s, however, Japanese firms had a large and rapidly growing stake in manufacturing concerns abroad, located largely in advanced countries, especially the United States. Japan consequently has become more concerned about TRIMs as the GATT talks have progressed. The major Japanese concern has doubtless been the potential for measures in the United States or Europe that might restrict the local activities of Japanese firms.

Japan today would be expected to have little interest in imposing TRIMs on non-Japanese MNEs operating inside Japan, for indeed compared to Japan's outward direct investment, foreign direct investment in Japan is minor. But despite Japan's apparent interests in disciplining TRIMs, Japan has not really emerged as a leader in advocating such discipline in the Uruguay Round. As with the United States, Japan's role in this regard seems as much a product of the negotiating history as of an assessment of current Japanese interests. That is, Japan seems willing to let the United States continue to play the role of leader on TRIMs discipline. It is an interesting question what the Japanese position might be if US leadership were to falter.

The European Community has long been both home and host to multinational firms, but between 1981 and 1990 the outward foreign direct investment position of the Community (that is, the stock of EC direct investments abroad) has grown significantly relative to the inward position. The vast bulk of the increase in overseas activities by European-based firms has been in North America. As a result, since 1987 the negotiating stance of Europe in the TRIMs discussions has stiffened, so that Europe has joined the United States as a hard-line advocate of prohibitions on measures likely to distort trade flows significantly. The European Community wants any discipline on TRIMs to be explicitly binding on regional and local governmental entities. This in part reflects a fear that individual states in the United States will pass legislation to regulate the activities of foreign investors.

Opposition to new restrictions on TRIMs has come primarily from the developing countries (see Abreu 1989). In 1981, with the New International Economic Order still an influential model, these countries formed a common negotiating bloc. To some extent they still negotiate as a bloc, but their common negotiating position on TRIMs is increasingly out of touch with the reality that the interests of different subgroups of developing countries are now sharply divergent.

For some developing countries, such as India, little has changed since the heyday of the New International Economic Order. These countries continue to have a modest presence of foreign firms, and those that are present operate primarily in import-substituting industries and are regarded with suspicion. These nations see TRIMs as a necessary tool to discipline the perceived excessive power of these firms.

Some highly indebted countries, in contrast, are revising their attitudes toward multinationals. Short of cash, and desperate to replace the capital flows they lost when new commercial bank lending was curtailed in the wake of the debt crisis, they no longer discourage foreign direct investment, but instead attempt to attract it through a variety of means, including privatization and debt-equity swaps. One might expect that these countries would correspondingly shift their negotiating position on TRIMs to one favoring a set of rules that would reassure firms and hence encourage direct investment flows. This has not yet happened, however. In the TRIMs talks, almost all the highly indebted nations continue to articulate the positions of the New

International Economic Order. Arguably these countries are thereby allowing the history of the process to trap them into a negotiating posture that is contrary to their current interests. They might, however, be persuaded to alter their position in return for other measures, as we suggest in the following section.

Finally, certain Asian developing nations with rapidly expanding manufacturing sectors, such as Thailand and Malaysia, have generally welcomed foreign investors but have also imposed performance requirements on them. These nations are reluctant to drop the use of TRIMs, especially given the historical concerns of these countries about loss of national sovereignty to Japan, which increasingly is replacing the United States as the source of foreign investment in the region. Yet at the same time these countries are also aware that if no progress is made in the TRIMs talks, the major home countries of MNEs might take actions designed to offset the effects of host-country performance requirements. (For example, the United States might in the future initiate a Section 301 action to limit imports from nations that subject foreign investors to export performance requirements.) The Asian industrializing nations thus might be willing to trade some discipline on TRIMs for assurances that such home-nation measures will not be forthcoming. These nations are likely to bargain hard, insisting, for example, on some change in the Section 301 provisions of US trade law and substantial reform in the GATT dispute settlement mechanism as the *quid pro quo* for such discipline. They can also be expected to resist any effort to link discipline on TRIMs with discipline on investment incentives.

Prospects for the TRIMs Negotiations

When the United States first raised TRIMs as an issue, it seemed very unlikely that any substantive agreement could be achieved. Given the developing countries' sharp opposition to any prohibitions, and only lukewarm support for the US position from other industrial countries, the best possible outcome seemed to be an essentially hortatory declaration that countries should avoid measures that prejudiced the interests of other parties, together with an inventory of such measures and provisions for consultation.

Now that the positions of other industrial countries have swung more strongly in line with the US position (while the official US position itself has remained steady in spite of changes in congressional attitudes toward foreign direct investment), and now that the interests and philosophies of many of the developing countries have shifted (although their negotiating stances have not), there is a more realistic prospect of achieving stronger discipline of certain TRIMs. However, this prospect depends very much on what is agreed upon elsewhere in the Uruguay Round.

Indeed, a strong agreement on TRIMs (which we define as one that prohibits at least six of the eight measures listed in the US proposal) as well as agreements on the other "new issues" might be possible if they are linked to all of the following US reforms:

☐ A credible scheme for phasing out the Multi-Fiber Arrangement, which limits the abilities of many developing nations to export textile and apparel products to the United States and other developed nations;

☐ Substantial measures to bring agriculture under GATT discipline in a way that serves developing nations' interests; and

☐ Reform of the GATT dispute settlement mechanism, accompanied by revision of Section 301 to bring its procedures more closely into line with GATT discipline.

We believe that these concessions would actually be consistent with US interests, but we also recognize the political problems that might result from their being offered. What is clear is that the degree of substantive progress in the "new issues" will ultimately be determined by the nature and magnitude of US (and other industrial nations') concessions in these politically charged arenas. If the concessions go sufficiently deep, it is quite possible that developing nations (perhaps led by Mexico) will come to accept a strong discipline on TRIMs.

It is equally apparent, however, that the "new issue" in which negotiations are most likely to falter in the absence of substantive concessions is the TRIMs exercise. Thus, it is not surprising that the Trade Negotiations Committee meeting in late July 1990, which achieved little progress in agriculture or textiles, also failed to reach agreement on the outcome of the TRIMs exercise. Instead, the negotiators face three alternative texts for consideration, reflecting the US position, the EC position, and the hard-line developing-country position.

Let us consider what would be the elements of an agreement to establish strong discipline on TRIMs. Such an agreement would almost surely contain the following:

□ A list of prohibited TRIMs containing at least the six categories on the US list agreed to by both the European Community and Japan;

□ A "standstill" clause banning the imposition of new TRIMs falling on the prohibited list;

□ A "rollback" mechanism, whereby existing TRIMs covered by the prohibited list would be phased out over some length of time consistent with the need for nations imposing them and the MNEs operating under them to adjust to the new prohibitions; and

□ A "grandfather" clause allowing certain existing TRIMs covered by the prohibited list to remain in effect following the phaseout period.

Obviously, a truly strong discipline on TRIMs would sharply curtail both the length of time allowed for rollback and the number of measures grandfathered. But some degree of lenience in these clauses would enable certain nations to sign onto the agreement whose internal political situations would prevent them from accepting an immediate ban on their existing TRIMs.

If the TRIMs exercise fails to achieve strong, universal discipline, even something short of this goal would be desirable and could still be salvaged. The first fallback would be a code on TRIMs to which a limited number of nations would subscribe.[2] The signatories should certainly include at least the United States, the European Community, and Japan. These might be joined (in decreasing order of probability) by certain member countries of the European Free Trade Association (EFTA), Canada, Australia, and perhaps even some of the newly industrializing nations (Mexico, for example). Because the United

---

2. The concept of a limited code is also discussed in Maskus and Eby (1990).

States, the European Community, Japan, the EFTA countries, and Canada are both host and home to more than 85 percent of the world stock of foreign direct investment, a code involving just these nations would cover the vast majority of worldwide operations of MNEs. The door should be left open, of course, for nonsigning nations to join the code at some future date.

A limited signatory code would contain all of the features of a strong discipline described above. Indeed, with a limited number of signatories, the list of prohibited TRIMS could likely be made longer, the number of grandfathered TRIMs fewer, and the rollback periods reduced from those that could likely be adopted under a universal agreement.

An alternative, and in our view less desirable, fallback position would be a general agreement on TRIMs discipline that contained strong "escape clause" language to allow some nations to continue to use TRIMs. The likely scenario here would be that certain developing nations would be given blanket exceptions so that they could continue to use these measures at will. Exceptions might be granted on a more limited basis to certain industrialized nations as well.

This alternative is less desirable than a limited code because it is unlikely that the exceptions would be revoked at any foreseeable time in the future. We do not see it as feasible, for example, that an acceptable graduation scheme could be worked out whereby developing nations would automatically "grow out" of their exceptions. The limited code, in contrast, would leave open the possibility of nonsignatory nations joining the code at some future date.

The least desirable fallback agreement would be a nonbinding declaration exhorting nations to refrain from the use of TRIMs when their effect is to cause prejudice to some other signatory nation. Such a declaration would fall short of even a minimally desirable outcome because it would simply be wrong in principle: one nation's TRIM does not generally cause readily identifiable harm to another specific nation, and it would be a rare case in which measurable "prejudice" could ever be identified as the result of a TRIM. The damage done by TRIMs is more subtle and, like lead poisoning, cumulative. If just one nation imposes one or a few such measures, the reduction of world welfare is very small, but if many nations impose many measures, the welfare reduction can be substantial. Remedy in that case would require a large-scale rollback of the offending measures, not a case-by-case approach.

In sum, we believe that a strong discipline on TRIMs applied universally is possible, but that it would require significant concessions in other areas on the part of the United States and the other major industrial nations. If such a comprehensive agreement proves impossible, the fallback position should be a code on TRIMs applying strong discipline to a limited number of signatories. This fallback should be achievable, and anything less would be undesirable.

Beyond the Uruguay Round

The greatest discipline on TRIMs that can realistically be achieved in the Uruguay Round is a list of investment measures that are prohibited as a condition of entry or for doing business in a country. This list might be supplemented by a list of additional measures that GATT contracting parties should avoid and whose use might be subject to challenge under the dispute settlement provisions. We see little probability that there will be any strong discipline on investment incentives or the linking of performance requirements to these incentives emerging from this round.

Many believe that a more comprehensive treatment of investment issues should be undertaken under the aegis of the GATT. This might be accomplished by means of a code on direct investment that would take into account the increasingly complex relations between international trade and international direct investment. Such a code could be negotiated in future rounds of multilateral trade negotiations or perhaps even in a separately convened negotiation on investment issues. Its desirable elements would include all of the following:

☐ *A code on rights of establishment.* This would spell out under what circumstances a foreign entity would be permitted to own and control a business enterprise within a host nation, and what limitations on such ownership and control could be placed on the investor by that nation. It would also cover such matters as to what extent the enterprise could employ citizens of nations other than the host nation.

☐ *A national treatment instrument.* National treatment as it applies to MNEs means that, once established, a foreign subsidiary of an MNE is subject to the same laws and policies of the host country as is a similar enterprise under domestic control. (This principle is sometimes defined as "treatment no less favorable than" that received by domestically controlled enterprises, but this definition opens the door to the foreign-owned subsidiary being accorded not merely equal but preferential treatment, something we do not believe "national treatment" should imply.) A national treatment instrument would spell out exactly what this principle means in practice, and it would list acceptable exceptions and derogations. There already exists a voluntary (i.e., hortatory) national treatment instrument within the Organization for Economic Cooperation and Development. This might serve as a starting point for negotiation of a more forceful instrument, but much strengthening would be required.

☐ *A code of host-nation rights and obligations regarding foreign investors.* Such a code would cover those rights and obligations of host-nation governments with respect to foreign investors that do not fall under the national treatment instrument. For example, it might subsume and extend whatever agreement on TRIMs comes out of the Uruguay Round.

☐ *A code on home-nation rights and obligations regarding foreign investors.* The main idea behind this code, much discussed but never formally implemented, is that there should be some limitations on the rights of a government to apply its domestic laws and policies to the overseas affiliates of MNEs headquartered within its territory. Without such limitations on extraterritoriality, it is difficult to see how host countries would be willing to accept the limitations on their own policies demanded by the national treatment instrument and the host-country code. The home-country code might also contain provisions analogous to TRIMs disciplines, such as prohibition of home-nation policies designed to prevent outward technology transfer.

☐ *A code on MNE rights and obligations regarding their foreign affiliates.* For over two decades the developing countries have sought a "code of conduct" for MNEs operating within their territories. Some of the developing-country demands in this regard have been quite extreme, and this perhaps has prevented industrial-country negotiators from seeing the many merits in such a code. Minimal requirements would include an enunciation of principles governing under what circumstances host-nation policy and law prevail or do not prevail over home-country law, when an enterprise faces conflicting demands from the two. Many MNEs would favor such an enunciation and understanding. The code might also place restrictions or prohibitions on certain types of business practices.

□ *Ancillary codes.* Ancillary codes might be negotiated to deal with such matters as taxation and transfer pricing, product safety standards, and environmental matters.

□ *Dispute settlement.* It would be desirable to institute special dispute settlement procedures for international investment. Under present GATT procedures, the dispute settlement process can be initiated only by GATT contracting parties (i.e., member governments). But MNEs, by their very nature, are to some degree anational; hence their interests and ownership may not be fully represented by any one nation-state. Thus, it would seem appropriate to allow firms themselves to initiate procedures to settle disputes that might arise between them and the governments of nations in which they operate (including the home nation). Firms should also be allowed to represent their own interests in these disputes rather than have those interests represented by a contracting party.

In addition, any code on international direct investment would have to take into account the relationships between international trade and investment so as not to create conflicts between the objectives of the code and the objectives of current trade law.

What are the chances that a code on international direct investment and MNEs will come about in future negotiations? We believe that the changing circumstances of international investment that we have outlined will ultimately bring about substantial need for the measures we have sketched. But, as we have already noted, the negotiating process, and the positions nations hold in this process, have certain momenta of their own. The question that remains unanswered is whether the momentum will shift in response to changing circumstances, and if so, how fast? Our best guess is that the momentum will change, but not quickly enough for major progress to be made on TRIMs in the Uruguay Round. If this is correct, investment issues could become the major focus for a future round of multilateral negotiations.

References

Abreu, Marcelo de Paiva. 1989. "Developing Countries and the Uruguay Round of Trade Negotiations." In *Proceedings of the World Bank Annual Conference on Development Economics*. Washington: World Bank, 21–46.

Davidson, Carl, Stephen J. Matusz, and Mordechai E. Kreinen. 1985. "Analysis of Performance Standards for Foreign Direct Investment." *Canadian Journal of Economics*, 18:876–90.

GATT. 1986. "Ministerial Declaration on the Uruguay Round." *GATT Focus*, 8 October.

Grossman, Gene. 1981. "The Theory of Domestic Content Protection and Content Preference." *Quarterly Journal of Economics*, 96:583–604.

Hart, Oliver. 1989. "Bargaining and Strikes." *Quarterly Journal of Economics*, 104:25–44.

Maskus, Keith E., and Denise R. Eby. 1990. "Developing New Rules and Disciplines on Trade-Related Investment Measures." *The World Economy* (forthcoming).

Williamson, Oliver E. 1981. "The Modern Corporation: Origins, Evolution, Attributes." *Journal of Economic Literature*, 19, no. 4 (December):1537–68.

Williamson, Oliver E. 1985. *The Economic Institutions of Capitalism: Firms, Markets, Relational Contracting*. New York: Free Press.

9

Intellectual Property

Keith E. Maskus

Intellectual property (IP) is an asset generated by the creation of new information with commercial or artistic usefulness. Like other assets, its economic value depends on the quality, uniqueness, and amount of the information supplied, along with the demand for its services. This value also depends importantly on the framework of legal protections accorded the owners of IP in its exploitation.

The protection of IP is an issue on the Uruguay Round agenda largely because current international protective standards are considered uneven and deficient by many IP creators, primarily those in the major industrial countries. Inadequate standards may significantly erode the returns to creative activity by encouraging the unremunerated exploitation of IP in the form of production and trade in counterfeit goods, unauthorized duplication and sale of copyrighted materials, and unapproved use of patented products or processes. Firms in information-exporting countries, notably the United States, claim that the costs of foreign IP infringement, in terms of forgone sales especially, are substantial (US International Trade Commission 1988). Given the growing importance of information-based goods and services in international trade, these costs could increase at an accelerating pace in the absence of improvements in protective standards. Further,

Keith E. Maskus is Associate Professor of Economics and Director of the Carl McGuire Center for International Studies at the University of Colorado.

limited protection may discourage some inventive and creative activities, leading to a slowdown in global growth and cultural development.

These arguments are not universally accepted. The contrary argument holds that to protect IP is to create monopoly rights that may be exploited to the detriment of information-importing countries. Harmful effects of IP protection could include high monopoly prices, onerous restrictions on the operations of licensees, and limited and expensive technology transfer, which could result in slower growth for such countries. Further, the evidence that greater and more harmonized IP protection would generate more global invention, and that positive net benefits from such induced invention would accrue to technology importers, is tenuous at best.

Accordingly, a clear tension over IP protection exists between what may be termed technology-exporting countries (TECs), which tend to favor the upgrading of international IP standards, and technology-importing countries (TICs), which tend to distrust this effort. The stark extremes in these views presented above capture the spirit of this debate but not its complexity. Important differences regarding IP policies have emerged within the TECs as a group, as the Uruguay Round negotiations reflect. Nor is there uniformity of opinion among the TICs, many of which are evidently poised to accept the usefulness of an international IP agreement, while others remain unalterably opposed. Moreover, many of the economic effects and welfare implications of changes in levels of IP protection are more subtle than this simple discussion suggests, depending, for example, on the form of the IP and its links to market structure and to overall trade and industrial policies (Maskus 1990). Nonetheless, much of the argument in the IP negotiations may be understood within the general confines of this characterization.

The Status of the Negotiations

By early 1990, draft IP annexes to the GATT had been submitted to the Negotiating Group on Trade-Related Aspects of Intellectual Property Rights by the United States, the European Community, Switzerland, Japan, and a group of 14 developing countries. Because strong differences among these proposals remained, the chairman of the negotiating group, Lars Anell of Sweden, simply assembled them into a composite document for the July 1990 meetings of the Trade Negotiations Committee, without prejudice to any of them.

There was no substantive change in this situation as a result of the July meetings. Some convergence in the positions of the developed countries emerged, but no important differences were addressed. This lack of progress was due primarily to factors outside the IP negotiations themselves, namely, the inability of the negotiators to move forward on an agricultural agreement, which effectively put all other negotiating areas on hold. An additional reason is that many IP issues still require lengthy examination and discussion at the technical level. The trade ministers were not in a position to endorse a negotiating process that retains substantial uncertainty about rather esoteric standards.

It is noteworthy, however, that the legal texts have been presented as prospective annexes to the GATT itself rather than as codes with limited country membership. The GATT annex approach is preferable on many counts, especially in that it allows for regular GATT dispute settlement and multilateral treatment, although this might be modified in some dimensions in IP cases. However, existing disagreements over the nature of such an annex make its eventual adoption problematic.

Negotiating Issues

The basic objective of the IP negotiations has been to develop a framework within which to discipline national IP policies or remove their trade-distorting effects, where those effects are harmful to the interests of various contracting parties. IP protection may be deemed unsatisfactory in either of two opposing respects. It may be considered deficient, as when a country fails to recognize foreign trademarks and thereby encourages exports of counterfeit products under identical or confusingly similar marks. Or it may be considered excessive, as when judicial or administrative procedures allow easy and uncompensated impoundment of legitimate imports accused of infringing local IP rights.

That varying levels of protection can influence international trade is beyond dispute. Less obvious is the appropriate definition of a trade distortion in this context. A country's view of the adequacy of international IP standards depends on its attitude toward the inherent rights in creative activity. Thus, for example, a system of compulsory licenses in the pharmaceutical sector may be deplored as an unwarranted intrusion on an inventor's natural right to trade and price his product or technology as he sees fit. Alternatively, it may be defended as an effective counter to the trade distortions associated with monopoly patents and as a means of securing any spillover economies from a new drug or manufacturing process. It is unclear that an internationally harmonized IP regime, providing protection at a level near that of the more protective TECs, would minimize distortions to trade, given that agreement is lacking about what features a truly undistorted system should entail.

At bottom this impasse seems intractable and therefore preclusive of a comprehensive IP agreement. Yet the fact that negotiations have proceeded to a point where a limited, yet substantive, accord may be attainable suggests that some common ground exists between the extreme positions. To oversimplify, this partial convergence may be attributed to growing respect for the "natural justice" approach to IP rights; to widening acceptance of the view that stronger IP protection can promote inward foreign direct investment, technology transfer, and domestic creative activity, yielding dynamic benefits; to expanding concern that major TECs are increasingly willing to treat foreign IP infringement as an actionable unfair trade practice; and to an emerging realization by some countries that limited and discriminatory IP protection may not be of sufficient significance to their development efforts to warrant continued resistance, when that resistance threatens the adoption of prospective agreements in other, more important areas of the negotiations. However, these factors clearly have not yet proved persuasive for some of the major developing countries that view their IP regimes as important development tools, notably India and Brazil.

The uncertainty surrounding the effects of stronger protection for IP rights makes it difficult to describe definitively an optimal outcome for the negotiations. A strong case can be made that failure to reach an agreement on IP within the GATT could significantly damage the international trading system. Such failure would preserve the status quo ante, in which natural protection schemes are based loosely on the limited standards and enforcement mechanisms of the various IP conventions directed by the World Intellectual Property Organization (WIPO). This system has proved largely incapable of disciplining even the most egregious forms of trademark and copyright infringement. Continued global reliance on the WIPO as the arbiter of protection regimes would invite growing numbers of unilateral and bilateral actions outside the framework of international obligations, which could contribute to fragmentation of the trading system. It would be naive to think that the United States and other like-minded nations would refrain from such actions in a world of growing IP infringement.

At the other extreme, a strong case also can be advanced that a fully harmonized international system of IP protection, with all countries providing complete legal safeguards to creators along the lines of the current US regime, could be harmful. To be sure, TICs would realize some benefits from greater foreign innovative activity, which could result in new products designed for their needs. However, it would result in substantial increases in the short-run costs to TICs in the form of large rents transferred to foreign IP owners, with little certainty of those countries procuring significant long-run benefits. Further, the presumption that standardized IP protection at advanced levels would stimulate innovation in each economy over some reasonable time frame is clearly false, and the existence of varying levels of economic and technological development across countries points to the desirability of differing national protection schemes, if not outright discrimination. Indeed, the GATT rarely insists on uniform levels of trade protection (as opposed to nondiscrimination), and to do so in the area of IP seems inconsistent and excessive.

Further, the legal and technical requirements for establishing and enforcing sophisticated IP systems may be excessively costly in some developing countries, particularly to the extent that doing so absorbs scarce engineering and entrepreneurial skills. Indeed, the greater the level of protection to which a country commits itself, the more difficult its effective enforcement will become. The new GATT machinery could as a result become burdened with large numbers of bilateral complaints, which in turn could result in escalating retaliation and fragmentation, much like that envisioned in the alternative scenario. Finally, one may expect numerous other welfare costs to accrue from markedly higher international standards for IP protection, including higher consumer costs in all countries. Again, it seems highly unlikely that a majority of TICs would endorse this outcome, or even that consensus on uniformly high standards could be reached among the TECs.

Thus, any IP agreement that is both feasible and likely to enhance world welfare must, in my view, lie between these extremes. The final negotiations must point to an accord that, either alone or in conjunction with the overall Uruguay Round package, provides an attractive balance of interests to most contracting parties and retains some sensitivity to divergent attitudes and development needs. Undue insistence that the agreement tilt heavily toward either extreme could easily jeopardize its adoption or its subsequent legitimacy. For example, US negotiators should recognize that a commitment by the developing countries to upgrade their levels of IP protection represents a GATT concession in the same sense that a reduced tariff does. Those countries would expect some balance of concessions in return, regardless of whether their initial deficient protections were considered violations of natural property rights in a broader sense.

WHAT FORM SHOULD AN IP AGREEMENT TAKE?

To flesh out particular aspects of this general principle, it is useful to consider the specific components that are likely to appear in any prospective IP agreement. The initial question is the appropriate form of the agreement: should it be done under GATT auspices, or should it take the form of strengthened WIPO conventions? Dissatisfaction with the WIPO among the TECs stems from the fact that its minimum protective standards are weak, that it requires little in terms of enforcement, that it provides virtually no meaningful dispute settlement mechanisms, and that membership in its conventions does not extend to all of the major IP–infringing nations.

The GATT provides an opportunity to overcome all of these perceived shortcomings. By tradition, the GATT largely has exempted IP laws from its disciplines, characterizing them as technical trade barriers akin to domestic development or competition policies. Recent practice has brought this approach into question, however. The enactment of the Subsidies Code suggests that many contracting parties consider the trade-related aspects of domestic policies to lie within the purview of the GATT, and the GATT panel report criticizing the discriminatory procedures under Section 337 of US trade law indicates that basic GATT obligations cannot be nullified or impaired by IP enforcement. Further, some GATT articles that explicitly mention patents, copyrights, and trademarks seem already to provide mild disciplines for border measures relating to IP rights. Accordingly, the argument made by some contracting parties that the GATT has no competence to erect IP disciplines carries little weight.

Within the context of a GATT agreement on IP, perhaps the least controversial issue is the adoption of basic principles of national treatment, nondiscrimination, and transparency, although nondiscrimination in some cases would involve a significant change from current practice. These basic principles are advanced in all of the negotiating texts now under discussion.

STANDARDS OF PROTECTION

More contentious is the formulation of the core provisions of the agreement, namely, those setting minimum standards of protection. Such standards involve delineating the rights of creators to control dissemination of their works, the term and breadth of such rights (including the designation of which works are subjects for protection), and the conditions under which such rights may be attenuated through, say, the issuance of compulsory licenses for patented products or the cancellation of trademark protection. The issue is fundamentally important, because once particular standards become GATT commitments, any failure to uphold them invites GATT sanctions. Accordingly, each country has an incentive to push for standards that it believes it will be willing and able to support through legislation and enforcement.

There remains a wide chasm on this score between the United States and the European Community at one pole, and several key developing countries at the other. The US and EC delegations continue to seek international standards commensurate with their own highly protective IP regimes. Thus, for example, virtually no products or processes would be excluded from patentability. The conditions under which compulsory licenses could be issued would be heavily proscribed, and the IP owner would be entitled to payment approximating the economic value of his asset.

The developing-country delegations, in contrast, advocate standards that would be little strengthened over current WIPO guidelines. No changes in standards would be required beyond ensuring that each country provides national treatment. Thus, the effective harmonization of IP policies desired by the United States would not materialize. Further, numerous products and processes would be excluded from patentability, compulsory licensing practices would be little constrained, and levels of compensation would be set at the discretion of the government compelling the licenses. Because these positions represent little change from the status quo, they cannot serve as the basis for a comprehensive GATT agreement if it is to have any meaning.

In fact, significant disagreements over standards remain even among the TECs. Some of these involve the unique IP problems created by the advent of newer technologies, such as copyright protection for software and *sui generis* protection for chip topographies and biotechnology products. Two other highly contentious issues are the European Community's strong preference for significant new protection of geographical appellations for wines, and the singular US view that patents should be granted on a first-to-invent basis rather than a first-to-file basis. These delegations also differ on the appropriate extension of copyrights to neighboring rights (which protect, for example, broadcasters, producers of sound recordings, and performers of works by others) and moral rights (which provide artists some control over the display and use of their work after its sale). These questions alone have some potential to derail an IP agreement.

It is evident that for an accord on IP standards to be reached, some of these positions must be softened, and language must be found that accommodates some national differences in IP practices. This prescription presumably points toward either an agreement with weak standards but wide membership, or one with stronger standards and limited membership. It seems clear that the United States and the European Community, without whose membership any IP accord would be essentially meaningless, will not accept the first outcome. Therefore, the standards issue alone appears likely to lead the negotiations toward, at best, an IP association among the industrial countries and perhaps some of the more important middle-income countries with strong prospects for future industrialization.

ENFORCEMENT

This conclusion is reinforced by consideration of the next component of an IP agreement, the provisions for enforcement of IP laws. To be meaningful, enforcement must allow for disciplining of both domestic production, to deter infringing activity that could displace imports, and trade in goods suspected of being illegitimate. That is, both internal and border measures must be available. Further, as part of a GATT agreement, access to such measures must be provided without discrimination between domestic and foreign litigants, and enforcement actions would have to be timely and transparent.

Full enforcement would require the establishment of seizure procedures by customs authorities; the implementation of judicial and/or administrative mechanisms for legal redress, including standards for proof and rights of appeal; the codification of civil and criminal penalties for infringement, including monetary compensation for damages; and the use of legal safeguards to deter abuse of the enforcement measures from becoming means of harassing and limiting legitimate trade in competing products. Given the range of enforcement mechanisms envisioned, such harassment is by no means a trivial concern. Indeed, it is easy to imagine scenarios in which the threat of legal action in an importing country could deter foreign exports and serve as a facilitating device for internationally collusive commercial behavior; strict standards in such a case could dampen rather than encourage legitimate trade.

Enforcement on this scale surely requires the presence of thorough legal and technical expertise with which to argue and assess competing claims. Such expertise is presumably lacking in many TICs, such as the poorest developing countries, and there seems little likelihood that their legal systems could readily be modified to handle the more technical cases of alleged patent and copyright infringement. In this regard, it is interesting to note that the submission of the group of developing countries allows for firm enforcement commitments on border measures in cases of imports that infringe most trademarks and copyrights. Because trade in counterfeit goods remains a principal IP irritant, this offer represents a substantive concession on the part of these countries in the interests of procuring an IP agreement. Speculation about the reasons for this concession presumably center on the relative ease of identifying certain trademark- and copyright-infringing goods and the recognition that such infringement is becoming increasingly annoying to interests in developed economies.

However, offers to upgrade enforcement mechanisms in other areas of IP have been less forthcoming; this may reflect both the technical difficulties in pursuing such enforcement and preferences for sustaining limited systems in the belief that they promote development. Moreover, these countries have made no pledges to erect and enforce disciplines against domestic production and sale of infringing goods. Again, because adequate enforcement is the second key feature of an acceptable IP accord, in the view of the TECs, this situation presents problems for the negotiations.

What Sort of Agreement Is Likely?

In principle, the hesitation of many TICs to join a strongly protective IP agreement could be overcome by the addition of provisions in their favor, but the prospects for such compromise are dubious. For example, the submissions by the United States and the European Community allow for the extension of technical assistance to developing countries in setting and enforcing standards and in improving the administration of their IP systems. It is unclear how generous this concession would be in practice and how welcome it would be in the developing countries. The US and EC drafts also provide for the possibility of negotiating longer transitional periods for poor countries to comply with the agreement. Many developing countries, however, clearly prefer language allowing special and differential treatment of their IP systems. In their view, their systems should be permitted to sustain long-lasting or permanent derogations from key provisions of the accord. Not surprisingly, delegations from the developed countries consider this notion to be a self-defeating loophole that would damage the integrity of any agreement.

Finally, some developing countries insist on provisions that would strike a balance between the rights and the "obligations" of IP owners. In brief, such language would open the door to GATT actions against perceived abuses of IP rights and restrictive business practices by private firms. Again, it is not difficult to understand why the developed countries are firmly opposed to this notion.

It is evident from this discussion of national interests and negotiating constraints that, if any IP agreement is to be reached, it will contain relatively strong protections as preferred by the major TECs. Such an agreement, however, would not be attractive to a number of significant TICs, and therefore the prospects for wide membership are limited. Reasonable forecasts suggest that, depending on the strictness of the minimum standards and enforcement requirements in the final package, some 40 to 50 GATT members might join the accord, including some important middle-income and Eastern European nations anxious to attract foreign investment and technology.

Adoption of the accord as a GATT amendment would require approval and accession of two-thirds of the contracting parties, or approximately 64 affirmative votes. Thus, if the major TECs view a GATT amendment as the desirable outcome, and if the head count offered above is accurate, a significant number of additional countries will have to be enticed to approve it. As was intimated earlier, some of the poorer developing countries may be willing to entertain such IP commitments in the GATT if other parts of the Uruguay Round package, especially in textiles, agriculture, and safeguards, are sufficiently attractive. It remains to be seen how willing the United States and the other TECs will be to effect such trade-offs for the sake of an IP amendment.

If cross-issue concessions are unacceptable, then an additional structural factor militates against the adoption of an IP amendment. At present the GATT places few IP obligations on any of its members. To write such obligations into the GATT is to make trade concessions; the greater the upgrading of its IP standards a country undertakes, the greater its GATT concession. In this view, those countries that already offer extensive IP protection are proposing to make relatively small concessions, while asking those countries with limited protection to accept major new obligations. It is difficult to envision a consensual balance of concessions and interests emerging from this process on its own.

In this analysis, then, the prospects for a GATT annex covering IP seem difficult at best. The remaining major possibility is the negotiation of a code on IP rights involving some dispute settlement mechanism in addition to standards and enforcement obligations. Like the Tokyo Round codes, a new IP code would presumably be open to accession but would not mandate the extension of nondiscrimination to nonsignatories. For example, one might envision the United States exempting code members from action under its Special 301 provisions (which are directed against countries that maintain inadequate IP protection) but redoubling its efforts to pursue perceived infringement elsewhere. In time, each country would need to calculate whether its interests lie in joining the code and upgrading its IP systems at the expense of its perceived development interests (and at the risk of absorbing GATT–sanctioned retaliation for failure to enforce its higher standards), or in remaining outside the code and risking retribution outside the confines of the GATT. Frustration over this apparent Hobson's choice may induce some developing countries to withhold their permission for the code to be adopted. In that event, it is conceivable that no IP agreement would be reached, even among like-minded GATT members.

Although the substantial problems discussed here imply that an IP accord of either kind will be quite difficult to reach, it is too soon to dismiss the possibility of success. Given the importance that innovative firms in the industrial countries place on IP rights, and given the interests of the developing countries in a well-functioning trading system, a desirable compromise agreement still could be achieved.

In my view, such an agreement would ideally consist of a GATT amendment that, in a manner consistent with the rationales for national IP policies, recognizes both the importance of rewarding innovative activity and society's interest in ensuring the effective dissemination of new information. In this light, strong provisions within the agreement for protecting against trademark and copyright infringement seem to be within grasp. Many developing countries are beginning to recognize that it is not clearly in their interests to allow such infringement, since the distortionary costs of inefficient resource use may outweigh the gains in lower prices and increased local employment (Maskus 1990).

Further, continued infringement would risk increased use of trade sanctions by the industrial countries. If the industrial countries could be persuaded to offer relatively modest concessions on market access and safeguards, along with long transitional periods for the poorest countries, it is not difficult to envision the emergence of acceptable articles prohibiting these forms of infringement. Because the bulk of reported losses from foreign infringement are in the areas of trademark and copyright (US International Trade Commission 1988), such an outcome should command the support of many significant IP–generating industries.

The more difficult areas include patents, especially for pharmaceutical and food products and processes, and protection for new forms of IP. Most developing countries understandably see little prospect for gain, even in a long-run, dynamic sense, from protecting these innovations, which will continue to be dominated overwhelmingly by foreign firms. For these countries to issue and enforce such protection and to forswear the use of compulsory licenses would be to adopt a major and risky change in their development and health policies. As already noted, such a change would represent a substantial trade concession, for which the industrial countries must be prepared to issue compensation.

It is possible to sketch a framework for a compromise on patents. The poorest developing nations would be exempted from its disciplines for a long period of time. Other countries would be expected to increase their protective standards over time according to a negotiated timetable under which minimum global standards would be strengthened. Gradualism of this sort would recognize the difficulties many nations would have in improving their enforcement capabilities. Some limitations would be placed on the justifications that could be used to issue compulsory licenses, and guidelines might be set within which firms and governments could negotiate over compensation. A panel could be empowered to review the actions of governments that claim to be acting to counter the abuse of patent rights by foreign firms. A number of other technical aspects of such an agreement would need to be addressed also.

A GATT annex along these lines should serve to upgrade substantially the level of foreign protection of IP rights, while largely respecting the needs of developing countries. Again, however, it seems that successful attainment of that goal will oblige each delegation to relax its current hard positions to some degree, to commit to potentially contentious changes in its own IP legislation, and to consider seriously its underlying dedication to IP in the overall Uruguay Round package.

After the Uruguay Round

Suppose that an IP annex were concluded and introduced into the GATT. Such an annex would likely incorporate high standards for the developed economies and perhaps also for major middle-income countries. Minimum standards, some temporary derogations from these, and relatively long transition periods likely would be allowed for developing economies. What new issues would then emerge over the near term?

Clearly, the initial problem would be to secure appropriate implementing legislation for the accord in each country that seeks accession. The potential difficulties in this process should not be underestimated. In the United States alone, Congress may have to revise Section 337, consider abandoning in part the Special 301 process, move to a first-to-file patent system, strengthen legislation on neighboring rights, and recognize legal protections for existing geographic appellations. Political acceptance of any or all of these changes would be difficult. Similar problems would emerge in other contracting parties, perhaps especially in some developing countries where opposition to upgrading protection for foreign creators of IP is entrenched.

Once these commitments are in place, it will surely be difficult for many contracting parties to enforce them rigorously, for technical as well as domestic political and economic reasons. It seems, therefore, that the GATT would need to supplement its technical assistance capabilities with an ongoing surveillance and notification mechanism. Moreover, given the near inevitability of frequent complaints about failure to enforce standards, the GATT must come to grips with the relationship of its principles to dispute settlement in IP cases. How feasible will it be to maintain nondiscrimination when governments begin to use the GATT to force adjudication of private disputes? What kinds of retaliation will be allowed in cases where dispute settlement fails? Given that other policies (tariffs and investment restrictions, for example) might be used to influence the value of an IP right, even if such policies are not actionable in their own right, would governments be allowed to take action against them under the doctrine of nullification and impairment? Questions of this nature will require clear thinking as operation of the agreement proceeds.

Under any reasonable scenario, a number of important TICs are unlikely to accede to the IP agreement. These countries will likely become growing targets for bilateral actions against their IP policies, particularly if infringing activity tends to gravitate into their economies. By not joining the agreement they would enjoy, in principle, continued exemption of their IP regulations from GATT discipline. But this exemption is liable to be of little practical help in deterring foreign sanctions. Thus, GATT authorities must ponder the implications of a limited agreement for the future cohesion of the trading system.

In this regard, it is not difficult to envision a tripartite IP system emerging over the longer run. First, countries lying outside the prospective annex may simply struggle to manage their trade relations with the major TECs as best they can. Some of them may find it advantageous eventually to join the IP accord if it appears their prospects for development have been stunted by their outsider status. Second, middle-income countries may adhere to the minimum standards in the IP agreement, providing substantive although not complete protection for foreign IP owners. Third, a small number of developed countries may wish to go beyond these minimum standards in their joint commercial relations, forming a *de facto* IP club with mutual guarantees of strong protection. One imagines that this general arrangement would be largely satisfying for IP providers in those countries.

Intellectual property will continue to grow in importance and complexity as information-based products and new forms of technology enter into international commerce. A GATT agreement on IP reached now will have far-reaching implications for the future distribution of the gains from this growth. It is clear that TICs will suffer short-term losses if they accede to the agreement. It is not clear that they will experience long-term benefits from such accession (although that possibility exists), in part because they will leave the field open to nonsignatories to pursue their own discriminatory IP policies. If these countries turn out to be losers on the IP front because of current concessions in the GATT, prospects for their future collaboration would be diminished. It may be sensible at this time for the TECs to consider whether an additional investment in the integrity of the GATT system, through concessions in other important areas, may be in their long-run interests.

References

Maskus, Keith E. 1990. "Normative Concerns in the International Protection of Intellectual Property Rights: Implications for the Uruguay Round." Paper presented at a joint conference of the National Bureau of Economic Research and the Centre for Economic Policy Research, Cambridge, MA, 2 August.

US International Trade Commission. 1988. *Foreign Protection of Intellectual Property Rights and the Effect on U.S. Industry and Trade*. Washington: US International Trade Commission.

10

Dispute Settlement

Robert E. Hudec

The GATT is a legally binding international agreement, as are, in most respects, the side agreements negotiated under its auspices since 1947. The rules of the GATT, however, are not directly enforceable in the domestic courts of most member countries. Unless and until GATT rules are enacted into domestic law, they impose no direct legal restraint on government officials.[1]

Enforcement of GATT law rests primarily on two lesser, but still quite powerful, sources of coercion: the moral and political force of international legal obligation, and the threat of trade retaliation, which the GATT can authorize in the case of violation. Both of these sources of coercion require that the GATT be able to make authoritative legal rulings on the actions of member governments. This is where dispute settlement comes in.

"Dispute settlement" is the term given to the GATT's procedure for adjudicating legal disputes between member governments. GATT Article XXIII gives the GATT membership, acting collectively, the power to issue legal rulings. Since the 1950s, GATT practice has been to refer legal disputes to an ad hoc arbitration panel of three (or

---

1. In the United States, some state courts have held that the GATT is directly applicable to state governments; there has been no authoritative ruling by the US Supreme Court on this issue (Hudec 1986).

Robert E. Hudec is Melvin C. Steen Professor of Law at the University of Minnesota Law School.

occasionally five) neutral individuals agreed to by the parties; usually these individuals are GATT representatives of neutral countries. The panel rules on the legal issue and writes a report explaining its ruling. The panel report is then referred to the GATT Council (the legislative arm of the GATT membership), and in the usual case the Council "adopts" the report, thereby making it an official ruling of the GATT. A similar dispute settlement system is provided for in each of the seven side agreements, or codes, adopted in 1979, except that the final power to issue a ruling is limited to the code signatories, which for most of the codes are the 30 or so most important GATT members.

If a legal violation is found, the GATT Council will call for compliance, and the case will then be kept on the Council agenda until compliance, or a settlement, is reported. Until recently the power to authorize retaliation has almost never been sought.

What Is the Problem?

At the outset of the Uruguay Round, almost every GATT government subscribed to the view that the GATT's dispute settlement procedure needed improvement. All governments spoke of the same general goals: to make it easier for governments to obtain GATT legal rulings, and to increase the effectiveness of follow-up pressures for compliance.

There was also general agreement about the core problem: like every other part of the GATT's decision-making process, GATT dispute settlement procedures are run by consensus. No decision is adopted unless everyone, including the defendant country, agrees. The defendant must consent to the creation of a panel, its members, and its terms of reference. If the panel rules against the defendant, the defendant must also consent to adoption of that ruling by the GATT Council. And, finally, the defendant must consent to any retaliation that is proposed in response to its noncompliance. In short, the defendant has the power to block the dispute settlement process at any point.

At present, this blocking power is held in check by a complex pattern of GATT traditions and understandings. These restraints are fairly effective. Almost every request for appointment of a panel is eventually honored (albeit with sometimes lengthy delays). Most panel rulings, but not all, are eventually adopted by the Council (again, with sometimes lengthy delays). Retaliation has not, so far, been much of an issue. These less formal restraints have allowed the GATT dispute settlement procedure to function reasonably well—well enough to produce a 300 percent increase in the volume of GATT legal proceedings during the 1980s.[2] Nonetheless, in a significant number of cases the procedure has been blocked or delayed, and the accumulation of such experiences, including a new outbreak in the past few years, has begun to impair the political credibility of GATT law in national capitals.

Blockage has occurred at all points of the process. Governments have refused or delayed their consent to the creation, terms of reference, or membership of panels with some frequency. In the absence of such obstruction, panels can be established and fully operational within three to four months after a complaint is filed. In the 25 panels actually created from 1987 to 1989, the average time from complaint to appointment of members was seven months.[3] Sometimes the result of blockage is merely delay, but on other occasions the defendant succeeds in extorting some legal or procedural concession in advance.

Over the years, the United States has probably earned the worst grades in this regard. For example, in a case challenging the US tax device called domestic international sales corporations (DISC), which lasted from 1972 to 1984, the United States refused to proceed unless companion cases involving other countries were tried at the same time, and unless the panel included tax experts. In Nicaragua's 1985 complaint against a politically inspired US trade embargo, the United States would not accept a panel until Nicaragua agreed in advance that the GATT could not examine national security claims. The United States did the same thing in three 1988 complaints: in an EC complaint

---

2. Prior to 1980, GATT averaged about 3 formal legal complaints a year, with about 1.5 legal rulings. In the 1980s, complaints averaged about 11 per year, legal rulings about 4.5.

3. The sample consisted of all GATT cases in which panel members were actually appointed in 1987–89. The complaint is the first public invocation of the dispute settlement process, usually before Article XXIII:1 consultations; appointment of members is dated from the official announcement. Calculations are based on unpublished data collected by the author.

about certain US sugar restrictions, the United States would not agree to a panel because of alleged EC foot-dragging in another case; in a Brazilian complaint about US Section 301 retaliation, the United States insisted on agreement that Section 301 itself could not be examined by the panel; finally, in an EC complaint about Section 301 retaliation, the United States refused to accept creation of a panel unless the European Community agreed to adjudicate the scientific basis of the EC anti-hormones regulation at issue, in the code forum chosen by the United States. US conditions were eventually satisfied and panels were appointed in all but the last case, which remains blocked as this goes to press.

The really critical use of the blocking power has been against adoption of panel legal rulings by the GATT Council. Out of 57 GATT legal rulings issued by panels between 1975 and 1989, one can identify at least 17 cases in which the power to block Council adoption of a panel ruling was used in a significant way.[4] On three such occasions, the blockage was ultimately supported by the rest of the GATT membership, and the ruling was, in effect, set aside as erroneous.[5] This has been, in effect, GATT's appeal process for claims of legal error.

In eight other cases, adoption of the report was simply blocked and left in limbo, usually with some support from other countries.[6] In most

---

4. If one were to count the number of separate panel reports containing legal rulings, the number would be 61. In two instances, however, there were three virtually identical rulings on the same legal issue at the same time involving a common party. Blockage occurred in both triads. To avoid making blockage look worse than it is, I have counted each of these unitary blocking episodes as one blocking of one ruling. Hence, the 61 rulings are reduced to 57.

5. The panel rulings were the 1976 ruling in three US counterclaims in the DISC case, in which a finding of GATT violation against tax laws in three European countries was set aside; the 1981 ruling in a US complaint against Spanish restrictions of the sale of soybean oil, in which a finding of no violation was set aside; and the 1982 ruling in a Canadian complaint against the US Section 337 remedy, in which a finding of no violation was set aside by "adopting" the panel report with an express reservation that the legal issue could be litigated over again.

6. These cases included four Article XXIII rulings: those involving EC subsidies on canned fruit (1985) and EC citrus preferences (1985), both blocked by the Community; a Canadian tax on gold coins (1986), which Canada blocked; and the US embargo of Nicaragua (1986), which Nicaragua blocked. The other four cases involved rulings under the Subsidies Code: on the EC subsidy on wheat flour exports (1983) and the US

of these cases, the dispute was eventually settled, even though the ruling itself was not accepted.

Finally, one can identify at least six other cases in which adoption of the panel report was blocked for several months or more before being accepted. In the DISC case, for example, the United States blocked adoption for four years while demanding that rulings in its counterclaim cases be adopted at the same time.[7]

Of 14 cases that were blocked but not overruled, the European Community was responsible for blocking 5, the United States 4, Canada 3, and Nicaragua and Korea 1 each.

There have been very few requests for retaliatory authority in GATT history, but even here the blocking power has raised its head in recent years. In 1988–89, the United States blocked two separate requests for retaliation authority, one by the European Community and the other by Canada, made after the United States had failed for almost three years to comply with a GATT ruling against its Superfund tax law.

Round One: The Midterm Agreement

At the outset of the negotiations, the majority of governments favored keeping the basic consensus requirement, veto power and all. In their view, it would be sufficient to adopt more rigorous procedures that would make the exercise of blocking powers more difficult. They argued that GATT law is not, and may never be, strong enough to club unwilling governments into submission. So, they contended, governments will actually submit to greater discipline if they know they have

---

countervailing duty proceeding on wine (1986), both blocked by the United States; on EC pasta subsidies, blocked by the Community; and on a Canadian countervailing duty action on manufacturing beef (1987), which Canada blocked.

7. In addition, a ruling under the Government Procurement Code on the EC value-added tax threshold (1984) was blocked by the Community during four months of rather intensive meetings. Canada succeeded for seven months in blocking adoption of a ruling involving its Foreign Investment Review Agency (1983). A ruling on the US Section 337 law (1989) was blocked by the United States for 10 months. Three identical panel reports on Korean restrictions of beef imports were blocked by that country for six months. As this goes to press, a late 1989 ruling on EC oilseeds subsidies is still being blocked by the Community.

an ultimate power to escape the process (much as escape clauses in trade agreements are said to encourage deeper tariff cuts.

The United States, on the other hand, pressed for greater restrictions on the veto power. At the beginning, its two main proposals were to grant the complainant an automatic right to have a panel appointed, and to establish a rule that the parties to a dispute cannot block a consensus when the GATT Council considers adoption of a ruling; the latter is usually referred to as the "consensus-minus-two" proposal.

These two contending positions were tested when governments agreed to conclude an "early harvest" agreement on dispute settlement at the Montreal midterm meeting in December 1988 (GATT 1989). The agreement, which was not actually approved until April 1989 because of an impasse on other issues, was adopted on a trial basis until the end of the Uruguay Round. On the whole, the midterm agreement represented a victory for the consensus requirement.

Most of the midterm agreement was devoted to the start-up phase of the procedure. Governments did remove a number of potential blocking or delaying points by agreeing to automatic, nonconsensual answers that would keep the process moving (GATT 1989). A 60-day time limit was set on the initial process of bilateral consultations, after which the plaintiff is allowed to request creation of a panel. Another time limit of about two months was set for the Council's decision to create a panel. Similar automatic steps apply once a panel is appointed: the panel's terms of reference are to be standard unless otherwise agreed, and if the process for selecting panel members becomes deadlocked, one party can request the Director General of the GATT to name the panelists.[8]

However, on the one really critical issue—whether the defendant's consent is needed to refer a complaint to a panel—the midterm agreement faltered. Instead of giving a clear yes-or-no answer, it merely said that "a decision to establish a panel or working party shall be taken. . . [by a specified date] unless. . . the Council decides otherwise" (GATT 1989, paragraph F:a) A clear affirmation of the right to a panel would simply have authorized the Secretariat or the Chairman

---

8. In addition, the agreement cleared up a number of time-consuming procedural issues involving participation or parallel complaints by other parties, and then set a six-month time limit from appointment of panel members to completion of the ruling.

of the Council to appoint one, without any Council decision at all. The ministers' ambiguous answer could not have been accidental. The issue was clear, had been debated for years, and had been clearly presented.

The midterm agreement did give a clear answer on the most important issue of all: whether to retain the consensus rule giving defendants the power to block Council adoption of adverse panel rulings. It clearly rejected the consensus-minus-two proposal and reaffirmed the consensus principle:

> The parties to a dispute shall have the right to participate fully in the consideration of the panel report by the Council, and their views shall be fully recorded. The practice of adopting panel reports by consensus shall be continued, without prejudice to the GATT provisions on decision-making which remain applicable. However, the delaying of the process of dispute settlement shall be avoided. (GATT 1989, paragraph G:3)

This text was identical to one that had been adopted by the GATT ministers in 1982, in response to an earlier consensus-minus-two proposal (GATT 1983, 15–16).

Round Two: The Current Negotiations

Despite the rather clear rejection of the consensus-minus-two proposal in the midterm agreement, the United States has returned to the microphone and is currently leading discussion of an even more far-reaching reform of GATT dispute settlement procedures. This time the proposal seems to have found support among most major governments.

This change in position seems to have been precipitated by the new version of Section 301 in the US Omnibus Trade and Competitiveness Act of 1988. The new law's message was that the US Congress had lost patience with the inefficacy of GATT rules and legal remedies, and had turned to threats of trade retaliation to protect what it regarded as legitimate US economic interests. More alarming, these unilateral Section 301 measures had produced some apparently very substantial trade concessions in 1989, cementing Congress's attachment to the new self-help policy.

Section 301 changed the negotiating dynamic. Instead of debating rather abstractly how much GATT dispute settlement should be strengthened, negotiators were now asking how much strengthening it would take to persuade the Congress to put these new unilateral remedies back on the shelf and return to primary reliance on GATT law.

The proposal now being examined calls for a procedure in which neither the defendant nor the GATT Council has any power to block a GATT lawsuit at any stage. Panels would be created automatically upon request, and panel rulings would become binding automatically, either directly upon being issued or, if the losing party wishes to appeal, upon review and affirmance by an appellate tribunal of legal experts. Under the proposal, if compliance is not forthcoming within a certain time, authority to retaliate is automatically available, subject to review by a panel as to its amount and character if challenged.

In May 1990, it seemed that the United States, the European Community, Canada, and Japan were prepared to go along with the basic elements of this proposal. Later reports suggest that EC support may now be fading (or possibly was never firm to begin with). Other delegations have also begun to talk about retreat here or there. In the background, many participants and observers are beginning to ask a more fundamental question: whether the GATT is really ready for such a radical change of procedure. An appreciation of the basic orientation of the negotiations requires an understanding of these more fundamental reservations.

THE CASE FOR MOVING SLOWLY

The current substantive law of the GATT has many imperfections. The GATT's rules on trade policy have been around for over 40 years, but they are still riddled with gaps, inconsistencies, and vagaries—the product of repeated political compromises that were never meant to make any legal sense. GATT rules on "new issues," such as services and intellectual property, do not yet even exist, and if experience is any guide, the first cut on these issues will have even less legal coherence than the GATT's current rules on trade. Governments have been comfortable with such imperfect rules, because they have never wanted them enforced too rigorously in the first place.

The present balance of legal and political elements in the GATT's dispute settlement procedure has evolved as a response to these imperfections, in an effort to extract legal discipline from this hard and rocky soil. The core of the process is objective legal analysis, provided mainly by an experienced and skillful Secretariat legal office, which came into existence in the early 1980s; the procedure has generally produced legal opinions of high quality, particularly since the legal office was formed. But the Secretariat, of course, can operate only behind the scenes. The real judges are the three (or five) GATT diplomats who serve as members of the panel. Although as a rule quite knowledgeable about the GATT, the individuals who usually serve in this role are seldom very "judicial" in training, experience, or professional independence. They do, however, lend a kind of political legitimacy to the process, filtering the Secretariat's legal opinions through the practical judgment of career diplomats. Review by the GATT Council, of course, supplies another political screen. These elements not only keep the system from overrunning its limitations, but also add political support and legitimacy to legal rulings once they are made—an important source of added power that often compensates for defects in legal and procedural foundations.

A SLOWER TIMETABLE

The question posed by the more judicial model currently being discussed is whether the GATT is really ready for it. Will governments submit to a process based entirely on objective analysis of the present GATT rules? Will such objective analysis have sufficient force to induce compliance in difficult cases?

Given a completely free choice, I would much prefer a more gradual process of reform, during which the three key elements of the GATT legal system—the substantive rules, the adjudication procedure, and the government commitment to compliance—could mature together toward a more judicial model. After all, the GATT's current dispute settlement procedure has achieved high volume, high visibility, and consistently high quality only in the past eight or nine years. Habits of obedience get built one case at a time, and these habits could still use a lot of toughening. The adjudication procedure itself needs to develop a broader-based legal capacity: more and better judges, an even stronger secretariat staff, and, ideally, a separate Secretariat Office of Advocate General that would be a party in all cases. Finally, the substantive rules of the GATT certainly need a great deal more work, which can probably only be stimulated in earnest by legal rulings exposing inadequacies.

A great many of the reforms currently being proposed could be adopted under this slower timetable. With regard to improving the GATT's substantive rules, the time is certainly ripe to create a standing GATT Articles Committee, charged with preparing textual revisions for consideration by the signatory governments. Another important source of substantive reform would be legal criticism by outside scholars and other professionals. To receive the benefits of such criticism, the GATT must first remove the excessive blanket of confidentiality that surrounds its law and its legal sources. This would be one of the most important contributions the Uruguay Round could make to improving the quality of GATT substantive law.

What is needed is public access to all relevant legal sources, following restriction for a year or two of sensitive documents pertaining to ongoing business, and with any ad hoc extensions beyond that time subject to automatic sunset provisions. Present GATT practice is very far short of this standard. Approved rulings are immediately derestricted, and Council summary records are usually made public in a year or two, as are most main document series. But many other documents of equal relevance remain buried forever, among them the actual texts of detailed legal arguments made to the GATT Council, most of which are locked up in a permanently secret "C/W" series. The code committees have stamped an even greater portion of their dispute settlement work "forever secret," including the "M" and "Spec" series that contain practically all the legal debates. The parties' legal briefs fall into a super-secret category; not even other contracting parties are permitted to see them. Worst of all, GATT practice allows member governments to prevent derestriction of any document they like, in perpetuity; some governments have used this authority to bury all documents pertaining to panel decisions that have been overruled or blocked. These cases are of absolutely critical importance to any coherent jurisprudence.

There is also much that can be done right now on the procedural side. There is no longer any excuse, for example, to require the defendant's consent before referring a legal claim to a panel; the ambiguity of the midterm agreement should be resolved in favor of an automatic right. To be effective, such a right must contain an unequivocal recognition that panels are the judge of their own competence, in the first instance. Otherwise, blockage will still be possible in most cases, simply by turning one's objections into an issue of the panel's competence.

Nor is there any reason to delay any of the reforms that would better ensure the accuracy and persuasiveness of panel decisions. Strengthening the panel's decision-making process begins with personnel. The Secretariat legal staff needs to be large enough to do its work under normal caseload pressure. Having better and more experienced panelists would also contribute. This means that certain governments must agree to allow the Secretariat to call upon particularly respected members of their delegations for more panel work; the GATT's budget for nongovernmental panelists must be adequate to support a similar pattern of panel assignments for them.

Governments seem to be agreed that the quality of panel decisions would benefit from copying the procedure adopted in the Canada–US free trade agreement, under which the panel submits a draft of its ruling on the merits, for comment by the parties, prior to issuing the final report. I would recommend having three separate stages, each building on the improvements made in the prior stage:

□ As is done at present, the panel would first submit a draft statement of the facts and a summary of the parties' arguments. The parties would submit proposed corrections.

□ The panel would then review and revise facts and arguments, prepare its draft opinion on the merits accordingly, and submit that draft to the parties. The parties would again submit comments and criticisms.

□ The panel would review the comments, revise accordingly, and only then submit its final report to the parties, to be circulated to all GATT members if the case is not settled.

Finally, there is no reason not to start cutting back on the all-important power to block rulings. The consensus-minus-two proposal strikes a balance that seems right for the present time. It would serve as a powerful symbol against blocking legal rulings, but in practical terms it would not really eliminate the defendant's ability to escape the process in the most serious cases, because of the relative ease of getting support from friends and allies.

THE APPEALS TRIBUNAL

The proposal that most clearly raises concern about the readiness of GATT law is the proposal to eliminate all Council review and to substitute, as a safety valve for legal errors, an appeals tribunal of legal experts. Error is a fact of life in every legal system, and means must be established for dealing with it. As we have already seen, the GATT Council has found errors in three panel rulings in the past 15 years; most governments have a few other rulings they would add to the list.

The form of tribunal most commonly discussed would be a standing roster of between 5 and 20 judges, chosen from among the most respected legal experts of the GATT community: veteran panelists and others of similar reputation.

Elimination of the GATT Council's review power is a perfectly appropriate goal in principle. Council review is often not very objective, as member governments often take positions reflecting their own interests. Most would not be qualified to sit on a jury. The problem is that, as GATT legal institutions are now structured, an appellate tribunal would confront a number of obstacles to making high-quality legal decisions. The only existing institution with the blend of legal expertise and political experience needed to do high-quality legal work is the GATT Secretariat legal office. But because of its close association with the initial panel decision, the Secretariat legal office will not be able to advise the appellate tribunal. Other staff can no doubt be found, but it is difficult to see how a new and untried appellate tribunal can assemble decision-making resources of similar quality.

Problems of quality will be compounded by the limited pool of prospective judges, who will continue to be needed for the primary panels. The shortage will be especially acute if every case is appealed.

No one has yet figured out how to keep every case from going to appeal. Even when defendant governments agree with a ruling and are willing to comply, domestic politics usually require that they fight to the bitter end. The problem could be further compounded if the selection process becomes politicized, as often happens when a standing body like this is created.

Finally, there is the larger question of whether governments are really ready to cooperate with such a rigorous legal system. One might think that governments would never agree to such a system unless they were prepared to abide by it. Alas, this is not so. Governments are perfectly capable of agreeing to commitments such as this because of the short-term benefits—reining in Section 301, for example—without focusing on their ability to carry out those commitments in the long run. GATT law is littered with the wreckage of such "expedient" commitments.

Added together, these difficulties pose a risk that the appellate tribunal might detract from rather than add to the speed and force of GATT adjudication. It may end up subjecting good panel reports to mediocre appellate proceedings that would discredit all parts of the process, producing endless legal wrangles where once there were definitive Council-approved rulings. This is, of course, only a risk. The GATT and its governments are served by many talented people. They could get lucky. Setting the appellate tribunal in place could conceivably precipitate the political will needed to make it function well.

As a matter of legal policy, it would not be wise to take the sort of risk involved in the appellate tribunal proposal, particularly since recent history suggests that several GATT governments may not be willing to work toward its success. In the real world, however, legal policy decisions are also subject to other political constraints. The need to correct the excesses of Section 301 is one such political constraint. The success of the entire Uruguay Round may depend on it. Unwise though it may be, the Congress is demanding a "great leap forward" in GATT dispute settlement as the price for correcting Section 301. If the Congress cannot be persuaded to accept a slower timetable, the great leap could on balance be the lesser risk.

It is not possible to form a judgment about these comparative risks from a vantage point outside the negotiations. I would nevertheless recommend three important conditions for making a decision about the proposed appellate tribunal.

First, Council review of panel rulings should not be abolished at this time unless really necessary for the successful outcome of the round. If an accommodation between Section 301 and the rest of the round can be made without such a radical reform, Council review should remain. GATT law is not as ready as it should be for the more formal judicial system that would have to replace it.

Second, if Council review of some or all panel reports is retained, there is no case for interposing an appellate tribunal into the decision-making process. Such an intermediate tribunal would not diminish the threat of vetoes by the parties to the case. Stuck between the first panel decision and a final political review in the Council, an appeals tribunal would have no real power and would become nothing but a source of delay and friction.

If it is necessary to abolish Council review and to substitute an appellate tribunal, the reform package should do everything possible to retain and enhance the primary role of the initial panel proceeding. It is here that the GATT's legal expertise lies, and the appellate process must be given the fullest opportunity to make use of it.

For example, a party seeking an appeal should be required to submit its claim of legal error, in the form of a petition for rehearing, before being allowed to make that claim on appeal. What is wanted here is the benefit of the panel's response to the claim, even if only to clarify how the panel's ruling relates to the issue. This will add time to the process, but its impact on the quality of the appellate process is definitely worth it. The rehearing stage proposed here, plus the extra draft-opinion stage proposed earlier, should together add not more than two months. The appeal process itself would add three months, probably in every case. Assuming six months for the basic panel decision (as the midterm agreement requires), the new procedure being proposed would require a total time of 11 months from the appointment of panelists to a binding legal ruling.[9] Since the start-up time, as noted above, should be at least three months shorter under the new rules in the midterm agreement,

---

9. I have computed the average comparable time for the 18 GATT panel proceedings since 1987 that produced adopted rulings. The average was 10.9 months from appointment of panel members to Council adoption.

the total time from complaint to final ruling under the post–Uruguay Round procedure will actually be shorter than before: about 15 months instead of 18. Another month or more could be cut off the start-up time in code cases by eliminating the "conciliation" phase, which has proved worse than worthless.

Likewise, it should be made clear that appellate tribunals exist to hear specific claims of legal error, not to retry the entire dispute. Issues should be framed precisely. As a rule, appellate tribunals should consider only those legal issues necessary to a resolution of the appeal. There should also be some formal recognition that appellate tribunals are not in as good a position as the original panel to assess quasi-factual legal issues of "reasonableness" or "necessity" or equality of commercial treatment. Some suggestion of deference to the panel's judgment on these issues would be in order.

THE RIGHT TO RETALIATE

Most GATT legal complaints are resolved satisfactorily once a favorable legal ruling is obtained, and the threat of retaliation is never pressed beyond the purely verbal stage. Practice has been changing over the past decade, however. The GATT itself has not authorized retaliation in any recent cases, but the United States has resorted to unauthorized retaliation on a number of occasions, the European Community has begun to respond in kind, and other governments have at least begun to talk about the possibility.

As noted above, there have been two recent episodes in which requests for GATT authorization of retaliation have been blocked. The third major leg of the new proposal being suggested by the United States is to remove the defendant's blocking power on this issue as well.

As a matter of legal principle, there really is no excuse for a defendant's ability to veto the plaintiff's right to such a remedy. There is, however, a pragmatic question about whether it is really necessary to force the issue at this time. An automatic retaliation provision is likely to generate far more concern about loss of sovereignty than it is really worth. The right to block is not, after all, a very important restraint on retaliation. Where there has been a failure to comply with a ruling of violation, a complaining government that finds its retaliation proposal blocked has a quite legitimate claim to resort to self-help. Smaller governments might well fear entering upon such uncharted waters, but this should not be a problem for the United States. If, therefore, other governments begin to draw back from an otherwise useful reform because of this final step, the GATT would lose little, if any, legal rigor by dropping the idea.

Round Two-and-a-Half: The "Nonviolation" Remedies

A further issue to be dealt with in the Uruguay Round dispute settlement negotiations is the GATT's procedure for dealing with restrictive government measures that lie outside the coverage of its legal obligations, but that arguably impact upon the balance of benefits under those obligations. Codes of international rules are contracts between governments. The political basis of such contracts is "reciprocity," a term that connotes not only a reciprocal balance of obligation, but, more important, a reciprocal balance of economic advantage. The long-term enforcement of such agreements depends on maintaining that balance. This reservation is expressed, in part, in termination clauses allowing governments to simply cancel a contract on rather short notice (for the GATT, 60 days) for any reason they like. Short of absolute termination, there is a gray area in which governments have to work out ways and means of dealing with imbalances of benefit caused by events not covered by the agreement's legal obligations.

CURRENT GATT REMEDIES

The GATT already has a procedure for dealing with reciprocity-upsetting events outside the scope of its legal code. Article XXIII provides that the contracting parties can investigate, rule upon, and make recommendations about two kinds of complaints: those about violations of legal obligations—the staple element of the GATT dispute settlement procedure—and so-called nonviolation complaints, concerning measures that are not in violation of the agreement. Article XXIII authorizes an investigation to determine whether the nonviolation measure has caused one of two reciprocity-impairing events: one in which "a benefit accruing to [the complainant] directly or indirectly under this Agreement is being nullified or impaired," or one in which "the attainment of any objective of this Agreement is being impeded." If the contracting parties find that such an event has occurred, they may issue a ruling to that effect, make a nonbinding recommendation concerning the situation, institute various consultatory procedures, or, if appropriate, release the complaining party—or parties on all sides—from whatever GATT obligations they deem appropriate.

The central idea behind this Article XXIII procedure is the recognition that there will inevitably be cases where measures not covered by the legal code have a reciprocity-upsetting effect, and that member governments will inevitably claim the right to bend or alter their GATT legal obligations in response. If the GATT did not offer a way of adjudicating these situations in a multilateral forum, including the power to alter GATT legal relationships in response to them, the stronger governments would simply impose their own adjustments unilaterally.

As sensible as the idea of GATT supervision of nonviolating actions may be, it is extremely difficult to carry it out in practice. Basically, such supervision requires giving the GATT a certain kind of lawmaking power—the power to impose new quasi-obligations, by a process of logically extending the sense, purpose, and policy of the legal obligations already consented to. Looking back, it is surprising that governments ever agreed to allow the GATT to adjudicate their behavior under the two open-ended standards quoted above.[10] It is not surprising that this remedy has not been developed very far in the GATT's first 40 years. There exists one rather impressive, if somewhat beaten-up, line of case law development involving GATT–legal measures that impair the commercial value of tariff concessions; the legal doctrine developed in these cases has been given the designation "nonviolation

---

10. Actually, it was not done without a rather colorful debate protesting this enormous grant of power. The story is told in Hudec (1990, 37–47).

nullification and impairment'' (NN&I).[11] But the broader reaches of Article XXIII authority over nonviolation measures have barely been scratched.

SECTION 301 REMEDIES

Over the years, the US Section 301 legislation has adopted an increasingly aggressive attitude toward measures which, although not in violation of the GATT, were thought to create reciprocity-upsetting impediments to US commercial interests. The Section 301 terminology for such legal-but-wrong measures is ''unreasonable.'' The policy of attacking these measures really began in the early 1980s, when the United States began to take a very broad position that the GATT as a

---

11. Article XXIII nonviolation doctrine has been limited to the first of its two broad tests, ''nullification and impairment'' of benefits accruing under the GATT.

The NN&I doctrine was first employed in two cases in the early 1950s. In a case involving subsidies granted by Australia, the panel ruled that an unanticipated change of direction in an established domestic subsidy policy impaired the value of an earlier tariff concession. A panel hearing a case involving German measures affecting imports of Norwegian sardines ruled that a change in an existing tariff policy toward competing products, known to have been relied upon when measuring the value of a concession, also constituted impairment. In theory, compensatory withdrawals could have been authorized in both cases, but the GATT first recommended correcting the impairing policy, and in both cases this was done.

In two 1985 cases, the United States obtained NN&I rulings against the European Community. In the 1985 canned fruit case discussed above, a panel found that a subsequent production subsidy impaired an earlier tariff concession. In the case that same year involving EC citrus preferences, a panel made the first ruling of nullification not based on the ''benefits'' of a tariff concession: the panel found that tariff preferences under an unapproved regional agreement, while not GATT–illegal, impaired the benefits of the obligation under GATT Article I to extend most-favored-nation treatment. In both cases, adoption of the panel rulings was blocked by the Community, but both cases produced settlements that corrected the offending practice.

In 1989 the United States obtained another NN&I ruling against the Community in the oilseeds case, which once again involved a production subsidy that impaired an earlier tariff binding. The Community, as already noted, has blocked adoption of the report, but has agreed to eliminate the NN&I practice.

For a full description of existing NN&I doctrine, see Hudec (1975). For an analysis of possible avenues of future development, see Hudec (1984).

whole was not producing balanced results for the United States, and that the imbalance could only be corrected by removing impediments to other international markets in which the United States had a greater comparative advantage: particularly in services, intellectual property, and certain high-technology industries. More recently, the United States has also begun to act against policies affecting the perceived imbalance in merchandise trade itself; an example is the Structural Impediments Initiative with Japan, which deals with such "unreasonable" impediments to trade as restrictive distribution networks, barriers to new retail stores, and lack of antitrust enforcement.

In the early 1980s the United States proposed to negotiate new GATT agreements to cover many of these barriers. When these proposals were rejected, Congress began to demand stronger action based on threats of trade retaliation under Section 301. In 1985, the United States began doing so, threatening trade retaliation in bilateral demands for liberalization of barriers to service trade, improvement of intellectual property protection, and correction of other "unreasonable" measures. Then came the Super 301 and Special 301 procedures, promising even more vigorous use of trade retaliation (through designation of specific countries as unfair traders, and of unfair practices regarding intellectual property, respectively) for the same purpose.

Trade retaliation is a violation of the GATT, except when authorized by the GATT in response to a legal violation or a finding of NN&I. Section 301 retaliation against "unreasonable" measures would have been GATT–illegal in almost every case in which it was threatened. The United States claimed such retaliation was justified by an underlying imbalance of reciprocity—a very broad sort of NN&I claim—but it was unwilling to submit that claim to the GATT for adjudication.

In retrospect, the type of imbalance the United States was claiming was so broad that it was probably beyond the capacity of the GATT to resolve by adjudication. Consequently, it can be argued that, in light of the refusal of other GATT governments to negotiate on these claims of imbalance, the only choice open to the United States short of withdrawal from the GATT was to engage in legal disobedience to communicate the intensity of its dissatisfaction. This was a one-time excuse, however. It cannot survive a Uruguay Round agreement establishing a new basic balance of reciprocity in response to these US claims.

THE NONVIOLATION ISSUE IN THE URUGUAY ROUND

The US Congress is still concerned about whether the Uruguay Round agreement will produce an acceptable balance of economic advantage; it is worried about likely gaps (which are sure to exist) in the new GATT agreements on services and intellectual property, and about the absence of GATT rules on structural impediments to merchandise trade itself, such as those claimed to exist in Japan. Congress would like to have it both ways. It would like to enjoy the benefit of all the new Uruguay Round rules, backed by effective enforcement, while at the same time having a free hand to use trade retaliation in violation of GATT obligations whenever it finds other "unreasonable" restrictions on US commerce not covered by GATT rules.

Not surprisingly, other governments have said they will not accept the obligations of the new Uruguay Round on those terms. They acknowledge that measures outside the GATT's rules may cause imbalance, but they insist that the only basis on which a GATT legal system can operate is a commitment by governments not to use trade retaliation except as authorized by Article XXIII. The whole round may depend on resolving this issue.

In the dispute settlement negotiations, the US concerns emerge in the form of questions about whether Article XXIII remedies for nonviolation measures can be made sufficiently "effective" to be accepted as an alternative to Section 301 remedies. Lurking behind this concern is the more basic issue of just how much "effectiveness" a government is entitled to ask for. The problem, after all, is government measures not covered by the rules—a subject no legal system can deal with as crisply and effectively as complaining citizens will want. If the United States wants to participate in a functioning legal order under the GATT, it will have to be ready to accept something less effective than its Section 301 "do-this-or-die" procedures. The issue is one of degree.

The basic structure of the Article XXIII NN&I finding, as presently understood, provides a meaningful remedy. The conclusion that benefits have been nullified or impaired is understood to mean that the balance of reciprocity has been upset, and that if the imbalance is not cured, the complaining party is entitled to withdraw obligations of its own to restore the balance. The right to make compensatory withdrawals is a right to retaliate. That right can be used to bargain effectively for correction.

In practice, there are two related weaknesses with the NN&I remedy as it now stands. First, since the remedy has not been used to any great extent, the substantive content of NN&I doctrine is not much developed. The core idea relates to situations in which unexpected actions or events upset reasonable expectations underlying a particular deal. "Reasonable expectations" is a familiar legal concept. Its application requires making a number of implicit normative judgments about the behavior of the parties, judgments that typically get built into the law gradually through case-by-case adjudication.[12] But, of course, one never learns the contours of these supplemental principles until actual cases are brought.

Second, it is doubtful that other GATT governments would agree to hand over this kind of lawmaking authority to panels or appellate tribunals without retaining some final, political control—not, at least, until the whole GATT legal system acquires a great deal more prestige than it now has. As a result, the NN&I rulings will most likely remain subject to Council review by consensus, including full blocking power for the parties involved. This is where the key judgment about "effectiveness" will have to be exercised. The bad news is that in the GATT's last three NN&I cases, a ruling favorable to the United States was blocked by the European Community (the canned fruit, citrus, and oilseeds cases). Moreover, there is a fair likelihood of such blockage in the future, because these equity-based NN&I rulings, totally detached from any legal text, cast long legal shadows that frighten governments. Now the good news: in each of the three cases, the impediment complained of was eventually removed after lots of shouting and one actual burst of unauthorized retaliation by the United States. In one case this happened as part of a broad-based settlement involving concessions on both sides, and in the other two simply by an eventual EC agreement to change. Also encouraging is the fact that the most recent case found both parties debating the legal meaning of one of the

---

12. For my own attempt to wrestle with the implications of "reasonable expectations" and other elements of this doctrine, see Hudec (1975, 1984).

"blocked" 1985 panel rulings. The power of precedent, it seems, is a part of the process that parties cannot block.

In addition to the Article XXIII NN&I doctrine, of course, the broad language of Article XXIII authorizes somewhat less coercive remedies against a broader class of measures: those whose effects may not be wrong enough, or specific enough, or clear enough, to warrant a judge-made remedy of compensation-cum-retaliation. These lesser remedies would include rulings of condemnation or remonstrance, recommendations of correction, and creation of various multilateral bodies to negotiate or investigate the matter. The contribution these multilateral remedies offer also has to be weighed in the "effectiveness" balance.

The possibilities are illustrated by a recent GATT dispute involving an EC claim that Japanese tariff rates and business practices were distorting world market prices for raw materials in the copper sector in a manner prejudicial to the Community. The issue was finally submitted to the Director General of the GATT, under an informal "good offices" procedure. The Director General designated a former GATT official to investigate and report on the matter. The report presented an adjudicatory-type objective judgment, concluding that the rather high Japanese tariffs were causing a market distortion due to certain factors in world copper markets, and affirming that no GATT legal violation was involved, but going on to recommend that Japan make a special effort to negotiate a reduction in its relevant tariffs.

In the end, it would seem that the United States has no choice but to surrender the core of its current Section 301 policy pertaining to trade retaliation against "unreasonable" measures if it wants a Uruguay Round agreement. The only question, really, is exactly how much of Section 301 must be excised, and what the United States can reasonably expect to obtain in exchange. The United States could demand that the Article XXIII nonviolation remedy be completely judicialized, with panel or appellate tribunal rulings becoming automatically binding. This might give Congress a stronger political excuse for cutting back on Section 301, but it would probably produce a weaker remedy for nonviolation matters in the long run. The United States itself could never live with this much delegation of lawmaking power, and it would probably be one of the first to bail out. As soon as that happened, the whole adjudicative process would be discredited.

A better answer is to leave Article XXIII nonviolation remedies subject to Council review by consensus, and to concentrate on improvements that will strengthen the quality of the process. Simple attention to the nonviolation process would have a strengthening effect, whatever its content. Specific decisions might include:

□ An affirmation that panels will be appointed to consider any claims, including claims involving broader issues beyond established NN&I doctrine;

□ An affirmation that governments understand the open-ended nature of the process, and the need for it;

□ Adoption of procedures flexible enough to permit panels to investigate such claims in whatever manner is most appropriate; and

□ Greater specificity about the types of remedial outcomes that are possible in nonviolation complaints.

If this were done, the Article XXIII procedure would probably merit taking an affirmative wait-and-see attitude—a judgment that it has enough potential power to warrant a good faith effort to make it work, but not enough to justify throwing away all parachutes. The key at this point will then be the precise surgery to be done on Section 301. The objective must be to strike a line that removes the core of the problem for other governments, but still reserves to the United States some threat and power to react if Article XXIII remedies fail.

The core problem with Section 301 is not its grant of domestic legal authority to retaliate in violation of GATT obligations. Every GATT government has such legal authority somewhere in its law. The core problem is Section 301's political commitment to violate the GATT whenever necessary to challenge "unreasonable" measures. Although Section 301 never actually requires trade retaliation in such cases, it does constitute a political mandate to do so, framed in legally binding statutory procedures that ensure that any deviation from the political mandate will expose the government to severe political sanctions. That political commitment destroys the reciprocity value of US legal obligations for other governments. That is what has to be eliminated from Section 301.

This can be done in varying degrees. The minimum condition, in my view, would be three major changes to Section 301: a provision authorizing the President (or the US Trade Representative) to take all Section 301 claims to the GATT, another making retaliation against "unreasonable" measures genuinely discretionary, and a third instructing the President to take into account both international obligations and the outcome of GATT dispute settlement proceedings as a condition of using Section 301 retaliation powers.

This solution would leave intact the basic Section 301 legal obligation to investigate and process claims about "unreasonable" measures. It would also leave the President with discretion to walk away from GATT proceedings, and with Section 301 legal authority to employ GATT–illegal trade retaliation if he so chooses. In the present context, retaining these Section 301 provisions would express a political reservation—some last-resort possibility of violating the GATT if Article XXIII fails. Some such reservation will seem a political necessity for Congress, while undoubtedly making life more difficult, politically, for other GATT governments. In reality, however, its message is really no more than that implicit in the commitment any government makes to an international legal system with as many gaps and imperfections as the GATT. It will not prevent the United States from making a good-faith effort to comply. Moreover, once the United States is actually drawn into the process of subjecting claims of "unreasonableness" to multilateral judgment, the reservation will become very difficult to invoke in practice.[13]

The Problem in Washington

US leadership on dispute settlement reform tends to obscure its own very serious compliance problem. There was a time when the Euro-

---

13. Governments sometime refer loosely to "repeal of Section 301" as a *quid pro quo* for reform of GATT dispute settlement procedures. I am aware of no ground for demanding removal of procedures requiring investigation, prosecution, and eventual retaliation against violations of obligations, so long as their procedures and time limits permit bringing such cases to the GATT, dismissing them when the GATT rules negatively, and completing GATT procedures before acting.

pean Community was the greatest sinner with regard to GATT dispute settlement. The United States has always run a close second, however, and has raced to the head (or bottom) of the list during the past five years. Today, it is the United States more than any other GATT country that imposes conditions on others before agreeing to panels, that blocks panels' adoption of adverse reports, that blocks requests for authority to retaliate, and, for good measure, that takes its time about complying with adopted panel rulings.

The long chain of bad behavior on the US report card shows a rather deeply rooted one-sidedness in US attitudes toward GATT legal obligations. The reforms now being proposed in the Uruguay Round will require a major change in the way Congress and executive branch officials think about GATT law. That must always be kept in mind. Everything else depends on it.

References

GATT. 1983. "Ministerial Declaration Adopted on 29 November 1982." In *Basic Instruments and Selected Documents, 29th Supplement*. Geneva: GATT, 9–23.

GATT. 1989. "Decision of 12 April 1989: Improvements to the GATT Dispute Settlement Rules and Procedures." Geneva: GATT, L/6489.

Hudec, Robert E. 1990. *The GATT Legal System and World Trade Diplomacy*, 2nd ed. Salem, NH: Butterworths.

Hudec, Robert E. 1986. "The Legal Status of GATT in the Domestic Law of the United States." In Meinhard Hilf, Francis Jacobs, and Ernst-Ulrich Petersmann, eds., *The European Community and GATT*. Deventer, Netherlands: Kluwer, 187–249.

Hudec, Robert E. 1975. "Retaliation Against 'Unreasonable' Foreign Trade Practices: The New Section 301 and GATT Nullification and Impairment." *Minnesota Law Review* 59, no. 6 (January): 461–539.

Hudec, Robert E. 1984. "Regulation of Domestic Subsidies under the MTN Subsidies Code." In Don Wallace, Jr., Frank J. Loftus, and Van Z. Kirkorian, eds., *Interface Three: Legal Treatment of Domestic Subsidies*. Washington: International Law Institute, 1–18.

11

Reflections on Restructuring the GATT

John H. Jackson

In a small book entitled *Restructuring the GATT System* (Jackson 1990), I recently explored the institutional problems of the current GATT system, with its very complex group of about 200 treaties, its uneasy provisional application, and the lack of firm constitutional underpinnings for its Secretariat and other institutions. In that book I suggested an approach to evolve the GATT into a World Trade Organization (WTO), by bringing into force, one would hope in the near future, a "mini-charter" influenced strongly by the failed attempt at such a charter in 1955, for an Organization of Trade Cooperation (OTC).

The basic idea of a WTO charter would be that, unlike the Havana Charter that was to have established the International Trade Organization (ITO), it would contain only organizational and institutional provisions; it would leave substantive trade obligations to the GATT, to the other GATT system treaty instruments, and to any new treaty instruments that result from the Uruguay Round negotiations. The GATT would remain in force, possibly becoming definitive rather than provisional, and the new organization would provide an institutional umbrella for the GATT and for other important trade agreements.

John H. Jackson is Hessel E. Yntema Professor of Law at the University of Michigan Law School. This chapter is adapted from his most recent book, Restructuring the GATT System, *published by Pinter for the Royal Institute of International Affairs, London (published in North America by Council on Foreign Relations Press, New York).*

Certain perplexing institutional issues will have to be faced in any event at the end of the Uruguay Round, if it is successful, to implement the results of this very complex and ambitious negotiation, whose scope extends to such new areas as services and intellectual property. To some extent, a WTO could solve the problem, or at least provide additional options for ways to implement the results of the round.

Since the publication of my book, a number of discussions have been held among many of the GATT member countries on the subject of a new institutional structure for the GATT system.[1] The government of Canada has formally proposed the development of a WTO and has discussed the idea with a number of its trading partners. A GATT meeting of trade ministers, held in April 1990 in Puerto Vallarta, Mexico, also took up the subject. The subject was again considered at a meeting in California in May 1990 of representatives of the United States, the European Community, Japan, and Canada. At the OECD ministerial meeting in Paris later that month, the ministers again discussed the future evolution of the GATT institutional structure, and included the following statement in the communiqué from that meeting:

> Ministers confirm their determination to achieve a far-reaching, substantive result in all areas of the Uruguay Round by the end of the year. Such an outcome should provide the basis for a commitment to strengthen further the institutional framework of the multilateral trading system, building on its contractual nature. This important question should be considered in due course, when the successful completion of the current negotiation has been secured.[2]

As we all know, the GATT is an anomaly in that it was never intended itself to be an international organization. The failure of the ITO to come into force required the GATT to assume a role it was not designed for. Nevertheless, the GATT has been remarkably successful, thanks to a series of pragmatic and able leaders over its 40-year history. The key question today is whether the GATT will be able, over its next 40 years, to cope with the new and different issues that are arising very quickly on the world economic scene.

---

1. There have also been several previous studies of and suggestions about the GATT institutional structure, among them an earlier study of my own (Jackson 1969) and those by Camps (1980) and Preeg (1989).

2. OECD Press Release Communiqué, Press/A(90)32, Paris, 31 May 1990, p. 11.

Institutional Problems of the GATT

The fundamental treaty structure of the GATT is flawed on several counts. The application of the GATT is still, after 40 years, provisional. This may not have any particular treaty meaning (the status of provisional treaties is not adequately covered in the 1969 Vienna Convention on the law of treaties, for example), but it is clear that the provisional nature of the GATT has had the effect of confusing many parts of the public, and even some government officials. The GATT rules are binding international treaty obligations, yet we still see statements to the contrary, even by officials or politicians who should know better. The GATT also was and continues to be a subject of some dispute between the Congress and the executive branch in the United States; this state of affairs is not particularly conducive to the efficiency and effectiveness of this international institution. Furthermore, "grandfather rights" still exist under the GATT, even though they were originally intended to be temporary.

A number of other institutional problems stem from this basic structural flaw in the treaty, including the problem of amendments, the relationship of the GATT to domestic law, the dispute settlement procedure, questions of membership, and problems of rulemaking and the powers of the contracting parties.

It is now considered very difficult to amend the GATT. The delay required by the treaty acceptance process, the difficulty in obtaining the required number of acceptances, the shift in bargaining power that has occurred as a consequence of the growth in membership, and the fact that even when an amendment is adopted, it does not apply to those countries that do not accept it—all these are reasons why the amending procedure has not been used for 25 years. This has caused a certain rigidity and an inability to develop rules to accommodate the many new developments in international trade.

One result of this rigidity in the GATT structure has been the development of an elaborate system of side treaties, which create some of their own problems.

A key problem is the relationship to the GATT of these many side agreements, which in most cases are stand-alone treaties, yet are intimately linked to the GATT treaty structure itself. It is unclear in some circumstances what this relationship is and whether an obligation contained in the side agreement will prevail over that of the GATT itself, or vice versa. In any event, since the side agreements tend to provide for a series of separate procedures for various matters including dispute settlement, there is a certain inefficiency in the potential for "forum shopping."

The relationship of the GATT treaty system to domestic law in a variety of GATT member countries is also very murky. This may be unavoidable, regardless of the basic treaty structure, since the national legal systems differ so widely. Nevertheless, more attention could be given to the possibility of establishing certain international treaty obligations with respect to how the trade and economic rules should be implemented domestically. Some attention has been given to this question in recent years, sometimes under the rubric of "transparency."

There are a number of troublesome problems with respect to membership, or "contracting party status," in the GATT and its large number of side agreements. A nation can become a "member" of the GATT or one of the side agreements in various ways. In some cases, territories that do not have full independent international sovereignty can become members. And in certain cases, former colonies can be sponsored for membership and enter the GATT with very little substantive commitment. This reduces the "terrain of reciprocity" and leads to criticisms of unfairness. The GATT also has an "opt out" clause (Article XXXV) under which an individual GATT contracting party can choose not to enter into a GATT relationship with certain other parties. This is a one-time-only option, exercisable only when one of the parties first enters the GATT. Nevertheless, in a number of circumstances there is an effective "opt out" provision at a later time, with murky legal results.

The powers of the contracting parties acting jointly, as defined in the GATT, are very ambiguous. Indeed, those powers are so broad that they could become the subject of abuse, although to date they have not. There are a number of unsettled and disquieting issues, such as the power of the contracting parties acting jointly to interpret the GATT agreement, and the relationship of actions of the contracting parties to some of the side agreements. Furthermore, the decision-making process leaves much to be desired. The so-called consensus approach has some inherent defects, but it has evolved to ameliorate some of the problems of a one-nation, one-vote structure, coupled with the ambiguity and terseness of the GATT text. For example, the GATT Council was created out of whole cloth by resolution of the contracting parties acting jointly and has no treaty status.

The dispute settlement processes of the GATT have been one of its more intriguing institutional evolutions. The treaty language on dispute settlement is very sparse indeed, but many decades of practice have resulted in a considerable amount of exegesis, and the elaboration of much of this exegesis in a Tokyo Round "understanding," as well as further efforts to improve the procedures during the current round. Dispute settlement procedures are intimately connected with problems of "effectiveness." There is considerable worry about whether the GATT procedures can stand up to some of the pressures now being imposed upon them.

Finally, a long-festering problem has been the relationship of the GATT to the other Bretton Woods institutions, the International Monetary Fund and the World Bank. This is one of the items explicitly flagged for negotiation in the Uruguay Round, and it certainly merits more attention, since the monetary questions are really only "the other side of the coin" of trade questions.

Principles of Organization

International institutions consistently pose some difficult and perplexing questions about the structuring of human affairs. National governments traditionally cling to sovereignty and often hesitate to relinquish any of that turf to international institutions. This reluctance is often related to the size and power of the nation concerned, and to the relative influence of key interest groups within the nation. Traditionally, smaller nations and weaker interest groups have been somewhat more willing to look beyond their national borders for institutional measures that would assist them to redress their relative lack of power.

There are sometimes exceptions. For example, the United States, after a period in the early part of this century in which it turned away from international ties, has since World War II been a leader in the development of international institutions. There are probably at least two reasons for this change in attitude. First, a wealthy nation such as the United States has a great deal at stake in the relative absence of armed conflict in a troubled and turbulent world. Second, the US Constitution already provides for a considerable amount of internal conflict and tension, and sometimes one part of the US government (particularly the Congress) may feel that its interests will be better protected if it hems in another part (e.g., the executive branch) by means of international obligations. Likewise, the reverse can be a motivation.

In any event, the concept of sovereignty is changing dramatically and, at least in the context of economic affairs, begins to lose most of its meaning, particularly in a world that has become so economically interdependent.

Different approaches to international affairs can be seen reflected in the different models of international institutions. Broadly speaking, there are two such models. The first is structured primarily as a forum for discussion and future negotiation. Institutions based on this model tend to have neither an abundance of concrete or precisely defined international rules or obligations, nor a mechanism for implementing or enforcing them. To some extent, the Organization for Economic Cooperation and Development (OECD) represents this model.

Institutions structured on the contrary model provide concrete and reasonably precise rules that their member governments feel are necessary to enhance the predictability of an uncertain world and the governments acting in it. In the area of economic activity many such institutions exist. Most prominent, of course, are the International Monetary Fund (IMF) and a number of specialized agencies such as the International Civil Aviation Organization, which deals with international transport activity, and the Universal Postal Union. Statements of the draftsmen of the ITO Charter indicate quite clearly that they intended to structure that organization on this model, with fairly precise rules and a mechanism for implementing or enforcing them. The GATT has been gravitating toward this model, although its troubled origins have made that more difficult to achieve than might have been the case under the ITO charter.

The question of the appropriate institutional model is central to the consideration of the constitutional problems and difficulties of the GATT system of today and the options for resolving them. Yet governments and even individuals are not always clear as to which model they prefer. During the last 15 years, for example, the US government has been articulating the need to improve the GATT dispute settlement process and rule implementation. Yet, in hard cases, the United States has been willing to subvert that process, by a variety of procedural devices or simply by refusing to comply with the results of panel procedures that go against it. In some of these cases, to its credit, the United States ultimately comes around. As this goes to press, however, there are a number of outstanding GATT judgments finding US actions inconsistent with GATT obligations, and several more procedures that have been started may end in similar judgments.

Other governments do not escape this criticism. The European Community has been one of the most ardent opponents of improvement in the GATT dispute settlement process during the last 15 years. However, this attitude within the EC has now apparently shifted toward support of an enhanced GATT dispute settlement procedure.

One can only sympathize with the plight of the trade minister of Canada who noted at the 1987 Geneva ministerial meeting which celebrated the 40th anniversary of the GATT that her government strongly supported the GATT's dispute settlement procedures, although its officials sometimes paused when expressing that view because Canada had lost its last three dispute settlement cases.[3]

Thus, even persons of good will and broad international perspective have ambivalent feelings about the fundamental nature that an international institution dealing with economic matters should take on. It is worthwhile therefore to examine more closely some of the policy objectives that relate to this fundamental question. In short, what are the arguments for each of the two models?

Rule-Oriented Versus Power-Oriented Diplomacy

Although the rules of international law may be somewhat less effective than those of domestic law, at least for those nations with stable legal

---

3. Statement by Mrs. Pat Carney, Minister for Trade for Canada, at the GATT 40th Anniversary Ministerial Round Table Discussion, Geneva, 30 November 1987.

systems and a generally effective central government, it is not always the case that domestic laws are implemented efficiently. It is important for the policy adviser and the statesman, as well as international lawyers and businesspeople, to accurately evaluate the real impact of international rules, recognizing that some of them (often the ones that do not reach the headlines) do have a considerable effect and influence on real government and business decisions (Henkin 1979, 38–88).

For example, despite cynical statements by members of Congress that GATT rules are "irrelevant," there are a number of proven instances in which congressional committees and their staff members have taken considerable trouble to tailor legislative proposals to minimize the risk of a complaint to the GATT. Not all of these efforts have been successful, but in other cases Congress has been persuaded to drop a proposal because of its inconsistency with GATT provisions. The US executive branch is also influenced by GATT legality arguments, although it too does not always defer to them.

Examples of congressional deference to GATT obligations include the case involving US domestic international sales corporations (DISC), in which a GATT complaint led to a change in the law replacing the DISC system with the present FSC (foreign sales corporation) system.[4] In another case, during consideration of the 1986 Tax Reform Act, certain congressional committees decided to add a customs users' fee to existing tariffs to partly fund the US Customs Service—a practice clearly contrary to the GATT. The committee staff persuaded the committees to redraft the proposal; nevertheless the law was later challenged and found incompatible with the GATT.[5] Finally, a very clear example of the persuasive power of GATT obligations involved the US "manufacturing clause": despite a GATT panel's finding that this provision of US law was GATT–incompatible, a bill (S.1822/H.R.4696) was introduced to make the clause a permanent part of US copyright law. In House hearings, US Trade Representative Clayton Yeutter argued:

> . . . . we have to be concerned about the fact that the manufacturing clause has been declared GATT illegal. Here we are attempting to strengthen the GATT, respond to

---

4. GATT, *Basic Instruments and Selected Documents.* 28 Suppl. 114 (1982).

5. *International Trade Reporter,* 4 (April 1987): 1450.

the criticisms of the GATT that exist throughout the world, including in this subcommittee, appropriate criticisms in my judgment, but how do we go about reaching that objective, which all of us share, if we patently violate GATT ourselves?. . . We have a definitive GATT decision against the United States on this clause. We have no defense whatsoever for the continuation of the manufacturing clause. How can we possibly go to other countries and say don't violate the GATT, if we cavalierly and flagrantly violate it ourselves?[6]

The bill did not pass, and the legislation lapsed.

The ability of nations to unilaterally apply such measures as antidumping or countervailing duties often has a powerful influence on potential transactions and even on government policy. The constraints on the nation applying those duties stem from the rules on those subjects in the GATT and its side agreements, and thus those rules have considerable utility in determining the likely response of an importing country to certain dumping or subsidy-like practices in an exporting country.

In addition to the question of evaluating the effectiveness of existing international rules, there are several important policy issues surrounding rule implementation, which often do not get explicitly addressed. First, should the international legal system be improved to make its rules more effective? Second, should new rules be added and made effective? At first blush, these questions might seem trivial. Indeed, most governmental and private practitioners would probably privately answer them in the affirmative. In practice, however, these same individuals may act differently. Objective observation of the workings of the international legal system, even as it pertains to international economic affairs, leads one to perceive that many in government and private practice are not always in favor of an effective international rules system (see, for example, Trimble 1985).

Why is there real (if sometimes concealed or implicit) opposition to effective international rules? Part of the reason can be traced to the persistence of older concepts of national sovereignty. But international rules also cause real difficulties for national leaders, making it harder to deliver on promises to constituents, for example. Several types of

---

6. US Congress. House Ways and Means Committee. *Hearings on H.R. 4696*. 99th Cong., 2nd sess., 1986.

situations lead even wise national leaders to cause their governments to break or consider breaking the rules.

One such situation arises when the international rule is patently unfair or bad policy, perhaps because it is outdated and not in tune with current practice and conditions. (The difficulty of amending GATT rules, mentioned earlier, sometimes gives rise to this problem). Bad rules can also arise when the current international rulemaking process is faulty—for example, the voting procedures of international organizations can give rise to rules that are unrealistic and that do not adequately recognize real power relationships (Jackson and Davey 1986, 273–76, 286–89; Schermers 1980, 681–83).

Another situation in which rules should arguably be breached occurs when reform of the rule is badly needed, but the international and national institutional system for some reason makes the reform impossible. It could be argued that the US departure from the currency par value system of the IMF in 1971 was such a case, as it led quickly to a major revision in the IMF Charter to allow floating exchange rates, something many eminent economists had been advocating for decades (see, for example, Triffin 1966).

Nevertheless, every departure from the rules carries some risks. It causes respect for the rule system itself to be weakened, and it makes it easier in the next hard case to depart from the rules. If rules are one tool for ordering or improving human affairs, then weakening a rule system tends to reduce the utility of that tool in all its contexts.

One way to explore these questions is to compare two techniques of modern diplomacy: a "rule-oriented" technique and a "power-oriented" technique. This perhaps puts the issue in too simple a dichotomy, because the observable practice of international institutions and legal systems involves some mixture of both techniques, but it is nevertheless a useful way to examine the policy issues involved. This dichotomy can be described as follows:[7]

In broad perspective one can roughly divide the various techniques for the peaceful settlement of international disputes into two types: settlement by negotiation and agreement with reference (explicitly or implicitly) to the relative power status of the parties; and settlement by

---

7. This discussion is adapted from Jackson (1978, 1979).

negotiation or decision with reference to norms or rules to which both parties have previously agreed.

Insofar as agreed rules for governing the economic relations between the parties exist, a system that predicates negotiation on the implementation of those rules would seem for a number of reasons to be preferred. The mere existence of the rules, however, is not enough. When the issue is the application or interpretation of those rules (as compared with the formulation of new rules), it is necessary for the parties to believe that if their negotiations reach an impasse, the settlement mechanisms that then take over are designed to apply or interpret the rules fairly. If no such system exists, then the parties are left basically to rely upon their respective power positions, tempered (it is hoped) by the good will and good faith of the more powerful party, cognizant of its own long-range interests.

All diplomacy—indeed all government—involves a mixture of these techniques. To a large degree, the history of civilization may be described as a gradual evolution from a power-oriented approach, in the state of nature, toward a rule-oriented approach. However, never is the extreme in either case reached. In modern Western democracies, as we know them, power continues to play a major role, particularly the political power of voter acceptance, but also to a lesser degree economic power, such as that wielded by labor unions or large corporations. However, these governments have passed far along the scale toward a rule-oriented approach, and they generally have an elaborate legal system involving court procedures and a monopoly of force, exercised through a police and a military, to ensure that the rules will be followed. The US government has indeed proceeded far in this direction, as the resignation of a recent President demonstrates. The history of England over the last thousand years also supports the hypothesis of evolution from power to rules. More recently, when one looks at the European Community, one is struck by its evolution toward a system that is remarkably elaborate in its rule structure, effectuated through a Court of Justice, albeit without a monopoly of force.

In international affairs, a strong argument can be made that to a certain extent this same evolution must occur, even though to date it has not progressed very far. The initiatives taken during World War II and the immediate postwar period toward developing international institutions is part of this evolution, but as with most evolutions there have been setbacks, and mistakes have been made. The history of international economic policy shows the same dichotomy between power-oriented and rule-oriented diplomacy. We have tried to develop rules, in the context of the IMF and the GATT. The success has been varied.

Nevertheless, a particularly strong argument exists for directing the progress of international economic affairs gradually and consistently toward a rule-oriented approach. Apart from the advantages that accrue generally to international affairs from such an approach—less reliance on raw power and the temptation to exercise it; a fairer break for the smaller countries, or at least a perception of greater fairness; the development of agreed procedures to achieve the necessary compromises—in economic affairs there are additional reasons for moving in this direction.

Economic affairs tend (at least in peacetime) to affect more citizens directly than do political and military affairs. As the world becomes more economically interdependent, more and more private citizens find their jobs, their businesses, and their quality of life affected, if not controlled, by forces from outside their country's boundaries. Thus, they are affected more and more by the international economic policies pursued by their own countries on their behalf. In addition, the relationships become increasingly complex, to the point of being incomprehensible even to the most brilliant human mind. As a consequence, citizens (at least those governed by democracies) assert themselves and require their representatives and government officials to respond to their needs and their perceived complaints. The result is increasing citizen participation, and more parliamentary or congressional participation, in the processes of international economic policy, restricting the degree of executive power and discretion.

This trend toward broader participation makes international negotiations increasingly difficult, if not impossible. The efforts of citizens to make their demands heard and have an influence impede a power-oriented negotiating process, which often requires secrecy and executive discretion in order to formulate and implement the necessary compromises. Consequently, the only appropriate way to turn seems to be toward a rule-oriented system, in which the various layers—citizens, parliaments, executives, and international organizations—all offer their inputs, arriving tortuously at a rule which, when established, enables business and other decentralized decision makers to rely upon stable and predictable governmental activity in relation to the rule.

Why Worry about the "Constitution"?

We sometimes hear it said that "the rules don't matter—as long as the participants have the political will to make the system succeed, it will." This perspective is shallow at best. A major purpose of human institutions is to prevent the disaster that occurs precisely when the "political will" to act constructively is absent. Institutions must be designed to withstand the worst-case scenario, not merely to operate under the best. Individuals and groups will always be tempted to undermine the system if they can obtain major short-term advantage by doing so.

Furthermore, the literature on negotiation and bargaining strategies, some of which explicates such strategies in the context of the "prisoner's dilemma" paradigm (Axelrod 1984), demonstrates that, in certain situations analogous to the conditions of international trade, participants will be tempted to take actions that seem to maximize their own returns only to learn that opposing participants do the same, with the result that both lose. The way out of the dilemma is to agree on a set of restraining rules.

Beyond these principles, however, there is a set of more general arguments that strongly support a rule-oriented constitution for international economic affairs. These arguments relate to the way economic affairs are conducted. The following words of former GATT chief economist Jan Tumlir express the matter very well:

> International trade as a large-scale activity requires careful planning and substantial investments, which can be recouped only over long periods of time. All long-term investments are highly sensitive to uncertainty, and foreign-trade-related investments doubly so for their outcomes may be affected by policy changes in several countries. The trade part of the international economic order can thus be understood as a set of policy commitments exchanged between and among countries in order to minimize policy-generated uncertainty and so to maximize the gains from trade. . . Historically, this set of commitments evolved as a series of contractual bargains. . . . Without the judge and bailiff in the background, contracts do not mean much (Tumlir 1986, 6, 20).

Reforming the GATT System: A Long-Term Perspective

Any attempt to improve the GATT system and to correct some of its problems can obviously choose from several different approaches. One is to try cautiously to remedy a few problems at a time, spreading the effort out over a number of years. This piecemeal approach has always had great appeal, since the easier issues can be taken up first, and there is less chance of broad opposition than might be the case with a more comprehensive approach. On the other hand, the piecemeal approach makes it harder to develop trade-offs across an array of problem areas in a way that can attract a coalition of constituencies (the basic rationale for large negotiating rounds), and the process often takes so long that the impetus for reform runs out of steam well before the task is completed.

Perhaps the step-by-step approach is the realistic and pragmatic one—the best that can be expected under the circumstances. Yet some converging trends in the GATT system suggest that there is some chance for a more fundamental reform. The following is a partial list:

☐ The Uruguay Round is vast and complex and is addressing several important "new issues," in particular services, intellectual property, and trade-related investment measures. It is unclear how some of the results of negotiations on these issues can be incorporated into the present GATT system. Thus, a certain amount of thinking about the institutional structure will be necessary to prepare for the end of the round.

☐ There appears to be growing concern about the relationship of some of the Tokyo Round codes to the GATT system.

☐ The entry or potential entry of certain new members will require some consideration of how the GATT system can embrace large economies structured on the basis of principles other than market economics.

☐ There is much concern about the dispute settlement process.

☐ Many other problems stemming from the weak constitutional structure of the GATT system have been increasingly recognized.

☐ The world economy is changing at an increasingly rapid pace, whereas the GATT system remains relatively rigid and difficult to adapt to many of the changes likely to occur. Thus it can be argued that a better "constitution" will be needed for the next decade or the next century, to address a large number of emerging new issues.

☐ National governments recognize that an international structure of rules and obligations can be useful in bringing about necessary internal change.

☐ World economic relations have changed dramatically in recent decades. The changes include a growing interdependence and speed of communication, greater impact of economic circumstances in one country on those in other countries, an increased incidence of risky unilateral actions by major trading nations, and an inability of the rules of the traditional GATT system to address new problems or structures effectively.

Even the convergence of all these forces, however, may not suffice to overcome a variety of negative, conservative political forces. These forces include those special interests that feel that national sovereignty leverages their influence on world events, at least when that influence is aimed at preventing change, and when international consensus rules give key governments the power to block proposed changes.

Yet whatever the practical likelihood that a broader or more fundamental set of recommendations might be implemented in the next few years, there may be some value in proposing such recommendations. They can become an inventory or checklist of possibilities, some of which can then be taken up independently. By setting these recommendations in the framework of an overall fundamental approach, potential inconsistencies among them can be thought through, and their longer-term implications can be better understood.

The basic approach would be to establish a new, simple treaty instrument that would explicitly create an umbrella organization for international commerce, with its focus on institutional and procedural issues; substantive rules and obligations would be left to other treaty instruments such as the GATT, which would be served and sheltered by the umbrella organization. A number of models for such an organization come to mind, including the 1955 draft OTC as well as other writings concerning services trade (see, for example, Jackson 1988), GATT dispute settlement procedures (Jackson 1979, 8–13, note 3), and the World Intellectual Property Organization.

The new treaty instrument would contain the organizational constitution for the new institution, which could be variously named, but which I have been calling (for simplicity's sake) the World Trade Organization, or WTO. Unlike the 1948 Havana Charter for an ITO, the WTO charter would not contain many substantive obligations. Those instead would continue to be expressed in the GATT and a number of other codes or agreements, all of which would be facilitated and served by the WTO structure. The design of this new charter should facilitate the gradual evolution toward a more prominent organization with broader constituency support and better public understanding.

This new treaty instrument could be part of a Uruguay Round final act, or one of the optional or required agreements listed in such an act, or it could be considered separately in later years after the Uruguay Round is completed. The substantive result of the Uruguay Round must be paramount, and any institutional restructuring should be viewed as ancillary and complementary to it—a capstone to the round, certainly not a substitute for it.

Very important to the success of the new treaty would be approval by key parliaments, especially the US Congress. This would avoid some of the ambiguity and undermining comments that have plagued the GATT for 40 years. Thus, consideration must be given to adequate discussion and preparatory consultation with such bodies. An important possibility with respect to the Congress would be to use the "fast-track" procedures for ratification, as part of a total Uruguay Round package or as a follow-up.

The WTO should be designed to avoid any "legal gap" in the GATT and related treaty obligations. The GATT would continue in force and, one hopes, graduate from its provisional status. There should be a smooth and gradual transition from the institutional arrangements now utilized by GATT to the new WTO institutions. At the outset the two institutions could exist in parallel, with the provision that actions by one operate legally as actions by the other, until sufficient membership in the new WTO is established. A GATT contracting parties' joint decision would help clarify this legal situation.

Membership in the WTO could include all of the present GATT contracting parties, plus the signatories of other GATT system agreements. In such a case, specific decisions under the GATT or other particular agreements would be made only by the parties to the agreement concerned, but all WTO members would have an opportunity to discuss the decisions and to be informed. Thus, it would be possible to include countries (and independent customs territories) in the WTO even if they were not (yet) parties to any of the substantive agreements. An overall objective would be to make the WTO a "universal organization." All GATT members could be provisional members of the WTO pending appropriate action by their parliaments or other constitutional processes. Alternatively, a small, select group of countries (those accepting important commitments) might be the initial members.

The structure of the WTO institutions should follow the GATT customs and practice developed over 40 years. Thus, a WTO Assembly would take the place of the "Contracting Parties acting jointly," and a WTO Council would be established following the format of the existing GATT Council. Provision for a smaller coordinating committee could be made, with the details of its membership and powers left open for future action. Although, as at present, the one-nation, one vote system would be the underlying legal principle, the principle of consensus would be followed to the extent possible.

The WTO charter would not only provide the institutional structure for the GATT and many other agreements, but would perform the role of an umbrella agreement for service trade agreements (Jackson 1988). Likewise it would define the relationship to the GATT of an intellectual property code. It would explicitly recognize the duty of the WTO to provide service and facilitation for these and other new subjects taken up by the Uruguay Round and later negotiations.

The WTO would inherit the powers, property, and tasks of the Interim Commission for the ITO (established in 1948 and still the legal entity for certain GATT purposes), as soon as the members of the commission approved (Jackson 1969, chapters 2 and 6). It would provide the umbrella for a unified dispute settlement procedure and for the trade policy review mechanism, as determined by the results of the Uruguay Round (probably reserving certain functions of that procedure to the various councils or committees of each of the other agreements). The details of each of these procedures would be merely inserted into the WTO charter as annexes. These procedures would be subject to evolution and revision by the WTO Assembly from time to time.

The WTO would also establish some explicit guidelines for the relationship of other treaty instruments to the umbrella. Finally, it could sometime in the future set up a smaller body to act as a more efficient guiding group for the organization, since the size of the GATT membership now makes such guidance difficult except through informal means, which are sometimes resented.

Except for those historically anomalous moments of extraordinary creativity (such as at the end of World War II), governments and diplomats seem to prefer the least dramatic approach that is feasible for the design of international institutions. As I have indicated, an alternative to the restructuring of the GATT through a new charter would be to think through and implement a series of small, step-by-step improvements in the GATT over a period of time. Obviously there are advantages and disadvantages to either approach. It should be remembered, however, that at the end of the Uruguay Round, the GATT contracting parties will necessarily face a series of important institutional issues. There is no way to escape most of these. If in fact the Uruguay Round is reasonably successful in solving a number of these issues, the aggregate of those issues results virtually in a fundamental new charter for the GATT, even if it is not given that name. Nevertheless, some of the issues above may be separated from others, and the contracting parties may be given certain options for how to proceed rather than face an all-or-nothing decision on one big final package.

However, there is always a likelihood that the Uruguay Round will not be quite so successful, and that certain parts of the discussions will be left over for later negotiations. In addition, some of the pieces mentioned above could be elaborated or embellished by further activity during the next decade, in pursuance of a step-by-step approach to reform.

Conclusion and Perspectives

The institutional problems facing the GATT bring the language of the *Wall Street Journal* to mind:

The key problem is that member nations, particularly the U.S., don't trust GATT's administrative machinery. . . . Instead there's a growing inclination for a do-it-yourself policy, a revival of unilateralism. . . . The GATT machinery has to be improved or replaced with something like the proposed International Trade Organization. The question is how to create confidence in the new procedures. (Clark 1989)

The old, comfortable procedures of diplomacy among a small group of similar nations will no longer suffice for the GATT. A rule-oriented "constitution" is evolving and is strongly needed. A successful completion of the very ambitious Uruguay Round will only reinforce that need. (The proponents of an intellectual property agreement in the GATT are among those who have made this quite clear.) In addition, successful completion will require some fundamental changes in the GATT "constitution." The critical question is whether those changes will be carefully thought through, or merely the result of the happenstance of the negotiation endgame.

References

Axelrod, Robert. 1984. *The Evolution of Cooperation.* New York: Basic Books.

Camps, Miriam. 1980. *The Case for a New Global Trade Organization.* New York: Council on Foreign Relations.

Clark, Lindley H., Jr. 1989. "Our Do-It-Yourself Trade Policy." *Wall Street Journal,* 22 September, p. A10.

Henkin, Louis. 1979. *How Nations Behave.* New York: Council on Foreign Relations.

Jackson, John H. 1969. *World Trade and the Law of GATT: A Legal Analysis of the General Agreement on Tariffs and Trade.* Indianapolis: Bobbs-Merrill.

Jackson, John H. 1978. "The Crumbling Institutions of the Liberal Trade System." *Journal of World Trade Law* 12:98–101.

Jackson, John H. 1979. "Governmental Disputes in International Trade Relations: A Proposal in the Context of GATT." *Journal of World Trade Law* 13:3–4.

Jackson, John H. 1988. *International Competition in Services: A Constitutional Framework.* Washington: American Enterprise Institute for Public Policy Research.

Jackson, John H. 1990. *Restructuring the GATT System.* New York: Council on Foreign Relations; and London: Pinter for the Royal Institute for International Affairs.

Jackson, John H., and William Davey. 1986. *Legal Problems of International Economic Relations,* 2nd ed. St. Paul, MN: West.

Preeg, Ernest H. 1989. *The American Challenge for World Trade: U.S. Interests in the GATT Multilateral Trade System.* Washington: Center for Strategic and International Studies.

Schermers, Henry. 1980. *International Institutional Law,* 2nd ed. Rockville, MD: Sijthoff and Noordhoff.

Triffin, Robert. 1966. *The World Money Maze: National Currencies in International Payments*. New Haven, CT: Yale University Press.

Trimble, Phillip. 1985. "International Trade and the Rule of Law." *Michigan Law Review* 83:1016.

Tumlir, Jan. 1986. "GATT Rules and Community Law." In Meinhard Hilf, Francis Jacob, and Ernst-Ulrich Petersmann, eds. *The European Community and GATT*. Studies in Transnational Law 4. Deventer, Netherlands: Kluwer.

Index

Index

A

Actionable subsidies, 97–99
Adjustment measures,
  and safeguards, 19, 79–80
  and textiles, 75
  worker assistance, 103
Aggregate measure of support (AMS), in
  agriculture, 13, 56
Agriculture, 11–14, 51–62
  Article XI, on import quotas, 54
  Cairns Group, 12, 56
  Common Agricultural Policy, 12, 51
  de Zeeuw, Aart, proposal by, 12, 60
  European Free Trade Association, 12
  export competition, 56–58
  export subsidies, 13–14, 55–58
  food security, 13, 55
  health and sanitary standards, 13,
   58–59
  at Houston economic summit, 57–58
  market access, 53–55
  and Montreal midterm review, 53
  Negotiating Group on Agriculture, 53
  oilseeds, 54–55
  post–Uruguay Round agenda for,
   61–62
  price supports, 14, 55–56
  and Puerto Vallarta meeting, 53
  status of Uruguay Round negotiations,
   12, 59–61
  subsidies in, 11, 13, 55–58
  tariffication in, 55
  tariffs, 13–14
  trade liberalization, 11–14, 22, 51, 56,
   60
  and Trade Negotiations Committee
   meeting (July 1990), 53
  and US Section 22, 14
  US–EC disputes in, 51–53
  use of hormones in beef production, 59
"Almost-all-or-nothing" approach, in
  Uruguay Round, 8, 43–44

Anticircumvention measures, in
  antidumping, 23, 24, 101, 119, 126
Antidumping, 23–25, 108–28
  Antidumping and Subsidies codes,
   23–24, 83, 89
  and anticircumvention, 23, 24, 101,
   119, 126
  and antitrust, 24, 121–22
  Article VI provisions regarding, 118
  and Article XIX safeguards, 23–24,
   82–83, 89, 109
  competition issues, 127–28
  and countervailing duties, 22–25, 109
  EC synthetic fiber case, 127
  enforcement, 24, 112–17, 121, 125–26
  Japanese Fair Trade Commission, 122
  Japanese policies, 123–24
  "like-product" issues, 122
  new issues, 117–18
  and Nordic countries, 114
  and petrochemical cartel disputes, 125
  post–Uruguay Round agenda, 124–28
  practices during the 1980s, 82–83,
   108–09, 116
  and price fixing, 109, 119
  proposals for reform, 116–24
  recidivist dumping, 119
  recurrent injurious dumping, 117–18
  'soft containment' approach, 114–15
  status of Uruguay Round negotiations,
   59–61, 123–24
  and subsidies, 83, 89, 95
  Sweden, 114
  Tokyo Round and, 112
  and trade liberalization, 109–12
  US policies and actions, 116–17,
   120–28
  See also Countervailing duties
Antitrust, and antidumping, 24, 121–22
Apparel. See Textiles and apparel
Appeals tribunal, in dispute settlement,
  191–94

Article III:4, and trade-related investment measures, 150
Article VI, on antidumping, 118
Article XI, on agricultural import quotas, 54
Article XVI, on export subsidies, 56–57
Article XVIII:B, on safeguards, 21–22, 88–89
Article XVIII:C, and local-content requirements, 151
Article XIX, 19–22, 79–87
    actions used in lieu of, 82–83
    and Puerto Vallarta meeting, 21
    and Section 201 (US), 19
    selective safeguards, 20, 79–80, 84–87
    and voluntary export restraints, 19–22
    See also Safeguards
Article XXIII,
    and dispute settlement, 180–81, 195, 199, 201–03
    and US–Canada negotiations on trade-related investment measures, 150
Article XXIV, on exceptions to most-favored-nation status, 7
Article XXXV, "opt out" provision, 29, 208
ASEAN, and subsidies, 97

B
Balance of payments safeguards, 21–22, 88–89
Bilateral trade arrangements, 5, 6–7
Brazil et al., draft framework for trade in services, 139–43
Brussels, December 1990 ministerial meeting in, 60–61

C
Cairns Group, 12, 56
Cameroon et al., draft framework for trade in services, 139–43
Canada, agricultural import quotas, 53
Canada–US trade agreement, as model for dispute settlement, 190
    Foreign Investment Review Agency, 150–51
    proposals for reforming countervailing duties, 104
    and proposed World Trade Organization, 206
    stance on permitted subsidies, 103
    US–Canada negotiations on trade-related investment measures, 150

Cartels, and antidumping enforcement, 125–26
Cartland, Michael D., draft framework on subsidies by, 23, 95–101
Committee on Anti-Dumping Practices, 95
Common Agricultural Policy (CAP), 12, 51
Competition, issues in antidumping, 127–28
Conditional most-favored-nation treatment, 33
Consensus, use of, in dispute settlement, 181
Consensus-minus-two principle, 185
Consultative Group of 18, negotiations on trade-related investment measures, 150
Consumer costs, of protection in textiles and apparel, 68–74
Counterfeiting, and intellectual property rights, 173
Countervailing duties (CVDs), 22–23, 100–09
    and antidumping rules, 22–25, 109
    Canadian proposals for reform of, 104
    in Cartland draft, 100–01
    reform of, 104, 106
    and safeguards, 22–25, 83
    and subsidies, 22, 23, 94–95, 99–101
    sunset provision, 100
    US International Trade Commission analysis of, 100
    See also Antidumping; Subsidies

D
de Zeeuw, Aart, 12, 60
Degressivity, 79–80, 103
Developed countries. See individual country
Developing countries,
    changes required of, 42
    and intellectual property, 164, 173–74
    and multinational enterprises, 155–56
    objectives in Uruguay Round, 41–42
    and subsidies, 103–4
    and textiles and apparel trade, 76–77
    See also Newly industrializing countries
Dillon Round, and EC policies on oilseeds, 54–55
Dispute settlement, 25–28, 33–35, 180–204
    appeals tribunals, 34, 191–94
    and Article XXIII, 180–81, 195, 199, 201–03

blocking power, 182
Canada–US agreement as model for, 190
consensus in, 181
consensus-minus-two principle, 185
cross-retaliation in, 26, 142
and Montreal midterm meeting, 184–86
nonviolation nullification and impairment doctrine, 196–98, 200–02
"nonviolation" remedies, 195–203
panel reports, 35, 181
procedures, 180–81
public access to GATT records on, 189–90
and reciprocity, 196
reform of, 34–35, 181–84, 190–91
relation to new issues, 25
and retaliation, 180, 194–95
and services, 142
and Secretariat legal office, 191
status of current GATT negotiations on, 25–26, 33–35, 185–95
subsidies and, 97–99
termination clauses in, 195
in trade-related investment measures, 162
US problems with, 182–83, 203–04
and US Section 301 remedies, 35, 186–87, 197–98, 202–03
Domestic international sales corporations (DISC), 212
Domestic law, relationship of GATT to, 3, 208, 212–13

E

Employment effects, of textiles and apparel liberalization, 74–75
Enforcement procedures,
of antidumping rules, 112–17, 125–26
cross-retaliation, 26, 142
for intellectual property, 33, 172–73, 177–78
Environmental issues, and subsidies, 106–07
European Community,
benefits of successful Uruguay Round, 47–48
changes required of, 40
Common Agricultural Policy, 12, 51
differences with US,
over agriculture, 51–53
over subsidies, 101–02
export restitution policy, 57
government procurement proposal, 17
multinational enterprises in, 154–56
objectives in Uruguay Round, 40
and rebalancing of agricultural tariffs, 13, 55
safeguards proposal, 84
and services, 134
and subsidies, 40, 94, 101–03
textiles and apparel proposal, 64
European Free Trade Association (EFTA), and agriculture, 12
Exon-Florio amendment, 27, 153–55
Export Enhancement Program (US), 57
Export restitution policy (EC), 57
Export subsidies, 96
in agriculture, 13–14, 57–58
Article XVI on, 56–57

F

Fast-track implementing authority, 3
Financial services, 26, 142
Foreign investment,
Exon-Florio amendment (US), 153–55
and intellectual property, 30, 31
international code covering, 160–63
trade-related investment measures and, 161
See also Investment
Free trade areas, 5, 6–7
Functioning of the GATT System (FOGS) Negotiating Group, 38–39

G

GATT Articles Group, and safeguards negotiations, 88–89
GATT Council, role in dispute settlement, 181
General Agreement on Tariffs and Trade (GATT),
difficulty in amending, 207
institutional issues, 4–5, 35–39, 205–24, 218–19
membership issues, 208–09
provisional nature of, 29, 207–08
relation to domestic law, 208
relation to other Bretton Woods institutions, 209
side treaties, 207–08
treaty instrument proposals for, 219–20
See also Institutional issues, specific articles
General Agreement on Trade in Services (GATS), 28–29, 130, 132, 135–6, 142–44. See also Services
Glass-Steagall Act (US), 26
Global quotas, in textiles and apparel, 15–16, 65–66. See also Quotas
Government procurement, 17, 45

Gray-area measures, 13, 83–84. *See also* Voluntary export restraints

H

Havana Charter, and International Trade Organization, 205
Houston economic summit, July 1990,
  and agriculture export subsidies, 57–58
  announcement regarding Uruguay Round, 1
  declaration on services issues, 28

I

Institutional issues, 4–6, 35–39, 205–24
  GATT relations with International Monetary Fund and World Bank, 38–39
  trade policy review mechanism, 36–37
  World Trade Organization, 37–38, 205–06, 220–22
Intellectual property, 31–33, 164–79
  compulsory licensing, 32, 170–71, 176
  copyright, 175
  and counterfeiting, 32, 173
  developing vs. developed countries on, 31, 164, 173–74
  enforcement, 32–33, 172–73, 177–78
  implementing legislation for, 177
  patents, 32–33, 176
  and post–Uruguay Round agenda, 177–79
  standards of protection, 170–72
  status of GATT negotiations, 165–66, 169–71, 173–77
  trademarks, 33, 175
  and US Section 337, 170
  and World Intellectual Property Organization, 31–32, 168, 169, 171
International Monetary Fund (IMF), 22, 38–39
International Textiles and Clothing Bureau, 76
International Trade Organization (ITO), 37, 205. *See also* World Trade Organization (WTO)
Investment, 29–31, 147–62
  incentives, 30, 98–99, 151
  local-content and export performance requirements, 30
  new issue areas, 27, 29–31
  and services trade, 27
  See also Trade-related investment measures; Foreign investment

J

Japan,
  and antidumping issues, 123–24

benefits of successful Uruguay Round, 47–48
  changes required of, 41
  and industrial targeting, 102
  and multinational enterprises, 154–56
  objectives in Uruguay Round, 41
  rice import restrictions, 14, 53, 55
  Structural Impediments Initiative (with US), 25
  and textiles and apparel, 64
"Japan problem," 47
Japanese Fair Trade Commission, and antidumping, 122
Joint Development Committee, and trade-related investment measures, 150

L

Labor, international movement of, and services, 132
Local-content requirements,
  and Article XVIII:C, 151
  and ASEAN, 97
  and export performance requirements, 30
  and prohibited subsidies, 96–97

M

Manufacturing clause, 212–13
Market access, 10–25
  in agriculture, 53–55
McFadden Act (US), 26
Montreal midterm review,
  and agriculture, 53
  and dispute settlement, 184–86
  Montreal Declaration, and services issues, 130
  US proposals regarding settlement dispute, 185
Most-favored-nation (MFN) principle, 6–7, 90
Multi-Fiber Arrangement (MFA), 14, 63–65, 67–68, 74, 76–78
Multinational enterprises (MNEs), 147–56
  developing countries and, 155–56
  European Community and, 155–56
  and Exon-Florio Amendment, 153–55
  Japan and, 154–56
  and Omnibus Trade and Competitiveness Act of 1988, 153–54
  and trade-related investment measures, 147–50
  US and, 153–56
  See also Investment

N

National sovereignty issues, 213–14

National treatment instrument, for trade-related investment measures, 161

Natural justice approach, to intellectual property rights, 167

Negotiating Group on Agriculture, 53

Negotiating Group on Non-Tariff Measures, 88

Negotiating Group on Subsidies and Countervailing Measures, 94

Negotiating Group on Textiles and Clothing, 87–88

Negotiating Group on Trade-Related Aspects of Intellectual Property Rights, 150–53, 165–66

Negotiating Group on Trade-Related Investment Measures, 151–53

Negotiation deadlines. *See* Domestic law

Newly industrializing countries (NICs), 42, 48

Nonactionable subsidies, 23, 100. *See also* Actionable subsidies

Nondiscrimination. *See* Selectivity of safeguards

Nonviolation, nullification and impairment (NN&I), 196–98, 200–02

Nordic countries, 53, 114

O

Omnibus Trade and Competitiveness Act of 1988, 153–54, 186

"Opt out" provision of Article XXXV, 29, 208

Organization for Economic Cooperation and Development (OECD), communiqué regarding Uruguay Round, 206

Export Credit Group, 105

May 1990 ministerial meeting, 57

Organization of Trade Cooperation (OTC), 205

P

"Pacific Five" countries, safeguards proposal, 85

Panel rulings, in dispute settlement, 35, 181

Patents, 32–33. *See also* Intellectual property

Performance requirements, and trade-related investment measures, 152

Permanent Group of Experts, and subsidy disputes, 97

Political and security concerns, in trade negotiations, 7

Price supports, in agriculture, 55–56

Producer-financed subsidies, in agriculture, 58

Puerto Vallarta meeting (April 1990), 21, 53, 206

Punta del Este meeting (September 1986), 14, 151

Q

Quotas

allocation mechanism, in textiles and apparel, 66

and effects on consumer costs in textiles and apparel, 72

expansion, under Multi-Fiber Arrangement, 67–68

R

Rebalancing, of EC agricultural tariffs, 13, 55

Reciprocity, 195–96

Research and development, and subsidies, 103

Retaliation,

and compensation, and safeguards, 20, 79–80

and dispute settlement, 26, 180, 194–95

Revenue effects, of textiles and apparel liberalization, 74–75

Rule-oriented versus power-oriented diplomacy, 211–18

S

Safeguards, 18–24, 79–91

adjustment measures and, 79–80

and Antidumping and Subsidies codes, 23–24, 83, 89

and Article XVIII:B, 21–22, 88–89

Article XIX, 19–22, 80, 83

balance of payments safeguards, 21–22, 88–89

and countervailing duties, 18, 22–25, 83

degressivity in, 79–80

GATT Articles Group proposal, 88–89

GATT restrictions on, 80–81

and gray-area measures, 18–20, 83–84

and International Monetary Fund and World Bank, 22

multilateral surveillance of, 21, 36–37, 79–80

Negotiating Group on Textiles and Clothing, proposals at Uruguay Round, 87–88

"Pacific Five" proposal, 85

prospects for reform of, 87–90

retaliation and compensation and, 20,
79–80
"safeguards complex," 18–24
Safeguards Negotiating Group, 79,
85–87
selective, 20, 79–80, 85
in Tokyo Round, 84–87
trade-offs with antidumping rules,
18–19, 109
and US Section 301, 83
and voluntary export restraints, 18–20
See also Antidumping; Article XIX;
Countervailing duties; Voluntary
export restraints
Safeguards Negotiating Group, 79, 85–87,
130
"Screwdriver" operations, and
trade-related investment measures,
152–53
Section 22 (US), and agriculture
liberalization, 14, 53
Section 201 (US), and Article XIX, 19
Section 301 (US), 4–6, 83, 97, 186–87,
197–98, 202–03
Section 337 (US), 170
Selective safeguards, 20, 79–80, 84–87
Senior Officials Group, negotiations over
trade-related investment measures, 151
Services, 130–45
Brazil et al. draft framework for trade
in, 139–43
Cameroon et al. draft framework for
trade in, 139–43
cross-border regulations, 133–34
desirable outcome of Uruguay Round,
136–45
differences between goods and, 130–31
and dispute settlement, 142
financial, 26, 142
General Agreement on Trade in
Services (GATS), 28–29, 130, 132,
135–36, 142–44
Houston summit declaration, 28
international regulations on, 132–135
labor, international movement of, 132
maritime transport, 29
and Montreal Declaration (1989), 130
no-exemptions policy, 29
and nonapplication provision, 29
and nontariff barriers, 133
proposals for reform of, 28–29, 136–43
special characteristics of trade in,
130–35
special and differential treatment
regarding, 138–39
surveillance of, 79–80

Treaty of Rome regulations on, 134
US draft framework on, 137
Short- and Long-Term Arrangements on
Cotton Textiles, 63–64
Smoot-Hawley tariff, and textiles and
apparel, 15
"Soft containment," in antidumping,
114–15
Special and differential treatment, in
services, 138–39
Structural adjustment. *See* Adjustment
measures
Structural Impediments Initiative (SII),
25
Subsidies, 22–23, 93–107
actionable, 97–99
in agriculture, 11, 55–58
and antidumping, 5, 83, 89, 95
and ASEAN, 97
Canadian stance on permitted
subsidies, 103
Cartland draft, 23, 95–101
and Committee on Anti-Dumping
Practices, 95
and countervailing duties, 23, 94–95,
99–101
developing countries' views on, 103–04
and dispute settlement, 97–99
EC stance on permitted subsidies, 103
and environmental issues, 106–07
Export Credit Group (EC),
involvement in, 105
German policy on, 101–02
and industrial targeting, 102
and local-content requirements, 96–97
maximum discipline on, 105–106
and Negotiating Group on Subsidies
and Countervailing Measures, 94
nonactionable, 23, 99, 100
Permanent Group of Experts, 97
post–Uruguay Round agenda, 106–07
prohibited, 96–97
and trade-related investment measures,
96–97
and US Section 301, 97
Subsidies Negotiating Group, 23
Sunrise industries, and challenges facing
GATT, 5, 27–28
Sweden, antidumping issues in, 127
Switzerland, proposal on textiles and
apparel liberalization, 64

T
Targeted Export Assistance Program
(US), 57
Tariff rate quotas, 15, 66–67, 73–74

Tariffication, 13, 15, 55, 67
Tariffs, 13–17
Tax Reform Act of 1986, 212
Technology-exporting countries, and
  intellectual property, 165
Technology-importing countries, and
  intellectual property, 165, 168
Textile, Apparel, and Footwear Act of
  1990, 74
Textiles and apparel, 63–78
  apparel sector, 75–76
  consumer costs of protection, 68–74
  developing-country proposals for,
    76–77
  employment and revenue effects of
    liberalization, 74–75
  and global quotas, 15–16, 65–66
  Multi-Fiber Arrangement (MFA), 14,
    63–65, 67–68, 74, 76–78
  proposals for reform of, 64–68
  protective legislation, 74
  and Punta del Este declaration, 14
  quantitative evaluation of liberalization
    proposals, 68–75
  quotas, 65–68, 72
  Swiss proposal, 64
  and tariff rate quotas, 66–67
  and Textile, Apparel, and Footwear
    Act of 1990, 74
  and trade liberalization, 14–16
Tokyo Round, 84–87, 112
Trade Negotiations Committee (TNC)
  meeting (July 1990), 53
Trade policy review mechanism (TPRM),
  36–37
Trade-related intellectual property rights
  (TRIPs), See Intellectual property
Trade-related investment measures
  (TRIMs), 96–97, 147–62
  in ancillary codes, 162
  Article III:4 and, 150
  Article XVIII:C and, 151
  code of home- and host-nation rights,
    161
  code of rights of multinational
    enterprises, 161–62
  code on right of establishment, 160
  Consultative Group of 18, 150
  dispute settlement in, 162
  escape clauses in, 159
  GATT ruling on Foreign Investment
    Review Agency, 150–51
  "grandfather" clause in, 158
  Joint Development Committee
    negotiations, 150
  local-content requirements, 30, 151

  and multinational enterprises, 147–50,
    153–56
  nonbinding declaration for, 159–60
  performance requirements, 152
  post–Uruguay Round agenda, 160–63
  prohibited subsidies and, 96–97
  proposals for reform of, 150–53, 157,
    160–63
  prospects for negotiations, 156–160
  at Punta del Este meeting, 151
  "rollback" mechanism in, 158
  and "screwdriver" operations, 152–53
  Senior Officials Group negotiations,
    151
  "standstill" clause in, 26–27, 158
  and subsidies, 96–97
  theory of, 148–50
  and world economy, 149, 153–56
Treaty of Rome. See European
  Community

U
US Congress, fast-track implementing
  authority, 3
United States,
  benefits of successful Uruguay Round,
    47
  changes required of, 40
  Commerce Department, and
    antidumping issues, 120
  differences with EC over prohibited
    subsidies, 101–02
  Exon-Florio Amendment, 153–55
  Glass-Steagall Act, 26
  International Trade Commission,
    analysis of countervailing duties, 100
  McFadden Act, 26
  noncompliance with GATT rulings, 211
  objectives in the Uruguay Round,
    39–40
  Omnibus Trade and Competitiveness
    Act of 1988, 153–54, 186
  proposal on antidumping rules, 116–17
  proposal on safeguards in Tokyo
    Round, 84–85
  proposal on textiles and apparel, 64
  Section 22, and market access, 14, 53
  Section 201, 19
  Section 301, 4–6, 83, 97, 186–87,
    197–98, 202–03
  Section 337, and intellectual property
    rights, 170
  Super 301 and Special 301, as remedies
    in dispute settlement, 198
  Tax Reform Act of 1988, 212

Textile, Apparel, and Footwear Act of
1990, 74
Webb-Pomerene Act, 128
Uruguay Round,
"almost-all-or-nothing" approach,
43–44
announcement at Houston economic
summit, 1
challenges facing, 4–7
extension of, 3, 43
key role of United States and
European Community, 44
and market access, 10–25
and new issue areas, 25–33
and newly industrializing countries, 48
and nonviolation issues, 199–203
objectives of developing countries,
41–42
objectives of European Community,
40–41
objectives of Japan, 41
objectives of United States, 39–40
OECD communiqué regarding, 206

US-Canada Free Trade Agreement, 27,
190

V
Variable levy, 53, 55
Voluntary export restraints (VERs)
in agriculture, 53
and Article XIX, 19–22
prohibition of, 20–21
and safeguards, 18
used in lieu of Article XIX safeguards,
83, 88

W
Webb-Pomerene Act, and antidumping
issues, 128
Worker assistance. See Adjustment
measures
World Bank, 22, 38–39
World Intellectual Property Organization
(WIPO), 31–32, 168 See also
Intellectual property
World Trade Organization (WTO), 37–38,
205–06, 220–22

POLICY ANALYSES IN INTERNATIONAL ECONOMICS

1   The Lending Policies of the International Monetary Fund
John Williamson/*August 1982*
$8.00   0–88132–000–5   72 pp

2   "Reciprocity": A New Approach to World Trade Policy?
William R. Cline/*September 1982*
$8.00   0–88132–001–3   41 pp

3   Trade Policy in the 1980s
C. Fred Bergsten and William R. Cline/*November 1982*
(Out of print)   0–88132–002–1   84 pp
Partially reproduced in the book *Trade Policy in the 1980s.*

4   International Debt and the Stability of the World Economy
William R. Cline/*September 1983*
$10.00   0–88132–010–2   134 pp

5   The Exchange Rate System
John Williamson/*September 1983, 2nd ed. rev. June 1985*
$10.00   0–88132–034–X   61 pp

6   Economic Sanctions in Support of Foreign Policy Goals
Gary Clyde Hufbauer and Jeffrey J. Schott/*October 1983*
$10.00   0–88132–014–5   109 pp

7   A New SDR Allocation?
John Williamson/*March 1984*
$10.00   0–88132–028–5   61 pp

8   An International Standard for Monetary Stabilization
Ronald I. McKinnon/*March 1984*
$10.00   0–88132–018–8   108 pp

9   The Yen/Dollar Agreement: Liberalizing Japanese Capital Markets
Jeffrey A. Frankel/*December 1984*
$10.00   0–88132–035–8   86 pp

10 Bank Lending to Developing Countries: The Policy Alternatives
C. Fred Bergsten, William R. Cline, and John Williamson/*April 1985*
$12.00   0–88132–032–3   221 pp

11 Trading for Growth: The Next Round of Trade Negotiations
Gary Clyde Hufbauer and Jeffrey J. Schott/*September 1985*
$10.00   0–88132–033–1   109 pp

12 Financial Intermediation Beyond the Debt Crisis
Donald R. Lessard and John Williamson/*September 1985*
$12.00   0–88132–021–8   130 pp

13 The United States–Japan Economic Problem
C. Fred Bergsten and William R. Cline/*Oct. 1985, 2nd ed. rev. Jan. 1987*
$10.00   0–88132–060–9   180 pp

14 Deficits and the Dollar: The World Economy at Risk
Stephen Marris/*December 1985, 2nd ed. rev. November 1987*
$18.00   0–88132–067–6   415 pp

15 Trade Policy for Troubled Industries
Gary Clyde Hufbauer and Howard F. Rosen/*March 1986*
$10.00   0–88132–020–X   111 pp

16 The United States and Canada: The Quest for Free Trade
Paul Wonnacott, with an Appendix by John Williamson/*March 1987*
$10.00   0–88132–056–0   188 pp

17 Adjusting to Success: Balance of Payments Policy in the East Asian NICs
Bela Balassa and John Williamson/*June 1987, rev. April 1990*
$11.95   0–88132–101–X   160 pp

18 Mobilizing Bank Lending to Debtor Countries
William R. Cline/*June 1987*
$10.00   0–88132–062–5   100 pp

19 Auction Quotas and United States Trade Policy
C. Fred Bergsten, Kimberly Ann Elliott, Jeffrey J. Schott, and Wendy E. Takacs/*September 1987*
$10.00   0–88132–050–1   254 pp

20 Agriculture and the GATT: Rewriting the Rules
Dale E. Hathaway/*September 1987*
$10.00   0–88132–052–8   169 pp

21 Anti-Protection: Changing Forces in United States Trade Politics
I. M. Destler and John S. Odell/*September 1987*
$10.00   0–88132–043–9   220 pp

22 Targets and Indicators: A Blueprint for the International Coordination of Economic Policy
John Williamson and Marcus H. Miller/*September 1987*
$10.00   0–88132–051–X   118 pp

23 Capital Flight: The Problem and Policy Responses
Donald R. Lessard and John Williamson/*December 1987*
$10.00   0–88132–059–5   80 pp

**24 United States–Canada Free Trade: An Evaluation of the
Agreement**
Jeffrey J. Schott/*April 1988*
$3.95   0–88132–072–2   48 pp

25 Voluntary Approaches to Debt Relief
John Williamson/*September 1988, rev. May 1989*
$10.95   0–88132–075–7   80 pp

26 American Trade Adjustment: The Global Impact
William R. Cline/*March 1989*
$12.95   0–88132–095–1   98 pp

27 More Free Trade Areas?
Jeffrey J. Schott/*May 1989*
$10.00   0–88132–085–4   88 pp

28 The Progress of Policy Reform in Latin America
John Williamson/*January 1990*
$11.95   0–88132–100–1   106 pp

29 The Global Trade Negotiations: What Can Be Achieved?
Jeffrey J. Schott/*September 1990*
$10.95   0–88132–137–0   72 pp

BOOKS

IMF Conditionality
John Williamson, editor/*1983*
$35.00 (cloth only)   0–88132–006–4   695 pp

Trade Policy in the 1980s
William R. Cline, editor/*1983*
$35.00 (cloth)   0–88132–008–1   810 pp
$20.00 (paper)   0–88132–031–5   810 pp

Subsidies in International Trade
Gary Clyde Hufbauer and Joanna Shelton Erb/*1984*
$35.00 (cloth only)   0–88132–004–8   299 pp

International Debt: Systemic Risk and Policy Response
William R. Cline/*1984*
$30.00 (cloth only)   0–88132–015–3   336 pp

Economic Sanctions Reconsidered: History and Current Policy
Gary Clyde Hufbauer and Jeffrey J. Schott, assisted by Kimberly
Ann Elliott/*1985*
$45.00 (cloth only)   0–88132–017–X   769 pp

Trade Protection in the United States: 31 Case Studies
Gary Clyde Hufbauer, Diane E. Berliner, and Kimberly Ann Elliott/*1986*
$25.00   0–88132–040–4   371 pp

Toward Renewed Economic Growth in Latin America
Bela Balassa, Gerardo M. Bueno, Pedro-Pablo Kuczynski, and
Mario Henrique Simonsen/*1986*
$15.00   0–88132–045–5   205 pp

American Trade Politics: System Under Stress
I. M. Destler/*1986*
$30.00 (cloth)   0–88132–058–7   380 pp
$18.00 (paper)   0–88132–057–9   380 pp

The Future of World Trade in Textiles and Apparel
William R. Cline/*1987, rev. June 1990*
$20.00   0–88132–110–9   344 pp

Capital Flight and Third World Debt
Donald R. Lessard and John Williamson, editors/*1987*
$16.00   0–88132–053–6   270 pp

**The Canada–United States Free Trade Agreement: The Global
Impact**
Jeffrey J. Schott and Murray G. Smith, editors/*1988*
$13.95   0–88132–073–0   211 pp

Managing the Dollar: From the Plaza to the Louvre
Yoichi Funabashi/*1988, 2nd ed. rev. 1989*
$19.95   0–88132–097–8   307 pp

World Agricultural Trade: Building a Consensus
William M. Miner and Dale E. Hathaway, editors/*1988*
$16.95   0–88132–071–3   226 pp

Japan in the World Economy
Bela Balassa and Marcus Noland/*1988*
$19.95   0–88132–041–2   306 pp

America in the World Economy: A Strategy for the 1990s
C. Fred Bergsten/*1988*
$29.95 (cloth)   0–88132–089–7   235 pp
$13.95 (paper)   0–88132–082–X   235 pp

United States External Adjustment and the World Economy
William R. Cline/*1989*
$25.00   0–88132–048–X   392 pp

Free Trade Areas and U.S. Trade Policy
Jeffrey J. Schott, editor/*1989*
$19.95   0–88132–094–3   400 pp

Dollar Politics: Exchange Rate Policymaking in the United States
I. M. Destler and C. Randall Henning/*1989*
$11.95   0–88132–079–X   192 pp

Foreign Direct Investment in the United States
Edward M. Graham and Paul R. Krugman/*1989*
$11.95

SPECIAL REPORTS

1 **Promoting World Recovery: A Statement on Global Economic Strategy**
by Twenty-six Economists from Fourteen Countries/*December 1982*
(Out of Print)   0–88132–013–7   45 pp

2 **Prospects for Adjustment in Argentina, Brazil, and Mexico: Responding to the Debt Crisis**
John Williamson, editor/*June 1983*
(Out of Print)   0–88132–016–1   71 pp

3 **Inflation and Indexation: Argentina, Brazil, and Israel**
John Williamson, editor/*March 1985*
(Out of Print)   0–88132–037–4   191 pp

4 **Global Economic Imbalances**
C. Fred Bergsten, editor/*March 1986*
$25.00 (cloth)   0–88132–038–2   126 pp
$10.00 (paper)   0–88132–042–0   126 pp

5 **African Debt and Financing**
Carol Lancaster and John Williamson, editors/*May 1986*
$12.00   0–88132–044–7   229 pp

6 **Resolving the Global Economic Crisis: After Wall Street**
Thirty-three Economists from Thirteen Countries/*December 1987*
$3.00   0–88132–070–6   30 pp

7 **World Economic Problems**
Kimberly Ann Elliott and John Williamson, editors/*April 1988*
$15.95   0–88132–055–2   298 pp

Reforming World Agricultural Trade
Twenty-nine Professionals from Seventeen Countries/*1988*
$3.95   0–88132–088–9   42 pp

8 **Economic Relations Between the United States and Korea: Conflict or Cooperation?**
Thomas O. Bayard and Soo-Gil Young, editors/*January 1989*
$12.95   0–88132–068–4   192 pp

FORTHCOMING

The United States as a Debtor Country
C. Fred Bergsten and Shafiqul Islam

Equilibrium Exchange Rates: An Update
John Williamson

Managed and Mismanaged Trade: Policy Lessons for the 1990s
Laura D'Andrea Tyson

Global Oil Crisis Intervention
Philip K. Verleger, Jr.

Economic Sanctions Reconsidered: History and Current Policy,
Revised Edition
Gary Clyde Hufbauer, Jeffrey J. Schott, and Kimberly Ann Elliott

Pacific Area Developing Countries: Prospects for the Future
Marcus Noland

Economic Policy Cooperation: Reflections of a Practitioner
Wendy Dobson

Currency Convertibility in Eastern Europe
John Williamson

US Taxation of International Income: Blueprint for Reform
Gary Clyde Hufbauer

**Reciprocity and Retaliation: An Evaluation of Aggressive
Trade Policies**
Thomas O. Bayard

Eastern Europe and the Soviet Union in the World Economy
Susan Collins and Dani Roderik

The Greenhouse Effect: Global Economic Consequences
William R. Cline

The Costs of US Trade Barriers
Gary Clyde Hufbauer and Kimberly Ann Elliott

Mexico and the United States: Toward North American Economic Integration
Jeffrey J. Schott and Gary Clyde Hufbauer

Energy Policy for the 1990s: A Global Perspective
Philip K. Verleger, Jr.

Financial Intermediation Beyond the Debt Crisis, Revised Edition
Donald R. Lessard and John Williamson

The Debt of Low-Income Africa: Issues and Options for the United States
Carol Lancaster

International Monetary Policymaking in the United States, Germany, and Japan
C. Randall Henning

The United States and Japan in the 1990s
C. Fred Bergsten, I.M. Destler, and Marcus Noland

The Outlook for World Commodity Prices
Philip K. Verleger, Jr.

Narrowing the US Current Account Deficit: A Sectoral Assessment
Allen Lenz

Korea in the World Economy
Il Sakong

Comparing the Costs of Protection: Europe, Japan, and the United States
Gary Clyde Hufbauer and Kimberly Ann Elliott, editors

The Future of the World Trading System
John Whalley

Export Disincentives and US Trade Policy
J. David Richardson

The Effects of Foreign-Exchange Intervention
Jeffrey A. Frankel

Third World Debt: A Reappraisal
William R. Cline

The New Tripolar World Economy: Toward Collective Leadership
C. Fred Bergsten and C. Randall Henning

Trade Liberalization and International Institutions: What More Could Be Done?
Jeffrey J. Schott

A GATT for Investment
C. Fred Bergsten and Edward M. Graham

International Adjustment and Finance: Lessons of 1985–1990
Paul R. Krugman

TO ORDER PUBLICATIONS PLEASE WRITE OR CALL US AT:

Institute for International Economics
Publications Department
11 Dupont Circle, NW
Washington, DC 20036
1-800-229-ECON; FAX: 202-328-5432
202-328-9000